DEXTER

and Philosophy

Popular Culture and Philosophy®
Series Editor: George A. Reisch

For full details of all **Popular Culture and Philosophy®** books, visit www.opencourtbooks.com.

Popular Culture and Philosophy®

DEXTER
and Philosophy

Mind over Spatter

Edited by
RICHARD GREENE,
GEORGE A. REISCH,
and
RACHEL ROBISON-GREENE

OPEN COURT
Chicago and La Salle, Illinois

Volume 58 in the series, Popular Culture and Philosophy®, edited by George A. Reisch

To order books from Open Court, call toll-free 1-800-815-2280, or visit our website at www.opencourtbooks.com.

Open Court Publishing Company is a division of Carus Publishing Company.

Library of Congress Cataloging-in-Publication Data

Dexter and philosophy : mind over spatter / edited by Richard Greene, George A. Reisch, and Rachel Robison-Greene.
        p. cm.—(Popular culture and philosophy ; v. 58)
    Includes bibliographical references and index.
    ISBN 978-0-8126-9717-9 (trade paper : alk. paper)
    1. Dexter (Television program) I. Greene, Richard, 1961 Sept. 2- II. Reisch,
  George A., 1962- III. Robison-Greene, Rachel, 1983- IV. Title. V. Series.
    PN1992.77.D49D49 2011
    791.45'72—dc22

                                                              2011008735

For Brandy Burfield

Contents

Acknowledgments

Working on this project has been a pleasure, in no small part because of the many fine folks who have assisted us along the way. In particular a debt of gratitude is owed to David Ramsay Steele at Open Court, the contributors to this volume, and our respective academic departments at UMass Amherst, Northwestern University, and Weber State University. Finally, we'd like to thank those family members, students, friends, and colleagues with whom we've had fruitful and rewarding conversations on various aspects of all things *Dexter* as they relate to philosophical themes.

Know Thyself?

GEORGE A. REISCH

The statistics are one in twenty-five. That means there's a good chance that there was one among my elementary school classmates, two in my high-school student council (which explains a lot!) and about eighty at the last meeting of the American Philosophical Association. Yikes.

Sociopaths are everywhere—at least according to psychologist Martha Stout who, in her book *The Sociopath Next Door*, formulates the one-in-twenty-five (four percent) statistic. The sociopaths Stout has dedicated her life to studying have three defining traits: they are incapable of feeling ordinary human emotions, like compassion, empathy, and love; they have no moral conscience and simply don't feel shame or guilt like the rest of us; and they easily hide this from those of us around them.

How do they do it? In large part, they don't. *We* do it. We are so confident that we know what other people are about, we do the work for them. As Stout puts it, "since everyone simply assumes that conscience is universal among human beings, hiding the fact that you are conscience-free is nearly effortless." When you're one of the one-in-twenty-five, living, working, and bowling with your friends, "the icewater in your veins is so bizarre, so completely outside of their personal experience, that they seldom even guess at your condition." (p. 1). The only good news is that most of these sociopaths are not vicious serial killers.

Hi, I'm Dexter. Welcome to Miami

Dexter, of course, is a sociopath and more—a serial killer with a complicated, tragic backstory that is progressively revealed to us, a killer who only kills other killers (Thank you, Harry!), and a serial killer who thinks, *a lot*. As his trademark inner monologues remind us every episode, Dexter reasons, analyzes, worries and—dear to any philosopher's heart—questions his assumptions and motives. That photographer sure looks like a killer and a good candidate for the plastic-wrap table, but is he really? (Oops, Dexter got that one wrong). Sergeant Doakes is getting *way* too close, but how can I, ahem, *take care* of this problem without violating Harry's Code? Now there's an ethical quandary worthy of Jean-Paul Sartre . . . oh, look, here comes Lila!

See, I'm even identifying with Dexter as I write. At least for that one hour each week, his problems are my problems. His stressed out workdays and fast-approaching deadlines are like mine. He's got his ominous flashbacks to his days in a shipping container; I've got recurring dreams about student council, or taking final exams in college classes I forgot to attend. Obviously, these involve different kinds of carnage and (vastly) different amounts of human blood, but Dexter remains a lot like us. Many have even had a Harry—a parent, teacher, or mentor who saw deeply into our youthful quirks, special talents, or tragic flaws and stepped in with some good advice, or some good rules to follow, that saved us from one or more of life's available disasters. And who among us has no Dark Passenger, even if it's just a thing for *Dancing with the Stars* or overlooking a couple of numbers on your 1040 form?

All this makes Dexter likeable. But, more than that, it makes *Dexter*—the show and the books—a welcome, comforting transfiguration of the real world of sociopaths described by Martha Stout. In the real world, we'd be like those in the cast—Debra, LaGuerta, Batista, or (speaking of Dark Passengers) Vince Masuka—all of whom neither have (nor want) to know the truth about Dexter. Their assumptions about him, reinforced by their daily perceptions and interactions with him, lock together into the veil, the cover, that he needs to thrive as a secret killer of killers and they need to get out of bed each morning in full confidence that the doughnut guy at work, Deb's *brother*, is not really some John Wayne Gacy.

Though they don't know it, these characters are living on the edge of a cliff. In fact, they fell off once receiving the news that their colleague Sergeant Doakes "was" the Bay Harbor Butcher (that Dexter—so good at managing the links between appearances and reality!). But I don't think many of them, or the show, will survive long if they were ever to learn that that nice, hardworking guy over in forensics is in fact, at his core, as cruel, heartless, and self-ish as any serial killer you can name. Of course we live at the edge of that cliff, especially if Stout is correct, and we too will take a big fall if someone close to us, or even that guy over in accounting with the ridiculous toupee and stupid jokes, turns out to be an illusion, a walking, talking shell of appearances, who felt nothing inside and wouldn't think twice about killing you if it didn't mean he'd probably lose his job and his freedom.

Look at What You've Been Thinking!

While one of *Dexter*'s rewards is letting us escape from that unpleasant thought about modern life (at least by letting Deb, La Guerta and the others shoulder the burden for a while), another is the front-row seat we get on all the psychological and philosophical complexity involved. While his true, hidden nature threatens to turn Miami Metro on its ear, and upend the lives of all the good, moral people (well, except for Quinn) who work there, it often feels like philosophy itself is strapped to Dexter's table, surrounded by competing theories of ethics, epistemology, and human existence, his knives about to slice into the assumptions underlying philosophy and its history.

If Dexter is so unlike us, why do we like him so much? Is this just a trick of the Hollywood light, or as the chapters in this book suggest, is Dexter's story a revealing window into our own world of Dark Assumptions about sex, death, aggression, and race? Or is Dexter best understood very differently as a *historical* monster, a man out of time, like a Roman warrior in downtown Miami or a brutal, punishing King thrown five centuries into the future?

What kind of ethics do Dexter and his assiduous devotion to Harry's Code really amount to? Good question. Some insist that Dex is a monster, no matter how good his doughnuts are. For other's he's a model ethical actor (except for all the blood, of course) who might be admired, if not quite emulated, by Immanuel Kant, himself. Yet others think all the blood Dexter spills is, all things considered, *a good thing*, and that our philosophers of law, ethics, and society could use a field trip to Miami and take very careful notes.

For others, the real Dexter is something else entirely. For all his self-criticism and search for understanding, he's not ultimately about ethics, justice, and morality. He's about aesthetics: Killing and looking *really good* when you do it—literally. There's a reason Dexter makes his killers see photographs of his victims before we cut to black. Dexter represents a way of life and can be seen as a superhero. In other chapters, Dexter emerges as a kind of artist, a Jackson Pollock addicted to red, or as a philosophical psychologist who shows us the real relationship between emotions and thought.

Perhaps the greatest significance of *Dexter* is the suggestion that the entire history of philosophy has been ignoring something very, very important. Socrates got the ball rolling with his famous quest for a person who truly possessed knowledge and his resulting injunction to "Know thyself." Of course, that's important. But it may be even more important for us to point our curiosity, or skepticism, and our philosophical tools in other directions—over at that guy in forensics, or maybe your logic teacher, your auto mechanic, your swim coach. You know, your yoga teacher may even *look* a bit like Dexter.

Unless, of course, you're one of the one-in-twenty-five. In that case, Socrates was spot on.

BODY PART I

Maiming and Necessity

1

The Killing Joke

JOHN KENNETH MUIR

Dexter Morgan, the unconventional protagonist portrayed by Michael C. Hall on Showtime's hit TV series *Dexter*, has frequently been cited by media outlets as the television heir to such notorious pop-culture serial killers and cinematic bogeymen as Hannibal Lecter (*Silence of the Lambs*) and Patrick Bateman (*American Psycho*).

In its original review of the series, *Daily Variety* noted that *Dexter* answers "the puzzling question of what Hannibal Lecter might do in his quieter moments." And, in an early first-season episode of the series originally aired in 2006, entitled "Return to Sender," Dexter actually adopts the name Patrick Bateman, M.D. as an alias; a deliberate homage to Morgan's colorful, anti-social predecessor.

However, if we look closer, Dexter's unique personality traits and special qualities may actually originate from a different literary and pop-culture tradition altogether.

Yes, Dexter Morgan is a serial killer, without question. But in every substantive way imaginable, he's also *a superhero*: a guardian who protects his turf, the city of Miami, from grave-and-gathering threats as assiduously as Batman patrols Gotham, Superman defends Metropolis, or Hercules upholds the honor of Thebes.

What Is a Superhero?

To see why Dexter Morgan might be a superhero—Miami's own Dark Knight—let's consider what a superhero really is. Without thinking about Dexter, I once gave the following definition of a superhero:

a character of extraordinary capabilities or powers who has a propensity to fight evil in all its forms, whether criminal, terrorist or demonic. For the most part, superheroes also wear unique or recognizable costumes that separate them from normal heroes, but even that distinction is not always the case. (John Kenneth Muir, *The Encyclopedia of Superheroes on Film and Television*, McFarland, 2008, pp. 7–8)

Consider how this broad definition applies to Dexter Morgan. At first blush it might be tempting to suppose that Dexter possesses no "super" powers at all; that he can't fly, for instance. Yet, Batman also possesses no overt super powers—just a super-wallet and super intellect, which permit him to invent and build miraculous vehicles and gadgets. Ditto the Green Hornet.

And the Punisher, an ex-Federal agent working against organized crime, also boasts no overt super-human qualities, only what Erich Lichtenfeld calls "a super arsenal."[1]

But a deeper inspection suggests that Dexter actually does possess an extraordinary capability, a "power." Indoctrinated by his foster father (James Remar) into the informal discipline called the "The Code of Harry," Dexter Morgan has honed the *extraordinary ability* to ferret out evil-doers, in this case, criminals.

This ability is a sort of "radar" beyond normal ken that permits Dexter to detect the black, monstrous truth roiling inside the hearts of murderers who, like Dexter himself, are able to successfully blend into mainstream society and escape legal sanction. Another way to describe this trait—Dexter's criminal-detect radar—is to evoke the famous tag-line of the early, 1930s superhero created by William B. Gibson, known as "The Shadow:" "*Who knows what evil lurks in the hearts of men?*" Answer: Dexter.

Another popular and long-lived superhero, Marvel's Spider-Man, possesses similar radar. His "spider senses" alert Peter Parker to dangers and threats in close proximity. Dexter's radar is also finely tuned. He can detect the truth about criminals hiding in plain sight, the shadowy truth behind monstrous men like Mike Donovan ("Dexter," Season 1), Matt Chambers ("Crocodile," Season 1), Jeremy Downs, or even Harry's Nurse ("Popping Cherry," Season 1). In "Popping Cherry," Dexter refers to his peculiar power as "*impeccable instincts*," but Dexter's ability to utilize this

---

[1] Erich Lichtenfeld, *Actions Speak Louder* (Wesleyan University Press, 2007), p. 306.

power (this radar) to target only wrong-doers clearly fits into the super-hero tradition.

So two aspects of my superhero definition have been fulfilled in *Dexter*. Dexter fights evil, destroying murderers the law can't touch, and he does so using a power that "mere" mortal men do not possess: the ability to see the truth of a man's soul just by looking. Even Deb recognizes this unique aspect of Dexter, noting in the first episode the amazing accuracy of his "hunches" regarding murder suspects. So, while it's abundantly true that Dexter cannot fly, spin webs, or telepathically communicate with sea-life (like DC's Aquaman), this alone does not disqualify him for consideration as a superhero. Powers come in all shapes and sizes.

Another element of this superhero definition suggests that a superhero is *differentiated from "normal heroes" by his very appearance*, by the gear he adopts or uses in his just pursuits; by the uniform or costume he wears while combating evils. Again, this is not always true of superheroes. For instance, Buffy the Vampire Slayer does not suit up in a recognizable costume to fight her demonic enemies on the Hellmouth. Steve Austin, the "Six-Million Dollar Man," similarly adorns no costume to battle his foes.

But oddly enough, Dexter Morgan does adhere to this quality of the super-heroic world, at least after a fashion. When he becomes, "The Dark Passenger" (his secret identity?), Dexter does adorn very specific gear, a costume of sorts. He dons *latex gloves*, so as not to leave fingerprints behind at a crime scene; he ties on *an apron or smock* to block blood spatter; and even, on many occasions, Dexter wears *a helmet with a glass visor*—a superhero's "mask," for lack of a better word.

Just as Batman battles criminals using an array of gadgets, from batarangs to bat-grappling hooks, Dexter, as Miami's "Dark Passenger," suits-up with a multitude of crime-fighting tools or instruments. In this case, those tools include plastic or *rubber sheets, duct tape, hypodermic syringes, a scalpel*, and rather disturbingly, a *drill*. To Dexter—much like Batman before him—these are *"the necessary tools of the trade*," per the pilot episode's dialogue.

In "Crocodile," the association between Dexter's accoutrements and the traditional iconography of the comic-book superhero is established visually, though without explicit comment, when a sheet of plastic billows like a roiling wave before him, not at all unlike Superman's majestic red cape. The wind, we must assume, is at both their backs.

On a much more *metaphorical* level, the series *Dexter* obsesses on the important superhero concept of the mask, a commonly featured wardrobe touch in the milieu of superheroes. Batman, Spider-Man, Daredevil, Captain America, Robin, Green Lantern, the Green Hornet, Hawkman, the Flash, Batgirl, and other popular examples of the superhero all wear masks that cloak their true identity from the public. But in the unusual case of Dexter, the "Dark Passenger" represents Morgan's true identity, and in day-to-day contact with his sister, Deb, and with his superiors and co-workers on the Miami police force, Dexter wears a mask of normalcy; hiding his secret identity, the Dark Passenger, from view.

In various episodes of the series, Dexter refers to the "face" or "mask" he must put on to hide his identity as a superhero/serial killer and function normally in society-at-large. Dexter calls this cloak *"the invisible mask of sympathy"* in "Crocodile" and notes that he enjoys Halloween in "Let's Give the Boy a Hand" because it is the time of year that *"everyone wears a mask, not just me."*

And when he must broach "normal" people (like Rita) in that episode, Dexter notes that *"it's time to put on my mask."* After that . . . *to the batmobile, Old Chum?*

Deeds Not Words

The roots of the popular superhero myth can be pinpointed in America's long-standing fascination with a much older genre: *the Western*. George Slosser, curator of the Science Fiction and Fantasy Collection at the University of California, Riverside, opined in the year 2002 that superheroes, like frontier cowboys before them, symbolize "the embodiment of the American myth of the lone, rugged individual who comes into society and cleans it up. We all want to do it, but we don't know how to do it. We live our everyday lives that don't allow for this kind of simplistic vision. So we cheer for it" (*Christian Science Monitor*, May 3rd, 2002, p. 13).

Roger Jewett and John Shelton Lawrence dig a little deeper in their work, *Captain America and the Crusade Against Evil: The Dilemma of Zealous Nationalism*. They explain that in "the modern superhero story of the American monomyth . . . helpless communities are redeemed by lone saviors who are never integrated into their societies and never marry at the story's end. In effect, like the Gods, they are permanent outsiders to the human community."

These two descriptors get us closer to understanding Dexter in the terms of superhero lore. It's easy to view his illegal night-time work as the Dark Passenger as being that of a "lone, rugged individual" who cleans up a dirty society, in this case, Miami. And, since law enforcement in Miami can't kill monsters like the Ice Truck Killer without Dexter's aid, it is indeed relatively "helpless" before such rampaging criminals. Just look at all LaGuerta's ill-fated press-conferences and busts, forever pinpointing the wrong perp (like Tony Tucci) for evidence that the world needs superheroes, and specifically that Miami needs Dexter.

This aspect of Dexter's world is part and parcel of the superhero myth, the idea that a vigilante (like Batman) *must be the one to save the imperiled town or city*. As Pramod Nayar explains,

> The superhero vigilante represents a symbolic escape-route for law enforcers; it is only by stepping out of the bounds of the law that the law can be upheld. Where the police, the judiciary, and the State cannot bring criminals to justice, the superhero steps in to do so by extra legal means, and violence. Violence is in fact so integral to the superhero comic book, and—there is blatant disregard for civil rights and a flirtation with fascism in Batman and other superhero books." (*Reading Culture*, Sage, 2006, p. 108)

In *Dexter*, Harry's Code is an explicit validation of this vigilante approach to justice; the approach of superheroes just like Bob Kane's Caped Crusader. During a flashback in the premiere episode, Harry informs a young Dexter that the *"police can't catch all"* the criminals, that there are some villains who always escape justice and yet must still be dealt with. He trains Dexter to be that man; the agent, outside the law, who can *"balance the books"* (per "Crocodile,") and bring about a sense of true justice. And, like the Dark Knight, Dexter prowls the night, closing—vigilante-style—unsolved cases.

And if violence is "integral" to the superhero genre, it's certainly integral to Dexter's world too. He overpowers, kills, and chops up the criminals whom the authorities can't catch. Dexter generally allows for no appeals concerning a criminal's civil rights, either, though in the case of young Jeremy Downs, he grants the boy a second chance because he senses something kindred in him. (A potential "boy-wonder"-style side-kick, perhaps? One who "sees" the world as Dexter does?)

Dexter, like many superheroes, is permanently an outsider too, one "never integrated" into society. The superhero, according to Warren Smith, is "usually a troubled, marginal figure,"[2] Ray Browne and Lawrence Kreiser agree that although superheroes "co-operate with and advance the causes of law enforcement institutions, they operate as outsiders without any legal authorization to use the force they exert."[3] This fits Dexter to a tee. Though he marries Rita in season three, his wife is eventually killed and Dexter returns— after that relatively brief interval of human companionship—to outsider status.

He periodically feeds clues to his sister, Deb, a recently promoted homicide detective in Miami, yet he never feels a part of the police despite his day job as a blood spatter analyst (*"Normal people are so hostile,"* he laments). Dexter perpetually remains an outsider, faking all human interactions. He notes that this unusual masquerade represents his *"burden,"* explicitly, but at the same time *his gift,* the thing that enables him to catch criminals. *"The inability to feel has its advantages,"* he notes in "Love, American Style." At least *"some of the time."*

This is a very Peter Parker way of looking at things. In Sam Raimi's *Spider-Man* (2002), Parker (Toby Maguire) laments his responsibilities as a crime fighter, and refers to his duty and capabilities as, explicitly both a "gift" and a "curse." Dexter's outsider status and radar are similarly, both a "burden" and an "advantage," as the dialogue points out. This is the crux of superhero-dom: the power to fight evil, and the fact that the power prevents real connection to those the hero protects.

Origin Stories: The Orphan Makes Good

Even Dexter's very lineage seems to qualify him for superhero status. Many of the greatest superheroes are orphans. Superman loses his father Jor-El and mother, Lara, when the distant planet Krypton explodes. Bruce Wayne, Batman, is orphaned when his millionaire parents are murdered. Peter Parker, Spider-Man, is also an orphan, one who eventually loses even his adopted father, Uncle Ben

---

[2] In Matthew Higgins and others, *Science Fiction and Organization*, Routledge, 2001, p. 181.

[3] Ray B. Browne and Lawerence A. Kreiser, eds., *Popular Culture Values and the Arts* (McFarland, 2009), p. 92.

Parker. In many cases, these famous superheroes heroes can interface with their parents only through flashbacks (in the case of Batman) or "stored memories" in the Fortress of Solitude (in the case of Superman). These father-son exchanges or *tête-à-têtes* appear frequently in superhero films, including *Superman: The Movie* (1978), *Superman II* (1981), *Batman Forever* (1995), *Spider-Man 2* (2004), and *Batman Begins* (2005).

Dexter is also an orphan, an abandoned child adopted by a kindly father-figure, Harry Morgan, who's also only accessible to Dexter in the present through memories and flashbacks. Specifically, Dexter was recovered by Harry at an egregiously bloody crime scene, and the traumatized boy had no sense of where he came from, or how he got there. He was a virtual amnesiac with no history or background, except that which Harry could imprint upon him. Many episodes feature flashbacks of Harry guiding Dexter to manhood, of "fathering" him in the ways of maturity and heroics.

In the article "Why Are There So Many Orphan Heroes and Superheroes?" Tracy Elli explains that a viewer or reader can

> evaluate orphan heroes and superheroes as a means by which angst, loneliness, and independence are emphasized. The comic-book-type superhero is usually one who suffers always, or at least most of the time. Particularly when such a hero must deal with the death of murdered parents, his mission in life may be to create a world safe for other children. Loss of even one parent can be intensely traumatic and forever alter a child's life, and superheroes may do all in their power to prevent this fate for other children. (<http//wisegeek.com>)

Taking this explanation as our cue, *the origin story of an orphan* boasts multiple purposes for the superhero, and thus for Dexter Morgan too. The story of a "tragic past" connects him to children— *always a symbol of tomorrow, or our hope for the future* in such dramas—and this is plain from the get-go with *Dexter*. When he confronts child-murderer Mike Donovan in the series premiere, Dexter immediately sets himself apart from such scum. "*I'm not like you,*" Dexter insists. "*I have standards.*"

Dexter's interactions with Cody and Astor reinforce his connection to children. He preserves their innocence as much as he can, and seems to relate to them better than to adults, perhaps because they don't wear the deceitful emotional "masks" that other adults often do. Children are exactly what they seem, innocent. Dexter does not have to navigate hidden emotions in dealing with them.

The proverbial heroic origin story and status as orphan also provides an important mystery or puzzle for the hero to solve: *where did he or she come from?* In *Dexter,* this mystery is enunciated in a season-long, multi-part story-arc, as Dexter Morgan discovers, step by step, the identity of his biological parents, and then the fact that he has a biological brother who shares his murderous predilections, though not Dexter's moral "Code" or sense of standards. In this case, that brother is the evil Ice Truck Killer who has been taunting him since the first episode began.

We already know that Dexter is a loner, but Dexter Morgan's status as an orphan deepens his angst and sense of loneliness. After he dispatches his villainous sibling, he arrives at a point where he has no one kindred in his life that he can really identify with. The Ice Truck Killer, his nemesis and his brother, has thus realized what author Katherine A Fowkes calls *"the shadow potential of all superheroes,"*[4] the capacity to use their extraordinary power for evil rather than good.

"Superhero stories," writes Sharon Packer, "show that a character can be a hero or a socially-phobic coward. They also show that heroes can direct righteous anger towards the social good or can misdirect it for the sake of evil, and become villains."[5] That's Rudy's journey, and it's amusing to note how the first featured *Dexter* "villain" is an amalgam of characteristics from Batman's famous rogue's gallery. Like the Riddler, the Ice Truck Killer leaves behind puzzles (photographs, actually) for Dexter to use as clues in apprehending him. And like Mr. Freeze, the Ice Truck Killer uses a "cold" conveyance (an ice truck), freeze-dries his enemies, and even leaves clues (like painted finger-nails) in blocks of ice.

The hero-villain relationship of Dexter and the Ice Truck Killer recalls the superhero genre in another fashion. It's the "I Made You / You Made Me" syndrome, or the *"two-sides of the same coin"* dynamic. Both Dexter and Rudy are sociopaths, and both are powerful or extraordinary, but Dexter—via the Code of Harry—*"controls the chaos"* inside himself, harnessing it to catch villains.

---

[4] Katherine A Fowkes, *The Fantasy Film* (Wiley-Blackwell, 2010), p. 129.
[5] Sharon Packer, *Superheroes and Superegos* (Greenwood, 2010), p. 233.

Rudy, on the other hand, uses his abilities with no sense of restraint and no sense of direction towards any social good. He kills innocents (prostitutes) and constructs a devilish game to draw out his sibling, Dexter. He just wants a playmate who shares his "hobby," and for a while it seems Dexter is actually tempted. But ultimately, in learning about his past as an "orphan," Dexter finds that there is no biological connection that can bring him peace. His family of origin is only the fulcrum for more pain and suffering, and Dexter ultimately chooses to destroy Rudy and rescue Deb. Metaphorically, Dexter selects Harry's family—and by extension, Harry's Code—over his biological family.

The Superhero Syndrome

Some people may look at Dexter Morgan and conclude that he's simply a very damaged human being, a very sick man who has found a socially-valuable (if illegal) outlet for his sickness. Those same people may be surprised to learn that there's also a narcissistic disorder or "superhero syndrome" in the DSM IV. Among the symptoms are a lack of empathy, a preoccupation with fantasies of power, a belief in one's "uniqueness" and a dependence on interpersonal exploitation.

Once more, Dexter fits the definition. He often notes that he can't love or feel empathy, but if he did, it would be aimed at Deb, Cody, and Astor. Also, Dexter occasionally fantasizes that the world knows of his exploits and champions him and frequently speaks of the fact that he doesn't fit in with "normal people," that he's "different." And as much as we may like Dexter, he's certainly exploitative on an interpersonal level. When Deb comes up with a behavioral profile that would target Dexter as the Ice Truck Killer, Dexter knowingly sends her in an opposite direction, playing on her insecurity and threatening her status on the job.

The Only Truly Decent Man Left on the Planet

In 1988, DC Comics published a tale called *Batman: The Killing Joke*, by Alan Moore. Today, gazing at *Dexter* with its splendid sense of humor and subversive social commentary, you must wonder if the series' producers are also telling us a kind of "killing joke."

Dexter feels no emotions. He *kills* people. He also breaks the law. Dexter even admires a good, clean kill on occasion (even of

innocent people; in the case of the Ice Truck Killer's handiwork).
And yet, he is undeniably the series protagonist, the "hero" of this
particular tale. As viewers, we root for him each and every week.

What message are the makers of this series attempting to trans-
mit here? Why have they elevated Dexter to the role of a superhero
when his behavior is so *anti-social*? Susan Amper starts to get at
this point:

> Our empathy for Dexter goes deeper than merely hoping he does not
> get caught. As Dexter grapples with life, we witness his struggle and
> sympathize. We can see ourselves in Dexter: his feelings of alien-
> ation, his wry take on the people around him and their incomprehen-
> sible behavior. But this is scary. If I identify with a serial killer, what
> does that say about me? (In Sara Waller, *Serial Killers,* Wiley-
> Blackwell, 2010, p. 105)

A way to ameliorate that lurking fear in the audience and foster
deeper identification with Dexter, is to associate him with the greatest of the great, the paragon of the heroic form: the superhero.

By providing Dexter a costume of sorts; by showcasing Dexter's
unusual "serial killer sense" or radar for pinpointing evil-doers, by
gifting Dexter a personal history as an orphan in keeping with
much of superhero lore and tradition, the writers and producers of
this clever TV drama allow the viewer to relax a little and see that,
in a certain context and from a certain viewpoint, Dexter is a laudable, even admirable figure, despite his narcissistic, anti-social tendencies. So there's no need to feel bad or afraid of the feelings of
"connection" Dexter's plight engenders in us.

There's also some extreme irony here, that so-called killing joke.
Dexter showcases us a world in which rampant, overwrought, out-
of-control emotion has caused the downfall or isolation of many,
many good people. The dramatis personae who orbit Dexter are all
psychologically damaged to one degree or another. Dexter recognizes this most clearly in Rita, in the first episode of Series 1, but
Deb is seen to be damaged too. She is so lonely and has such low
self-esteem that she ends up constantly pursuing the wrong man.
This almost gets her killed. She's the walking-wounded, perhaps
because she feels Harry always preferred Dex.

Likewise, LaGuerta is so driven by the emotion of ambition that
she can't see straight; she can't connect to other people in a meaningful fashion. Another detective, Angel feels things so passion-

ately that he cheats on his wife and loses the most important relationship in his life. And Doakes—J. Jonah Jameson to Dexter's Peter Parker—is an abrasive, hostile, closed-off personality who breaks the rules, and denigrates others. He's suspicious and almost paranoid.

It's no wonder that these men and women can't solve crimes, or mete out justice. Dexter's capacity to be separated from his emotions literally makes him a superhero in such company. Where the others are prone to emotional outbursts, Dexter is pretty stable by comparison. He alone can see *dispassionately* the way things are, and "who" people really are under their masks, under their veneers.

Because he lacks emotionality, but boasts a moral code, Harry's Code, Dexter truly is the last decent man in Miami, one who understands something important about life; something that America has forgotten in its post-911 rage and anxiety: *Justice is blind. Justice is impartial.*

The pursuit of justice is not about passions; that's merely vengeance. On the contrary, the "killing joke" is that Dexter, a sociopath who feels nothing beyond "the surface," is ideally suited to mete out justice because he doesn't feel love or hate, amity or enmity. Unclouded by the human concerns and passions of those around him, Dexter is an impartial moral arbiter. Where others are clouded by their passion, Dexter's lack of emotionality, lack of belonging allows him to be reasonable, rational and, like *Star Trek*'s Mr. Spock (another outsider), even logical.

Perhaps Dexter is indeed the Superman for our day and age: an outsider to humanity who can comment objectively upon it, and act in its best interest. No, he can't leap tall buildings in a single bound, but he's definitively immune to the toxic passions that infect our national discourse, divide us into Red States and Blue States, and celebrate uncontrolled emotions and unreasoned, vitriolic arguments and soundbites. In his unique way, Dexter is a champion for truth and justice—even if his clinical approach to punishing evil is not precisely the American way.

2

Dexter's Pointy Ears

ABROL FAIRWEATHER

Dexter's a perfect case study in emotion precisely because he doesn't have any. This may not be exactly the right way to put it. Lots of things don't have emotions, but are not for that reason great resources for understanding them. Consider your coffee maker, the book in your hand, perhaps your favorite pet, though the latter may be an interesting borderline case depending on your pet preferences. These non-emotional items are not as fruitful case studies because they are so unlike us in so many other ways that the differences we see in them and ourselves could be due to the fact that they are made of plastic or paper, as much as their lack of emotion.

But Dexter, aside from killing lots of killers (let's call this *meta-killing*), is a pretty normal guy. He drinks beer, has a job, gets laid; the stuff of life, the kind of life typical of members of our species in the twenty-first century. It's these two facts together that make Dexter a particularly interesting case study in emotion. He appears to have in place all the things that give rise to emotions in regular folk like us; he just doesn't have the emotions. This is clearly true of the 'early Dexter', which will be the Dexter of interest here, though things get more complicated in Season 5, and are maybe even getting emotional! So, the differences we see between him and ourselves are most likely explained by his lack of what we have: emotion.

You may not know many actual people who're quite like Dexter, but you probably know at least one Vulcan that is: Spock. Yes, the guy from *Star Trek* with pointy ears. Just like Dexter, Spock reasons quite well, he is able to make decisions concerning what matters and what ought to be done in light of his values. But he does all of this without having the emotional feelings that humans like Captain Kirk or you and me would have if we were doing what Spock does. Moreover, it appears that Spock is quite successful as Kirk's advisor precisely because of his lack of emotion. That is what allows him, like Dexter, to do his thing and do it so well.

There are differences between Spock and Dexter. Being Vulcan rather than human, Spock's pointy ears make him look a good bit different than Kirk and Bones, and not just in the way that Dexter looks anatomically different from Maria LaGuerta, Deb, and Rita (because they are girls), or Vince Masuka, for that matter. Spock also did a lot less serial-killing! But, these differences need not stand in the way of fruitful comparison. Ironically, we will see that much can be learned about us good ol' emotional types—assuming you will continue to have any emotions by the time you're done reading this chapter—by looking further into these two unemotional types.

Dexter's Loss Is Our Gain

Dexter's traumatic past is our philosophical opportunity. Because young Dexter sat in a large pool of his mother's blood watching her being mutilated and destroyed by a chainsaw wielding drug dealer, he doesn't have emotions. Sad though this may be, it presents a nice philosophical opportunity. Because Dexter is still so much like the rest of us, we can see what effects emotions themselves, rather than other aspects of our being, have in us by seeing what effects are lost when they are absent in Dexter.

John Stuart Mill would approve of our philosophical methodology. From a moral point of view, Mill would examine the consequences of Dexter's meta-killing. As a Utilitarian, he would ask whether Dexter's meta-killing is improving the balance of pleasure over pain for the citizens of Miami, and perhaps for the world as a whole. This is a very interesting moral question—is Dexter making the world a happier place? Of course, his victims will feel considerable pain as they sit neatly wrapped and prepared on their death table viewing pictures of their own victims while looking up at Dexter's stubbly, smiling face, and receive that little slice on their cheek right before the knife plunges into their chest. But, their pain just counts as one factor, and the preservation of their future would-be victim's lives would certainly balance that out, and then some. On the other hand, the homicide division of Miami Metro will have a lot of unsolved murders if Dexter keeps murdering their murderers. And we have to consider the raw pleasure Dexter himself gets from the killing as well.

While this is an interesting approach, we're going to steer clear of morals and use a different approach to understand emotion through Dexter, one based on Mill's Method of Difference. Roughly, this tells us that if we want to understand the cause of a certain phenomenon E, we look for two kinds of cases. One where E is present and a number of other factors (A, B, C, D) are also present, and second where one of these other factors (A, B, C, or D) is not present and neither is E. We can figure out the causal effects of some phenomenon by deleting only it from a situation and then seeing what else is deleted, because this tells us what is present due to the presence of that factor itself, rather than other variables in the situation as a whole.

Let's apply this to our favorite meta-killer. Because emotions are missing in Dexter, something else (E) is missing in him as well. Whatever this something is, we have it, precisely because we have emotions. We want to know what this something else is and Dexter is just the guy to learn from. Whatever this something else is, Dexter doesn't have it.

The Spock Problem

Imagine yourself almost as you are now. You have beliefs about how the world works, you have values and judgments about what matters, you have a body and can move around, *but you have no emotions*. Now ask yourself: What else would be missing from my life because my emotions are missing? Spock, Dexter, and the philosopher Robert Nozick will help us figure this out. Spock, while showing no emotion and being very, very rational, reliably advised the very emotional Captain Kirk on the important decisions facing the starship *Enterprise*.

The philosopher Robert Nozick offered a thought experiment called "The Spock Problem."[1] Nozick uses Spock to ask whether we regular, emotional folks would actually be better off being like Spock; being rational, having beliefs and making value judgments, but having no emotional feelings that come from them. This is how

---

[1] Robert Nozick, *The Examined Life* (Simon and Schuster, 1989).

you just imagined yourself at the beginning of this paragraph. You are all in the same boat now! Like Spock, you and Dexter can have non-emotional feelings like pain and pleasure, tickles, itches and toothaches. Dexter, like Spock, is also pretty darn good at what he does, presumably because he is not hindered by emotions. Unlike Spock, Dexter is a bit cooler, has better luck with the ladies, and loves killing killers, but these don't seem to be relevant differences for the point at hand. The "problem" Nozick poses is to explain why we wouldn't be better off without emotions.

Notice the following interesting point about the Spock Problem: while it seems obvious that oodles and oodles of important things would be missing from life if your emotions were missing (for example having friends), you couldn't be emotionally bummed out by the fact that you don't have friends because we're imagining that you don't have emotions to begin with! As my friend used to say, "If I had feelings, that would really hurt." Saying why an emotion-less life would be a poorer life is surprisingly difficult. Your lack of emotion cannot cause you any emotional troubles!

What, then, does Nozick say about why the Spock-like life is an impoverished life? Nozick concludes that emotions connect us to the world of value much as vision connects us to the world of shape and color. Emotions are *value perceptions*. When we see a red ball, we know redness and roundness directly by being acquainted with roundness and redness, rather than abstractly knowing them through descriptions of redness and roundness that we read in a book (one which is neither red nor round).

Nozick says that external values actually create an internal replica of themselves inside of us when we respond to situations emotionally. The value of what we take pride in comes to dwell within us and we are directly, experientially knowing it when we are proud. We feel the value of what we are proud of (such as neatly slicing someone's jugular) when we feel pride, and this is what makes the feeling of pride important. Simply put, emotions connect us more deeply and directly to value than mere reasoning can ever do. With emotions, we feel our values.

If Nozick's right, Spock doesn't have this kind of access to value. He can judge that certain events of the Starship were good, but he can't feel that goodness. Unlike Spock, you feel the good-ness of good things, and the badness of bad things when you have emotional responses to them. Since values vary, people will have experiential confrontations with value on different occasions and in different ways. Perhaps this is a way in which emotions will also cause conflict. But, despite these differences and potential conflicts, we all experience value when we have emotions, and this is why they are important to us.

The Dexter Problem

How do these reflections apply to Dexter? This is *The Dexter Problem*. It appears that Dexter feels neither remorse nor love, nor does he experience deep bonds of friendship, regret, pride, shame, or disgust. He doesn't feel these things in his relationships with Rita, Deb, or Trinity. Does Dexter feel emotions about his favorite pastime, killing killers? This is complicated. If we take Dexter at his word, he has no emotions and thus no emotions about killing killers. On the other hand, he only feels satisfaction when he kills killers and he sees a moral imperative to do so. Perhaps killing is the only time he gets to feel emotion. When Miguel Prado asks Dexter what it feels like to kill a killer, he says "justice." So, he definitely feels something. But is it an emotion?

To say that Dexter does not feel emotions is not to say that he feels nothing at all. This is an important point in understanding the nature of emotions. Dexter feels tired, he feels behind on duties, he enjoys the sun on his skin when he's on his boat, and he sure seemed to enjoy some sexual lust with his "short-lived" girlfriend Lila. And he enjoys killing. This does not show that Dexter actually has *emotions*, it just shows that there is a basic difference between emotional and non-emotional feelings. Understanding what emotions are will require knowing just what marks the difference between the two, the subtle difference between an emotional feeling and a 'mere feeling', as we might call it. To understand that difference better, we need to understand Dexter a bit better.

When Dexter is killing, he sometimes thinks about the fact that he's taking the life of a human being, and the impact on the lives of other human beings his killing will have. When at home with Rita, he thinks about how much she really loves him, or when he's at work, about how Deb really needs and trusts him. He also realizes that he does not have anything close to kindred or appropriate feelings towards others in these situations. Most of us would naturally feel some sort of regret, shame, or fear if we acted in ways that undermined the things we value, or didn't show an appropriate response to the things we value, and some sort of pride or self-respect when we do. This is the part that Dexter does-n't have. He often has the thoughts that an emotionally equipped member of the species would have, including relatively accurate beliefs about what he is doing, and values much like decent folk have, but no emotional reaction or feeling follows from them. This is essential to being Dexter. Most of us wouldn't be able to do what Dexter does precisely because we would have the emotional feel-ings normally aroused by the beliefs and values Dexter has.

Emotional feelings are thus ones that 'run through' our beliefs and values, feelings imbued with and saturated by an often com-plex web of cognitive states, including beliefs, values, judgments, perspectives, construals, and ways of seeing the world. Mere feel-ings, or non-emotional feelings, do not depend on or run through our beliefs and values. Dexter's non-emotional feelings of pleasure while having a beer on his boat are due to the way his body reacts to the warm sun and cold beer. On the other hand, were we to feel guilty for killing Miguel, that emotional feeling of guilt would be explained by our beliefs and values. Likewise, we feel pride in things only if we believe that we did them and that they are valu-able things to do. This is a very different kind of feeling than a tickle or an itch, or the pain of being bludgeoned by a baseball bat. That would be painful no matter what our beliefs and values may be, but pride is a feeling we have only when certain beliefs and values are in place. And so, one interesting thing about Dexter is that he often believes the things we would believe when we have emotions, but he doesn't have the emotional part. He has the beliefs that connect us to emotional feelings, but he doesn't con-nect to the feelings.

This small difference not only helps us identify what is unique to emotional feelings, it also shows us something essential to Dexter's success. Dexter wouldn't be nearly as good of a killer if he had the affective, emotional connections to his victims, his wife, and sister that most people would have. Maybe that's what pre-vents most people from being meta-killers. This is somewhat sur-prising because we often think that violence comes from an excess of emotion and lack of reason, as with crimes of passion, hate and vengeance. In Dexter, it seems to be the opposite; he kills because he is too rational and not emotional.

Dexter is thus better off because he has no emotions, and pre-sents a particularly compelling version of The Spock Problem. At least, given his current life plan to kill as many killers as he can, he is plainly better off than he would be if he had emotions. It might be that he would have a different life plan if he had emotions, but this may just emphasize that he is better off without them. Harry, his dad and mentor, would certainly agree.

As Goes Dexter, So Go We?

If this is true of Dexter, how can we be sure this is not also true of us? Perhaps we too would be better off without emotions. We really *could be* more like Dexter if we wanted to. Since emotional feelings are tied to beliefs and values, we can affect our emotional life by affecting our beliefs and values. We are not simply passive receivers of emotions, but have an indirect control over which emotions we have by controlling what we believe and value. If you simply stopped thinking about your ex-boyfriend or ex-girlfriend, or stopped caring about them, you wouldn't have emotions about them. You are then becoming more Dexter-like by having fewer emotions.

Perhaps we would become less emotional by becoming more Buddha-like and cultivating a detached perspective on our own mental life. There is much about human psychology we would have to examine to know how far we could take either emotion-eradication strategy, but it seems possible that we could become more Dexter-like if we made a goal of it. Dexter did not need to go through the training and discipline we would have to go through. He presumably had this done for him when those drug dealers killed his mom with a chainsaw in front of his little eyes and left him sitting in a pool of her blood. We would take different paths to the summit, but it looks like there is a path we could travel to get there too.

The question now is whether this would be desirable. We could be like Dexter, but should we? Dexter is pretty cool, in a science-geek kinda way. His wife is hot (so long as she lived), kids are cute, job is exciting, he's in good shape, and most importantly, his dreams have largely come true—he kills lots of killers. While this might not appear to be a laudable life project to most us, perhaps that is because we're hindered and small minded due to our emotions.

Anyway, who are we to say? Whatever floats your boat. The important question is whether we, like Dexter, would be better positioned to achieve our important life aims if we didn't have emotions, or if there would be something essential and valuable missing from our life. That is, what value, if any, do emotional feelings bring to our life?

The Good Life and The Dexter-like Life

Remembering Nozick's answer to the Spock Problem and Mill's Method of Difference, perhaps we can now say clearly what is missing from Dexter's life. Dexter intellectually recognizes the value of Rita, Deb, and his kids, but he doesn't *feel* their value. Nozick says that feeling value is itself something valuable, and Mill would add that this is the 'something else' that would be missing when emotions are missing. Fair enough, but does Dexter *feel* the value of meta-killing? When he tells Miguel that killing killers feels like justice, it sure sounds like a value perception. On the other hand, he might just be reporting that he believes he is doing the just thing, and he enjoys certain non-emotional pleasures in the process, since, as he often tells us, he has no emotions. It's a subtle difference, but an important one. For Dexter, since meta-killing is an act of justice, knowing the justness of meta-killing directly and experientially, perhaps through the emotion pride, would be even better than the meta-killing alone. Taking Dexter at his word and assuming that he has no emotions, poor Dexter's life is deprived of this kind of value. His life is deficient compared to the same life lived *with* emotion.

This seems to answer one of our main questions. What's the unique benefit that emotions bring to life? Feeling our values, rather than just knowing them abstractly. In the process, we seem to have an answer to the other main question: why not be like Dexter? Because we would not be feeling our values, we would just know them as abstractions. This also explains why we think of emotions as deep. Not only do emotions contain a sometimes large range of our beliefs and values in them, thus containing much of who we are, but we become more deeply immersed in our own values when we respond to the world emotionally. We actually experience our values. This shows us something valuable that we have (assuming you have emotions) but that Dexter does not.

I think Dexter can strike back here. Simply to show that there is a kind of value that the emotional life has which Dexter does not have is not to show that the former is a better life than Dexter's. He gets to be a top notch meta-killer, which those fettered by emotion either would not be able to pull off or would be mediocre at were they able to muster it at all. Because of the supreme importance of killing killers for Dexter, he would hate himself if he gained emotions and became unable to kill killers because of these emotions. Even if he got the extra value of feeling the value of his relationship with Rita and his kids, that his job is cool and he has a great sister, the inability to kill killers would presumably outweigh these. So, even if emotions bring some form of value to our lives, the value of what we get by not having them may be greater. Still, Dexter would have to admit that if he were able to continue to kill killers *and* have emotions about his success in doing so, then his life would be better than it currently is.

That may be the main question for Dexter, and points to the main question for the rest of us. Whether emotions are worth it will come down to whether we could do what matters most to us, and to do it well, if we were fully emotional. If we could, then the emotional life would be the better life because we will feel its value. If we could not, well, odd as it may sound, we might be better off being more like Dexter.

3

Dearly Damaged Dexter

DANIEL HAAS

Dexter Morgan is an uncomfortable character to root for. We're first introduced to him as he drives down the Miami strip, eagerly anticipating the coming night ("Dexter." Season 1). After weeks, perhaps months, of stalking a potential target, his hard work is about to culminate. He is going to kill Mike Donovan, husband, father of two, and leader of a successful boy's choir.

Many of the murders in Showtime's *Dexter* are played for laughs, but the Donovan murder is different. It's a cold horrific affair, one of the few times where the audience is really reminded that Dexter is a sadistic psychopathic killer who enjoys the suffering of his victims.

First, Dexter car-jacks Donovan by wrapping fishing wire around his neck and forcing him to drive to an abandoned warehouse. Once they're inside, Dexter throws Donovan against a wall and starts screaming, "Open your eyes and look at what you did." Donovan, clearly terrified, keeps his eyes closed. Dexter continues in a flat, emotionless voice, "Look or I'll cut your eyelids right off your face."

Donovan opens his eyes to see the rotting corpses of three little boys. You see, Donovan is a pedophile and a murderer and Dexter has recovered the bodies so that Donovan can be shown exactly why he is about to die. Crying, Donovan begs, "I couldn't help myself. Please, you have to understand."

Dexter smirks and says "Trust me. I definitely understand. See, I can't help myself either." He pauses. "Children, I could never do that. Not like you. Never, ever kids. I have standards." Dexter gives Donovan a sedative and prepares his body for the kill, which involves strapping him to a table and wrapping him in plastic-wrap. Dexter takes a blood sample from Donovan's cheek, a trophy of his latest kill. "Soon, you'll be packed into a few neatly wrapped Hefties, and my own small corner of the world will be a neater, happier place. A better place." He then proceeds to cut Donovan's body into pieces which will later be dumped in the ocean off Miami's shore.

I reproduce the scene to illustrate that Dexter is unquestionably a sadistic killer. He stalks, tortures, terrorizes, and brutally murders a person roughly every other episode. And he enjoys it. Yet there's something sympathetic about him. I hope I'm not alone in this, but I find myself rooting for Dexter to catch his victims and hoping that the Miami police never discover his real identity. After all, most of the people he kills are serial killers or rapists who deserve to be punished for their crimes. And Dexter really can't help himself. He's got a Dark Passenger compelling him to kill. So, it's not really his fault, is it?

But hold on. If I say that Dexter isn't really morally responsible because he can't help himself, well then what about all the killers that he stalks and kills? Current brain science seems to show that biology and childhood experiences play a causal role in determining whether or not someone becomes a psychopath. If that's true, then aren't the Trinity Killer and the Ice Truck Killer just as compelled to kill as Dexter is? And surely we want to say that the Ice Truck Killer is morally responsible for his psychotic behavior. What is moral responsibility anyhow? And is there a sense in which Dexter is morally praiseworthy for his decision to kill only other killers?

You're a Killer, I Catch Killers

You might think that it's just obvious that psychopaths, such as Dexter and the menagerie of serial killers he murders, are morally responsible for their actions. After all, they're running around Miami killing people. They're doing something wrong and that's all there is to it. They should be locked up and made to pay for their crimes.

Well, okay, I can sympathize with you on that. But there are many different kinds of responsibility. If a three-year-old child steals a chocolate bar while shopping with her parents we wouldn't really say that she's deserves to be held morally responsible for stealing. She's too young to understand that taking the chocolate without paying is wrong. Yes, she is causally responsible for causing something bad to happen, but is that the same as being morally responsible? This is a good teaching opportunity for her parents, but a child is not necessarily an appropriate target for moral blame. So, what makes moral responsibility difference from other kinds of responsibility?

First, there's a difference between legal and moral responsibility. Something can be illegal without being morally wrong. For example, in an early episode of Dexter ("Let's Give the Boy a Hand," Season 1), we find out that Dexter's girlfriend, Rita, has a neighbor with a yippy dog. The dog barks through most nights and keeps Rita and her children from sleeping. Rita eventually gets fed up and confronts her neighbor. She asks her to do something about the dog but her neighbor refuses. She says that the dog is her ex-boyfriend's, she doesn't really like it, and that she's just going to let it stay in her backyard and bark all it wants. Rita also learns that the dog is never taken for walks and is rarely fed. She also has really good reason to think that if the Humane Society or the police were called nothing would be done about the dog, as there are no obvious signs of animal abuse. Rita responds by breaking into her neighbor's yard, stealing the dog and giving it to a family with two young children that she knows will take care of and love it.

Now, what Rita did is unquestionably illegal. She broke into her neighbor's home and stole her pet. But it is not clear that she did something morally wrong. After all, she rescued an animal from abuse, gave it a good home, and she protected her children. It actually sounds as if she's done something morally right and that she deserves to be praised for her action.

Likewise, something can be morally wrong without being illegal. For example, cheating on your significant other is morally wrong but it's not illegal. When Dexter cheats on Rita with Lila, he does something morally wrong but he's not breaking any laws ("Dex, Lies, and Videotape," Season 2). And if we, as a society, decided that every moral transgression ought to be illegal, well, we'd all be in prison.

Serial killers are clearly breaking the law. And Dexter is just as legally responsible for murder as any other murderer would be. Even if many viewers admire his vigilante justice he's still legally on the hook for his ever-growing body count if he's ever caught. And I'm not trying to suggest that he should get off the hook for his crimes. While serial killers might fail to be morally responsible for their actions there are clear legal and pragmatic reasons for locking them up.

People can be responsible for their actions in both an attributive sense and an accountability sense.[1] It is easy to conflate these two notions of responsibility so we need to be careful. To attribute responsibility to someone is to make a factual judgment about what they have done or perhaps what kind of character they have. When we make this kind of judgment, we're saying that someone is causally responsible for an undesirable state of affairs or performed poorly at an assigned task. The little girl who steals a candy bar from a store is responsible for theft in an attributive sense. We can surely hold serial killers responsible for their actions in this way. Their actions clearly cause the death of their victims.

But we haven't said anything about whether or not the little girl deserves to be held accountable for her actions. While we attribute responsibility for stealing a chocolate bar to her, it's a further move to say that she is accountable for this theft and that she ought to be blamed and punished for stealing the chocolate bar because that is what she deserves. This second notion of responsibility is responsibility as accountability. To say that someone is accountable for their actions is to judge that the person ought to account for their behavior. It is to treat the person as deserving of sanction or retribution if they did something wrong or, if they did something right, it is to acknowledge that the person is deserving of praise. And there's at least some reason to think that for Dexter, the Ice Truck Killer, and other psychopaths, it would be unfair to hold them accountable for their actions in this sense.

I've Always Sensed There Was Something Off about Him

While it's possible that not all serial killers are psychopaths, many serial killers satisfy the criteria to be diagnosed as psychopaths. And there are several things that psychopaths are incapable of that might make it unfair to hold a serial killer who is also a psychopath morally accountable. First, serial killers might not be capable of being motivated by moral concerns. Psychopaths do not experi-

---

[1] Gary Watson, "Responsibility and the Limits of Evil: Variations on a Strawsonian Theme," in *Agency and Answerability: Selected Essays* (Oxford University Press, 2004), p. 226.

ence moral emotions such as guilt, regret, or empathy.[2] The exact cause of their impoverished emotional understanding is still unknown but the cognitive sciences have identified brain abnormalities and genetic sources as likely causes.[3] Note that these all are causal factors that the psychopath is in no way responsible for.

We're told over and over that Dexter and his brother do not feel anything. In one of Dexter's first inner monologues he tells us "I don't know what made me the way I am but whatever it was left a hollow place inside. People fake a lot of human interactions but I feel like I fake them all and I fake them very well. . . ." When describing his sister, Dexter tells us "She's the only person in the world that loves me. I think that's nice. I don't have feelings about anything but if I could have feelings about anything at all I'd have them for Deb."

Even his dating decisions are made without emotion. He decides to date Rita, a single mother of two who's the survivor of domestic abuse. Her abusive past has left her afraid of intimacy and sex, which suits Dexter well because his impoverished emotional life leaves him incapable of maintaining relationships that require emotional depth and intimacy. One of the running themes in Dexter and Rita's relationship is Dexter's attempts to fake emotional intimacy with Rita despite his lack of feelings.

The fact that psychopaths typically have an impoverished emotional life has led some philosophers to claim that they are incapable of being motivated for moral reasons. One reason for thinking that the average psychopath lacks the ability to be motivated by moral concerns is that psychopaths can't feel empathy. They can understand that people guide their behavior by moral demands and that moral norms give reasons for why it is wrong to hurt people, but they do not feel any of the emotions that tend to motivate other people to act on moral norms. For example, they lack the ability to feel compassion for the suffering of others. And often, they can accomplish their own goals best by ignoring moral demands. Without the ability to experience the emotional component of moral demands, psychopaths have a hard time seeing why

---

[2] Patricia Greenspan "Responsible Psychopaths," in *Philosophical Psychology* 16:3 (2003), p. 418.

[3] Georgie Ann Weatherby, Danielle M. Buller, and Katelyn McGinnis, "The Buller-McGinnis Model of Serial Homicidal Behaviour: An Integrated Approach" *Journal of Criminology and Criminal Justice Research and Education* 3:1 (2009).

moral demands ought to take precedence over other sorts of demands.

Like the businessman who says "I understand that it is morally wrong to harm the environment but this is business and I stand to make lots of money by harming the environment," the psychopath finds it impossible to set aside her own wants and needs in order to muster motivation to act on moral reasons. The businessman is unlike the psychopath in one crucially important respect. When he decides that moral obligations are less important than his economic success, it is not because he suffers from a brain abnormality. It's because of a moral failure that is directly attributable to his values and priorities. The psychopath, by contrast, lacks moral motivation, not because of a failure to properly prioritize the various demands that are placed upon him, but rather because of a physical inability to feel the emotions necessary to motivate himself to act upon moral demands.

The Ice Truck Killer is clearly like this. He's very bright and can understand the reasons people do moral things, like refraining from killing other people. He just doesn't feel any motivation to act on moral reasons. He understands that it is morally wrong to kill people but he just does not care and cannot bring himself to care. And he thinks his little brother, Dexter, is making a silly mistake by allowing himself to be constrained by Harry's Code. "You're trapped in a lie, little brother, the same lie they tried forcing me into," he tells him. "But you're not alone anymore, Dexter. You can be yourself with me . . ." And what the Ice Truck Killer has in mind by this is "a killer without reason or regret."

There's also reason to think that many serial killers are compelled to kill by irresistible desires. This is definitely the way Showtime portrays its serial killers. The second season's story-arc for Dexter involves him dealing with his murderous impulses as an addiction which eventually evolves into identifying with himself as a killer. He joins a drug addiction support group and spends much of the season struggling to "stay clean." Many of the serial killers we've seen in the series also experience their impulse to kill as an unwanted addiction. The Ice Truck Killer describes his desire to kill as a "hunger that is never satisfied." Dexter's Season 4 nemesis, the Trinity Killer, was compelled to recreate tragic deaths from his childhood again and again. He doesn't want to keep doing this and we see him building his own coffin at one point during the fourth season. He's thinking of killing himself to stop the cycle, to stop the irresistible homicidal urges he has grappled with for decades.

Psychopaths look as if they're incapable of being motivated by moral demands through no fault of their own. Many of the serial killers we see on *Dexter* look as if they suffer from an irresistible urge to kill. Many ethicists have argued that it would be unfair to blame someone if they couldn't help but do what they did. If serial killers really are incapable of doing other than what they do, then it looks as if they shouldn't be held morally accountable for their crimes.

A Little Bird with a Broken Wing

There's a second kind of ability that serial killers lack that could exempt them from being held morally accountable. When we learn about the tragic history of Dexter and his brother, Brian Moser, we note that their psychopathic behavior has deep roots in tragic early-childhood events that they were not responsible for. Dexter and his brother did not choose to have their mother brutally murdered in front of their eyes and they definitely did not choose to spend days locked in a shipping trailer sitting in her blood. Yet it's easy to see the traumatic, character-warping effect this tragic event had on the two boys. When forced to remember that event ("Truth Be Told," Season 1), Dexter thinks, "A buried memory forgotten all these years. It climbed inside me that day. And it's been with me ever since. My Dark Passenger . . . something nameless was born here. Something that lives in the deepest darkest hole of the thing called Dexter."

In flashbacks to a time before their mother's death, Dexter and Brian look like normal, rather sensitive little boys. Brian even compassionately puts a bandage on his brother's hurt knee. To oversimplify a complex psychological story, we might say that even though the brothers were predisposed to develop psychopathic tendencies they could have grown up to be productive, well-adjusted members of society. But their tragic childhoods combined with preexisting genetic dispositions caused them to become sadistic killers.

And if we flash-forward a few years in each child's life, it looks like it is sheer luck that placed Dexter in the care of Harry Morgan, the cop that discovers Dexter and Brian at the scene of their mother's murder ("Born Free," Season 1). In a show of compassion for the suffering child, Harry carries Dexter away from the bloody crime scene and takes him home to live with his family, eventually adopting him. Dexter was only three at the time of the murder and fortunately, was too young to really understand what had happened. His brother calls him "a little bird with a broken wing." Harry raises Dexter in a loving family and Dexter has a relatively normal childhood.

Brian was not so lucky. He was never put up for adoption. He was more severely traumatized by the incident, probably because he was old enough to understand what was happening and to vividly remember the horrific event. He ends up in a mental institution diagnosed with anti-social personality disorder. At twenty-one he is released and goes on to become the Ice Truck Killer.

What really distinguishes Dexter from his brother is that Dexter was raised in the loving home of Harry and Doris Morgan and educated in the Code of Harry by his adoptive father. When Dexter's father sees signs of psychopathic behavior in Dexter, such as killing small animals like dogs and cats, he realizes that there's a good chance that Dexter will grow up to be a killer. Harry loves his adoptive son and decides to train the boy so that he will know what police look for at crime scenes and be able to avoid getting caught. He also teaches Dexter a Code that ensures that the person he is killing is a 'bad' person such as a serial rapist or killer. Reflecting on his upbringing ("Popping Cherry," Season 1) Dexter thinks, "I am lucky. Without the Code of Harry I would have surely committed a senseless murder in my youth, just to watch the blood flow."

It's a matter of mere luck that Dexter and Brian end up as they do. Neither played any role in becoming a psychopath. This was something that happened to them. Furthermore, the fact that Dexter kills other serial killers and Brian kills prostitutes is ultimately because of factors beyond either of their control. Brian kills prostitutes because they're easy prey and maybe because his mother was also a prostitute, while Dexter kills serial killers because his adoptive father taught him to. Neither killer plays a role in developing the motivations that guide their behavior. And in Dexter's case, the values that make him in some sense more admirable than his brother are those that he was indoctrinated into by his adoptive father.

You Can't Help What Happened to You. But You Can Make the Best of It

All of us undergo some degree of childhood indoctrination by parents, our education, our culture and other sources. This gives us character-traits that influence how we interact with the world and values and beliefs about right and wrong and the way the world is. Much of this is positive. We are usually taught that we're members of a moral community and that other people are also members of that community who should be treated with respect. We learn that others are intrinsically valuable and we learn to emphasize with their needs.

This all happens before we develop critical thinking skills and before we gain an ability to reflect on what we're learning. In significant ways each and every one of us are passive when it comes to what values and beliefs about the world we initially adopt.

Some of us are unlucky, like Dexter and Brian. Traumatic childhoods can twist and break us. And if we truly come out of our childhoods so damaged that we are incapable of being motivated by moral reasons or of emphasizing with the suffering of others, then it might be unfair to treat us as fully morally accountable agents. We've become something else more akin to a genuine monster or a rabid dog. And the serial killers that Dexter grapples with are indeed monsters. Deadly, yes. Do they need to be locked up? Clearly. But morally accountable? Probably not. Like the rabid dog the serial killer does not deserve to be held morally accountable.

But Dexter is a more complicated creature than your average psychopathic killer and his moral standing is just as complicated. The supportive environment his adoptive family provided and the moral code that Harry indoctrinated Dexter with leave Dexter with the ability to respond to moral demands. Whereas the Ice Truck Killer indulges in murderous behaviour that targets innocent individuals, Dexter has managed to direct his psychopathic tendencies so that he only targets other serial killers. While Dexter's behavior is still morally problematic, some might think he deserves at least a little praise for using his own deficiencies to protect the general public from other monsters.

Dexter is not merely performing actions that are more desirable than those of other serial killers. He actually evaluates the code that Harry gave him. He questions it, even thinks about abandoning it, and eventually decides to embrace a modified version of Harry's Code. This shows that Dexter has the ability to critically reflect on his moral beliefs and values and modify them if he finds they are mistaken. Paradoxically, this gives us reason to think that Dexter is more morally accountable for his murders than more mundane psychopaths. This is because he can appreciate that what he's doing is wrong. It is true that he can't help himself but he recognizes that there are good reasons why he shouldn't be allowed to continue to kill people. At one point he even decides that he should turn himself in and atone for his crimes. It would be fair to hold him morally accountable for failing to turn himself in.

At the same time, the justification that he gives for not turning himself in is tied to the exact sorts of concerns that someone might think make him praiseworthy. Dexter, despite all odds, has built deep relationships with his sister Debra, Rita's children, and to a lesser extent, Rita. He cares about their well-being and for all intents and purposes really does value them. And he reasons that turning himself in would cause these people immense pain. Considering the effects his actions would have on someone else, putting the needs of others ahead of his own, and emphasizing and showing compassion for another human being are huge achievement for Dexter. The growth he goes through in his quest to become more human is admirable, perhaps even praiseworthy.

I confess that I'm conflicted about this, and I can imagine a lot of readers thinking that I'm trying to have my cake and eat it too. Does Dexter deserve *some* moral praise? If so, it's probably not for following Harry's Code. Even Dexter recognizes that he should be locked up and made to atone for his murders even if he's murdering people that deserve to be brought to justice. No, if Dexter does deserve moral praise it's because he strives to be a better person, he genuinely loves his family, and is trying to be more human. Maybe that's not enough, for the hard-hearted moralists out there. And maybe they're right. But I think many of us can find something admirable, and perhaps even praiseworthy in Dexter's quest to become a better human being. As Dexter himself puts it, "Score one for the little wooden boy . . ."[4]

---

[4] This one's for my dad, Dale Haas.

4

Can We Blame a Man with No Choice?

NICOLAS MICHAUD

Dexter Morgan walks into a warehouse; it is deserted, dank, and dark. On a table before him is a naked man. The man is bound to the table by plastic wrap and he struggles weakly against the bonds that press and stretch his flesh, making him look like a baked ham at a butcher's shop. Dexter walks up to the table and, while the man begs for his life, makes a small cut on the man's cheek using a scalpel. Dexter collects a drop of blood welling up from the incision onto a glass slide. All the while, the man's begging has no noticeable effect—regardless of the terror in the man's eyes, or the reasons from his lips, Dexter begins to cut the man into pieces. Although we do not see the gore, we are very aware of what takes place. Dexter doesn't laugh, and he doesn't cry, he just smiles as the man dies.

How is it that we can watch these events unfold and yet not think of Dexter as an evil man? When we watch the show *Dexter* we regularly see scenes like this, and yet we are not bothered. It seems we think that what Dexter is doing isn't really that bad; as a matter of fact, it might be a good thing because the baked-ham man that Dexter just killed is also a murderer.

Dexter generally only seeks to kill serial killers. He restricts himself to killing people who purposely murder other human beings. But, this isn't the sole reason why we absolve Dexter: Dexter has a compulsion. There's a sense in which he must kill. Try as he might, due to the traumatic events of his childhood, Dexter cannot stop himself from indulging his morbid murderous streak. He does attempt to divert that impulse into only the most positive possible ways, but, nevertheless, it is a compulsion that drives him. It seems that Dexter lacks the ability to do other than kill. So, for this reason, too, we absolve Dexter and treat him as a sort of hero—a generally good guy who has an unfortunate burden to bear.

How Much Control Does Dexter Have Over the Butcher's Knife?

The standard philosophical verdict, then, is to say that because Dexter cannot do other than kill, he cannot be blamed for his actions. When we think about moral responsibility, it seems pretty reasonable to say that if Dexter is going to be blamed, he should be able to choose from among at least two options, in his case, to kill or not to kill.

Dexter's case is tricky, because it does seem as if he has the ability to choose to kill or not kill particular kinds of victims (guilty ones as opposed to innocent ones), and so it does seem that he has the ability to do other than kill a particular person. But, I think if we take a step back we can see that Dexter lacks the ability to not be a serial killer. He might try, and there are moments when he seems to hang up his butcher's apron, but he still inevitably returns to killing; his compulsion drives him. So it seems fair to say that Dexter does not have the ability to be other than a serial killer. If he doesn't have the ability to be otherwise, it doesn't seem reasonable to blame him for it.

This idea, that we should only blame people when they have the ability to do other than what they're doing seems pretty convincing for most of us. It is the reason we tend to absolve kleptomaniacs, those who have a mental disorder compelling them to steal. And the reason why, if someone holds a gun to our head and tells us to steal something, we think we should not be blamed for stealing. Some believe that the kleptomaniac had no real choice but to steal, and we argue that if someone holds a gun to our heads that we had no real choice either. We only can reasonably blame others when they have a choice not to do what they are doing. If their only option is to do what they are doing, then why blame them?

If we have no choice but to do what we are doing, then we shouldn't be blamed. Dexter has no choice but to be a serial killer, so we shouldn't blame him for being a serial killer. What does he have a choice to do? He has a choice as to which victims he murders. Given this fact, we can blame him for choosing the wrong victims and praise him for choosing the right victims. As a matter of fact, that's exactly what we do when we watch the show. We don't damn him for being a serial killer. We feel that is something he cannot help; it makes no more sense to blame him for being a serial killer than it makes sense to blame a cheetah for having a need to eat meat. On the other hand, we recognize that his compulsion does not drive him to kill one kind of person, he has a choice: He must kill, but whom he kills is up to him. Being a generally good guy, he chooses to kill people who kill innocent people. Since it seems that he has an actual choice, to kill an innocent person or kill a guilty person, we praise him when he refrains from killing the innocent and kills the guilty instead. But we don't blame him for killing in general, because he has no option other than to kill.

Does Inevitability Absolve Us?

I've just argued that people can't be blamed for what they do when they have no real choice but to do what they do. But the philosopher Harry Frankfurt (best known for the best seller, *On Bullshit*) disagrees. Frankfurt maintains that *even when we cannot possibly do other than what we in fact do*, we can still be held blameworthy for our actions—specifically when what we do is the result of the fact that we want to do it.[1] Dexter's killing clearly falls into this category. And we'll see that Frankfurt provides us with a very persuasive argument as to why even those people without options can still be held worthy of blame or praise.

Frankfurt's argument made debatable what everyone thought had been settled. It was pretty widely accepted that people are only to blame for their acts when they have more than one option, and if they have only one option, then they cannot be blamed for taking that option. Frankfurt, though, presented a series of famous counterexamples. Frankfurt gives us examples where we would agree that a man, let's call him "Dex," is unable to do anything other than what he does and is still blameworthy. I am going to call this the case of "Dex kills Deb." We will see how even though Dex has no choice, he can still be blamed in at least once circumstance.

---

[1] Harry G Frankfurt. "Alternate Possibilities and Moral Responsibility," *Journal of Philosophy* 66:23 (1969).

Imagine that "Dex" is seriously considering killing "Deb." Also imagine that "Brian" is able to control Dex's actions. Perhaps he can do this using hypnotic suggestion, magic, mind-control devices, whatever best suits our fancy.

Imagine that Dex walks into Deb's house and does not even hesitate to kill her—he just steps right in and does it. Brian looks on in pleasure, but does nothing. He doesn't have to use his power to force Dex. Dex walks in to Deb's house and kills her because he wants to do so. Dex had no choice but to do as he did (because if he had decided not to do it, Brian could have still made him do it), but don't we still want to hold him morally responsible?

Compare this with a case where Brian does exercise his power and forces Dex to kill Deb. There seems to be a significant difference here. In either case, Dex is going to kill Deb. The important difference, however, is that, in the second case, Dex kills Deb because Brian forces him to, not because he wants to. In the first case Dex kills Deb because he wants to, so Brian doesn't have to use his mind control. But here is a clear case in which Dex has only one option (to kill Deb), and yet can still be blameworthy—if he does it because he wants to do it and not because he is forced!

To make Frankfurt's point clearer, imagine that you have serial killer tendencies. You are driving along and see a man step in front of you on the road. What you don't know is that your steering wheel has locked. If you try to swerve your car, your car will just keep going straight. The broken steering wheel will prevent you from doing anything other than drive straight. So, you have no other options—you will hit the person on the road. The only real question is whether you want to hit the person or not. Well, since you have serial killer tendencies you don't even try to turn the wheel. You just gleefully keep driving straight and mow the person down. Do you think you should be absolved? After all, your steering wheel was broken and you couldn't turn if you had wanted to! Well, what Frankfurt is going to say is, "You didn't even try to turn! Yes you had no other option, but that doesn't absolve you, as you did what you did not because you had no choice, but because you wanted to do it!" To Frankfurt why we do what we do is very important.

Judge Frankfurt Rules Dexter Guilty

Well, it does seem that Dexter enjoys being a serial killer. As a matter of fact, he seems to think that he's doing good work. Perhaps he has some moments of regret now and then and wishes he could live a normal life, but, for the most part, he seems to be pretty happy removing evil people from the world. In other words, his status of being a serial killer is not one that has come about only because he has a compulsion. Yes, it's true that if Dexter tried to give up killing, he would fail. His illness is such that he must kill other people, but does he really try not to do so? It seems that in most cases there is no attempt at restraint, or regret. As a matter of fact, his biggest concern is getting caught. Dexter kills people not because he has to do so, but because he wants to.

This is a serious problem, then. Dexter, by Frankfurt's argument is still blameworthy for being a serial killer. Some might argue, in Dexter's defense, that Dexter truly hates his compulsion, which might well be true. Nevertheless, Dexter does not hate it enough to truly prevent himself from acting as he does. I recognize that a compulsion is very possibly impossible to fight, but if he turned himself in, for example, he would likely be unable to kill again. From this we can conclude that his status as a serial killer is something that he is, at the very least, unwilling to give up his life or freedom to change. So, according to Frankfurt, even though he has no choice, he's still to blame for being a serial killer. Why? Because Dexter is not a killer simply on account of his compulsion; he's a killer because he wants to kill people he thinks are bad.

One option, if we want to defend Dexter, is to argue that he lacks the ability to want to not be a serial killer. If that's true, then Dexter lacks the capability to try to turn himself in or otherwise stop himself from killing. In this case it seems that Dexter has no choice but to want to be a serial killer, and so he's a serial killer because of that fact. To be clear, this means that not only does he want to be a serial killer, but he also cannot even form the desire to not be a serial killer.

There are two levels of compulsion then. Level One is the compulsion to kill, which leaves room for wishing you didn't have that compulsion. Level Two is the compulsion to have the Level One compulsion, and so you cannot even try to change the Level One compulsion because you're compelled to want to have it. But, is the fact that Dexter is a serial killer only the result of his compulsion? If it is, then according to Frankfurt we should not blame Dexter. If, on the other hand, Dexter is a serial killer not just because of his compulsion, but also because he wants to be, then Dexter is to blame.

Frankfurt is pretty strict. He's only going to acquit Dexter if Dexter's being a serial killer is the result of just his compulsion. But I think Dexter kills not just because of his compulsion. I think he wants to want to be a serial killer. Consider the lesson Dexter learns from his failed attempt at rehab in Season 2. Early in the season, he treats his 'killing problem' as an addiction and tries to fight it. This doesn't last long. Well before the end of the season we find Dexter killing again. It doesn't seem to be because he succumbed to his addiction. He is empowered to kill. It appears that he wants to want to kill. So he does not have the Level Two compulsion. He is capable of not wanting to be a serial killer, but he does not turn himself in because he'd rather be a serial killer than be in prison, or executed. I recognize that this conclusion is debatable. Some of you may think that Dexter truly does have the Level Two compulsion. Let's grant for a moment that he does, because this leads to an interesting dilemma.

Any Way You Slice It

If it's true that Dexter has a severe compulsion, and therefore, even by Frankfurt's arguments is not blameworthy, it's because being a serial killer is the result of compulsion—a violation of human will. Serial killers, in general, then would fall into the category of people who do what they do only because of their compulsion. They do what they do not because they want to, but because they have no other option. The fact that they have no other option is the entire reason why they do what they do. Well now, Dexter has a problem. Dexter kills serial killers because they are guilty. They are people who choose to kill innocent people, from his perspective. But if they are also compulsives, like himself—and let's assume that some of them are—shouldn't they also be absolved?

If we absolve serial killers, they are in effect innocent. Yes, they kill, but they don't do it because they want to do it, they do it because their brains are such that they must be serial killers. So not only do they lack the ability to be anything other than serial killers, they are serial killers only because of their illnesses. If this is the case, then, even by Frankfurt's strict argument, we have to absolve them. This means, though, that Dexter is going around killing innocent people. If that's the case, then he's breaking Harry's Code and is himself a guilty person, and is thereby required by the Code to remove himself from society, whether by killing himself or through some other means.

Well, the other horn of the dilemma is to say that serial killers are blameworthy. There could be many reasons why we say this. We might argue that they still enjoy what they do, or that they have more control than we think they have, or they still do what they do, in part, because they want to do it. If serial killers really didn't want to kill humans, we would at least see them try some other options. They could go hunting, or play really violent videogames or something else to fulfill their murderous lusts. And we could argue that if they lack the ability to try to do otherwise, they can't not want to be serial killers. Well then, they still want to be serial killers. So even if that want is not something they can control, it is still a bad want.

If that last argument is true, even in the most extreme case, Dexter can't control wanting to be a serial killer, but he is still guilty for acting like a serial killer as a result of that want. The want is beyond his control, but it's still bad, and he, thereby is bad for fulfilling a bad desire. When you think about it, it makes sense. Think of a really good person, someone like Mother Teresa. She probably couldn't want to be an evil person. Her genetics or her brain or something prevents her from even being able to form the desire to do evil. So when we praise her for being a good person, we're praising someone who has no choice but to want to be a good person. What really matters is what she does with that want. Does she let herself fulfill her desire to be good, or does she try to hold back for other selfish reasons?

Well Dexter may not be able to control his want, either. He wants to be a serial killer, and he lets himself be one. Now, granted, he does try to fulfill that want in the most productive means possible, but that doesn't change the fact that he wants to be a serial killer and acts like one too. So from this argument's perspective, if serial killers are not absolved due to their compulsion, neither is Dexter.

So it seems that Dexter has a dilemma. Either

#1. Dexter agrees that serial killers, like himself, are compulsives and compulsives are absolved of their crimes because they could not even want to do other than they do

or

> **#2. Dexter agrees that serial killers are still blameworthy because they want to be serial killers, and act to fulfill that want.**

If he agrees with #1 then he must agree that he is killing innocent people and if he agrees with #2 he agrees that serial killers are to blame and by the same token he's also to blame.

Almost Caught!

After months of careful planning Dexter walks into a dimly-lit room at Princeton University. Silently, he walks behind a plush leather armchair, syringe in hand, ready to kill again.

"Sit down, Dexter" says Harry Frankfurt.

Caught by surprise, Dexter freezes where he is.

"You cannot find a way out of this dilemma, Dexter. So you might as well sit down. Killing me will accomplish nothing."

"Unfortunately, Dr. Frankfurt, you know too much," replies the unusually perturbed Dexter.

"Well, let's talk about it, Dexter." Frankfurt's chair swivels around and Dexter can now clearly see the face of his nemesis. Dexter thinks to himself, "Why not?" and sits down to discuss the dilemma.

"Let's be reasonable, Dexter," the Professor says, "we both know that killing me is not part of your usual M.O. In fact, if you kill me you will just be proving my point.

"You mean that if I kill you, given the fact that you are not a serial killer, I am demonstrating the fact that I am not a compulsive who can only kill serial killers, . . . that I have a choice?

"Correct."

"But, Professor Frankfurt, if I were to kill you, wouldn't I also be showing that I am a compulsive about being a serial killer itself, that I cannot want to be anything other than a serial killer?"

The professor looks at the syringe in Dexter's hand and knows he has a problem. Dexter begins to stand up.

"Wait!" Dr Frankfurt implores. "But Dexter, are you sure?" Are you sure that you cannot want to be other than a serial killer? Are you sure that you're so compulsive that you're willing to kill anyone who gets in the way of your being a serial killer, like me and Doakes?"

"Well, Dr. Frankfurt, it seems that I only have two choices: I am either a compulsive who is so compelled that he is not fully a person capable of making free decisions—not so much a person as a machine—or I am blameworthy because I want to be a serial killer and that want is a free choice. I think I like option #1 better" he says as he begins to raise the syringe. "Either I'm killing innocent people and am innocent myself, or they are guilty and I too am guilty."

As Professor Frankfurt asks one more question, he pointlessly raises his hands to defend himself, "But Dexter why is it that you are willing to kill me, an innocent person?"

"Well that should be obvious to you, Professor Frankfurt . . . because, otherwise, I am guilty."

Later that night, out on his boat, Dexter watches the pieces of Dr. Harry G. Frankfurt sink down into the depths and realizes that in choosing the first prong of the dilemma, because it was a choice, he's still guilty . . . and smiles the emotionless smile of the truly free.

5

What Dexter Doesn't Know Can Hurt You

RACHEL ROBISON-GREENE

You've been called for jury duty. Don't worry, it won't take long. The cases you will consider are not arduous civil suits or petty misdemeanors, so your charge certainly won't be boring. The crimes under consideration are the most ghastly kinds of murders. What would your verdict be in the following cases? The jury instructions are simple: in each case the life of the defendant is on the line, so to be justified in finding him or her guilty, you must be sure.

Case #1. Suspect: Jamie Jaworski. Jaworski runs a truly disgusting rape and torture website. The distinctive devil tattoo on his arm is present in one of the online videos featured on the site. There is violent pornography in his house. Jaworski fell in love with a married mother of three who is now missing.

Case #2. Suspect: Jeremy Downs. Downs is a teenage boy who was institutionalized after killing a young man four years ago. He claimed that the boy he killed tried to rape him and that the murder was retaliation. Another boy of a similar age ends up dead and the wound patterns are very similar.

Case #3. Suspect: a nurse at a local hospital. The nurse gives off "killer vibes." A sick man doped up on drugs reports that she is giving him too much medication. She keeps a scrapbook of deaths that occurred at the hospital where she works.

Reasonable Doubts

If the verdict you came to is that, based on the evidence, you can't be sure that any of the defendants are guilty, I'm not surprised. A good defense attorney would rip these cases to shreds. There may be enough evidence to make their guilt probable. But Dexter's Code requires certainty. As he says "My father taught me one thing above all others—to be sure." This certainty requirement ensures that he only kills the bad guys.

What is certainty? Let's consider two different definitions. The first is that to be certain is just to have a particular kind of feeling. To have certainty is to feel sure that your belief is true. Cops on crime shows operate on this definition all the time when they pursue a particular perp because they "feel in their bones" that they have the right man. The problem with this definition is that we can feel this way even when we're wrong. I'm sure every one of us has felt sure of something that turned out not to be the case.

The other sense of certainty demands a lot more from us and finds its most famous expression in the work of seventeenth-century philosopher René Descartes. In his *Meditations on First Philosophy* Descartes attempts to find one thing that he can believe beyond any doubt. This means that nothing can possibly call into question the truth of that belief. He raises doubt by considering whether his beliefs hold up in the face of various skeptical hypotheses. For example, his senses may be deceiving him as they do in the case of a mirage or an optical illusion. This hypothesis calls some beliefs into doubt, but others remain steadfast. He considers that he might be dreaming and all of the things he thinks he is experiencing are actually just products of his imagination. Since this hypothesis still leaves plenty of beliefs immune to doubt, he considers the possibility that an evil demon might be deceiving him, tricking him into believing all of the things he presently believes, though his beliefs are in fact false. One can be certain of only the beliefs that stand up to this kind of scrutiny.

This certainty requirement for knowledge is . . . ahem . . . certainly not foreign to contemporary popular culture. Scenarios from movies like *The Matrix* and *Vanilla Sky* involve skeptical hypotheses that force us to think about what we really know about the external world. After all, we may actually be plugged in to some fancy machine and all of our experiences might just be programmed algorithms whirring around in the body of a supercomputer.

Typically, however, we don't tend to think that certainty of this type is required for day-to-day knowledge. Dexter knows where he docks his boat *Slice of Life*. Astor and Cody know that Rita is their mother. Brian Moser knows how to amputate a human leg, and so on. If you think this is true—that we can know things about our day-to-day lives without ruling out *Matrix*-style counterexamples— then you're an infallibilist rather than a fallibilist about knowledge. An infallibilist believes that knowledge requires certainty. A fallibilist believes that we can have knowledge, even in cases when we fall short of certainty in the Cartesian sense.

There is no reason to believe that when Harry tells Dexter to "be sure," he wants his son to be able to rule out the possibility that an evil demon is tricking him into believing everything he believes. More plausibly, Harry is advising Dexter to know that someone is guilty before killing them.

Traditionally, for a person to have knowledge they must have a belief, the thing they believe must be true, and they must be justified in holding the belief that they hold. This is a view that traces back to Plato and the majority of philosophers today still accept it (though a number of them add additional requirements). Each of these requirements is intuitively appealing. Let's start with belief.

In Season 1 Lieutenant La Guerta does some sloppy detective work. She looks at the neatly wrapped body of one of the Ice Truck Killer's victims. There is a difference between this body and those of previous victims. In the past, the dissection of body parts has been symmetrical. If the upper right leg is cut into two pieces, then the upper left leg will be cut into two pieces and so on. Not so with the most recent victim. One leg is cut into more pieces than the other. La Guerta surmises that the killer was interrupted before he was finished—there must be a witness! Track down the witness and it's only a quick jump to tracking down the Ice Truck Killer.

Now, as Dexter and Debra point out, it's clear to anyone who gives the matter any thought that no one interrupted the killer while he was cutting up the body. If this had been the case, the killer would not have had time to wrap the parts. Deb and Dexter, therefore, believe that there was no witness. The available evidence justifies the belief that there was no witness. And, in fact, it's true that there was no witness. But LaGuerta does not know it because she doesn't believe it. Knowledge requires belief.

Let's move on to the second requirement for knowledge. In order for a person to know something, the thing they believe has to be true. A great example of this is when Deb comes to believe that Neil Perry is the Ice Truck Killer. He inserted himself into the investigation early on by claiming to be a witness, which is common for serial killers. Traffic violation records show him to be present at two of the crime scenes. He knows things about the crimes that were never released to the public. A dead body is buried in the backyard of his unbelievably creepy double-wide trailer home. He even confessed for Pete's sake!

As it turns out, however, Perry is in it for the notoriety and has never killed anyone. When LaGuerta brings a severed head into the interrogation room to spook him, he practically passes out. This is certainly not someone who could make super-killer Dexter Morgan feel like "a student in a master class" ("Circle of Friends," Season 1). Deb believes that Neil Perry is the Ice Truck Killer. She is justified in believing it. But Deb doesn't know it because it isn't true. Knowledge requires that that one's belief is true.

Knowledge also requires justification. It isn't enough to merely have a true belief. Consider Astor's claim in the first part of Season 5 that Dexter is, in some way, responsible for the death of her mother. As it turns out, there is some truth to her allegation. Dexter pissed off Trinity and Rita paid the price. But Astor certainly doesn't know this. Her accusations are just the angry, desperate attempts of a hurt pre-teen to find someone to blame for a death she doesn't understand. She believes Dexter's to blame and it is, in some sense, true that Dexter is to blame, but Astor doesn't know that Dexter's to blame. Knowledge requires justification.

Justification admits of degrees. A person can have some justification for their belief and still fail to have knowledge. For example, imagine that Masuka goes to a strip club and forms the belief that one of the strippers is "warm for his form." He forms this belief because she smiles at him when he tips her and spends more time near him than anyone else when he starts whipping out the big bills. Masuka has some evidence for the belief that the stripper is hot for him, but nowhere near enough justification for his belief to count as knowledge.

Bodies of Evidence

The question of what exactly constitutes justification is a hot topic in philosophy, and there are several competing models of what counts for justification. It's difficult to say exactly what model

Dexter is thinking of, though it is clear that he does have a model, some sort of theory which tells him when he is justified in believing that a suspect is really guilty.

This isn't a mere philosophical question for Dexter. Without some idea of how he is justified in believing his victims are guilty, he can't follow his Code. We'll consider two main theoretical families. The first consists of internalist theories of justification. There are strong and weak versions of internalism. According to strong internalism, for a person to be justified in believing something, it must be the case that they are aware of their justifiers. Something is a justifier if it provides some reason to believe that the proposition under consideration is true. In other words, in order to know something, the reasons you have for believing it must be reflectively accessible to you.

At least some of our intuitions should support this view. Imagine that a friend approaches you and says, "Dexter gets the chair in the last episode of the series." First you are ticked off that they revealed such an important spoiler about one of your favorite shows. But then you start pressing your buddy about how they came to know Dexter's fate. Did plot summaries get leaked on the internet? Did a writer or cast member spill the beans? "Oh, I don't know what leads me to believe that. But don't get me wrong. I'm not just speculating. I know he gets the chair." I'm sure you would find this maddening. At least at first blush it seems that if a person truly knows a thing, they should be able to tell you the reasons they have for believing it.

This is arguably the theory of justification that the court system operates under. Judges and juries expect witnesses to testify not just to what they know, but also to the reasons they have for forming the relevant beliefs. Dexter is quite familiar with this system. While on the stand testifying in a murder trial, he reports that he has investigated two thousand one hundred and three cases. And that isn't give or take. So he clearly knows how the game is played. As a scientist, he realizes that he has to look beyond initial appearances when investigating crimes. Recall the "cokehead murders" from Season 1. All outward appearances indicate that the crimes were motivated by drugs. The victims were drug dealers and their associates. Doakes quickly forms the belief that they were killed by rival dealers and he demands that Dexter write exactly that in his report. But Dexter points out that the science doesn't support this conclusion. It tells him that this was a crime of passion. The main target was not the dealer (who was dispensed with in a quick and sloppy way). The primary victim was the dealer's girlfriend, who was killed much more elegantly. Dexter suggests that the killer is a jealous ex-boyfriend. Additional investigation into this hypothesis is necessary.

He claims to be even more diligent about gathering evidence when it comes to determining the guilt of his victims. In fact, he says "My Code requires a higher standard of proof than your city's laws, at zero cost to the taxpayer. If you ask me, I'm a bargain" ("There's Something about Harry," Season 2). But is this really true? Dexter often proceeds without evidence that would be necessary to procure a conviction in court. Consider the investigation he does into the case of Jeremy Downs. As we saw earlier, the only real evidence he has on Downs is that he killed someone before and the knife patterns on the most recent victim are very similar to those involved in the murder four years ago. He also witnesses Jeremy taking a teenager off into a swamp to see an alligator, which is how he lured away his first victim. But, I would point out, this may not be merely a ruse. After all, there is actually an alligator in the exact spot where Downs brings the boy. Dexter practically steps on it. There's hardly enough evidence to know that Downs is killing again, though there may be enough to make this conclusion probable.

Dexter goes after Downs, presumably to mete out his form of justice. But the cops beat him to the punch. Masuka lifted a print from the alley where the boy was killed and the department sweeps in to make an arrest. This evidence, which actually ties Downs to the crime scene, was evidence that Dexter didn't have when he decided to attempt an abduction of Jeremy at the park.

There are many cases in which Dexter abducts his victims before he even has all of the pieces of the puzzle. Early in Season 1, he abducts Jamie Jaworski at a construction site. Jaworski is real scum. He operates a website featuring rape and snuff films. A young wife and mother named Jane Saunders goes missing and Dexter suspects Jaworski. The department pursued a case against him, but it was dropped because of a faulty search warrant. We see Dexter thumbing through a case file, but all it contains are a bunch of glossy photographs. He doesn't even know how the murder was committed. When he has Jaworski strapped to the table, he says "Talk to me about Jane Saunders." Jaworski replies "Alright, I did her." But Dexter has to ask "How?" Jaworski replies "A snuff film. And I'm not sorry." Dexter responds, "Of course not. And now I'm not sorry either." How can Dexter possibly have the justification that strong internalism requires if he doesn't even know how the murder was committed?

This happens again in Season 2 when Dexter tries, unsuccessfully, to kill a practitioner of voodoo named Jimmy Sensio whom he suspects of poisoning people to create the appearance of a successful death curse. Dexter did do some actual science in this case and was able to ascertain that all of the victims were poisoned. But he doesn't even know how the poison was administered. Again, he has to ask his victim while he is strapped to the table. The absence of this crucial information would most likely lead to an acquittal in court, if the case even ever made it to trial. After all, how can you be sure that a person poisoned someone if you don't know whether or not they had the means to administer the poison? What Dexter is doing is like asking a killer for a vital piece of evidence related to determining their guilt while they are strapped to the electric chair. What is Dexter going to do if he finds out his victim couldn't possibly have committed the crime, let him go? Doing so would present a real problem for following one of Harry's other rules—don't get caught.

But maybe Dexter doesn't violate Harry's Code by not having all the evidence available to reflect upon. Perhaps this is not the right account of justification anyway. The courts arguably require something more than knowledge. Detectives may know that a suspect is guilty, but fail to obtain a conviction in court. Though there is some intuitive support for strong internalism, there are also reasons to believe that it is too strong. It may be that there are some things that we know, even if all of our evidence isn't currently available to us.

Consider the case of "super-cop" Frank Lundy, who has been investigating the Trinity Killer for years. On the basis of his extended investigation, spanning numerous states and inquiring into multiple murders, he comes to believe that Trinity always operates in sets of three murders (actually, it turns out to be four, but at least we can say that Lundy knows that Trinity operates in sets of at least three). He may not be able to, at any given time, call up all of the evidence he has for this belief. But it might be enough simply that he is capable of calling it up if absolutely necessary. If this is the case, then weak internalism fits the bill quite well. According to this view, in order for a person's belief to be justified, it must merely be the case that they are capable of becoming aware of their justifiers.

This, however, can't be the theory of justification that Dexter is operating in accordance with either. It isn't as if he has some additional information about Downs or the others that he just can't call up to his conscious mind at the moment. He didn't have strong enough evidence to begin with.

If this isn't Dexter's account of justification it's no great loss, because there are some problems with this view as well. Consider the case of a child who knows where the cookie jar is kept. Imagine that the child is so young that they do not yet even have the concept of memory or evidence, but when they want a cookie they push a barstool up to the cabinet and find what they're looking for every single time. The child isn't even capable of calling up her justifiers. She doesn't even have those concepts, yet it seems that she knows where the cookies are.

There's another, typically internalist theory that doesn't quite fit into the category of either strong or weak internalism as I have described them here. The coherence theory of justification is a view that also requires a sort of internal, reflective evaluation, but this evaluation concerns whether the belief one is thinking about adopting coheres with the other things one already believes. A given belief is justified to the extent that it coheres.

Is Dexter operating in accordance with the coherence theory of justification? Perhaps. Consider his investigation into Jonathan Farrow in Season 4. The department finds blood and a fingernail in Farrow's apartment. The fingernail turns out to belong to a woman whose arm was found inside the body of an alligator. Dexter forms the belief that Farrow is a killer. This belief coheres with all of his other beliefs at this point. So, he decides to kill Farrow.

This case, as loyal Dexter viewers might now recognize, points to a serious problem with coherence theory. The beliefs we have might be internally consistent, but this doesn't mean that such beliefs will be true. As it turns out, Farrow is innocent. If we have no reason to believe that our beliefs will be true if they are internally consistent, why do we care about coherence?

Hey Dex, Is Your Spidey-Sense Tingling Yet?

We might want to move in a different direction entirely. By contrast to internalist theories of justification, externalist theories hold that not all justifiers need to be cognitively accessible to the believer. One of the most prominent externalist theories is reliablism.

According to this view, a belief is justified if it is the product of a reliable belief producing mechanism or process. Imagine that your son is out playing with his friends and you hear them all talking. Your son tells a big whopper of a lie. You know that it was your son and not one of the other children that lied because you can reliably pick out the sound of his voice. It seems plausible that many, perhaps even the majority of our beliefs are formed in this way.

This view is initially promising as a candidate for the way Dexter might be justified. As John Kenneth Muir points out in another chapter of this book, Dexter's ability to recognize other serial killers is so amazing it's like a superpower. Recall the flashback to Dexter's first human victim, the nurse who tried to kill his father. All it took was a look passed between the two of them for Dexter to report to Harry, "She's . . . like me."

The problem is, Dexter's overall methods are not all that reliable. Dexter himself claims that using his spidey-sense alone is not sufficient for determining the guilt or innocence of his potential victims. He says, "My instincts are impeccable, but I have to be sure of my prey" ("Popping Cherry," Season 1).

Just as very few lawyers would win case after case employing the courtroom techniques that Perry Mason employs (in fact, many would probably be disbarred), few vigilantes would be successful if they employed the standards that Dexter employs. As Daniel Malloy points out elsewhere in this book, a significant amount of moral luck is involved in the show. Dexter happens to kill guilty people most of the time, but, given his investigative techniques, he could just as easily have killed innocent people. Sure, he does the occasional DNA test or background check, but he's much more likely to carry carving tools than fingerprint powder and luminal along with him on his little outings.

More than a Feeling?

I don't think it's unusual that, in one episode Dexter seems to have one notion of justification and in another episode he acts according to a different notion altogether. He slashes all across the conceptual space. Perhaps this is because Dexter's Code did not initially come from him, it came from Harry. The poor boy just wanted to kill things; he didn't understand the deeper philosophical foundations for his father's lessons. Perhaps Harry didn't either. He was just trying to make the best of a bad situation.

The fact that Dexter's theory of justification is all over the map points to the conclusion that, when he claims he has to be certain, he is employing the first sense of certainty we discussed in this paper. Certainty for Dexter is just a particular kind of feeling. He looks like a coherentist in some moments, a strong internalist in others, and a reliablist in still others because employing one method makes him feel certain at some moments and other methods at others.

But, as we said at the beginning, this view of justification is not sufficient for knowledge, Feeling certain often has nothing to do with actually being right. If this is so, Dexter doesn't have justification sufficient for knowledge of the guilt of many of the people he chooses to kill. Would he want to know this so he could change, or would he rather satiate the cravings of his Dark Passenger in blissful ignorance so long as he feels justified? He could potentially hurt a lot of innocent people. He could have one strapped to his table right now. "Tonight's the night. And it's going to happen again, and again . . ."

6
Dexter the Self-Interpreting Animal

BRIAN GREGOR

What does it mean to be human? This is the central question of philosophical anthropology. It's also a question that Dexter poses in a fascinating way. The *Dexter* TV series suggests that being human is not simply a matter of being a member of the species *Homo sapiens*; Dexter is clearly a human in a biological sense, but is he human in the deeper sense of the word? And what might that deeper meaning be? This question arises throughout the series as Dexter wrestles with his own humanity (or lack thereof). As to what this humanity might be, the series leaves us with more questions than answers: just the sort of territory where philosophy feels at home.

Riffing on Aristotle's famous definition of the human being as a "rational animal," the philosopher Charles Taylor defines the human being as a "self-interpreting animal." To be human is to interpret oneself, to work out one's sense of identity as a self. Who am I? What am I doing here? Where am I going? How should I live? It's human nature to ask these questions, to examine our lives and represent ourselves in art, stories, and other cultural expressions. But Taylor's point is not merely that we examine and represent ourselves. More profoundly, our identity as selves—our very being as humans—comes into being through self-interpretation.

We're used to thinking about our identity, our humanity, our "self," as something we have, pretty much like we have a head, limbs, and organs—as an interpretation-free fact, an object, a thing among other things. But Taylor maintains that self-interpretation does not interpret some "thing" that is already there, just waiting to be interpreted. Rather, self-interpretation brings our selves into being. Humans are different from other kinds of life. At a certain point of maturity, plants and non-human animals have fulfilled their potential. They are what they are. They are all they will ever be. But the human being is more than biological; although we reach a point of biological maturity, we never arrive at a final point where we simply are what we are. Who knows what new twist might lead us to re-evaluate the meaning of our lives? We're like stories whose endings are not yet written.[1]

In a particularly philosophical moment, Harry explains this to the young Dexter: "When you take a man's life, you're not just killing him. You're snuffing out all the things that he might become" ("Popping Cherry," Season 1). As human beings, we're always becoming, until the day we die. Our identities are always in process. Who we are—our very being as humans—is always growing, developing through our self-interpretations.

Those of us who know and love Dexter will recognize the truth of this. Dexter is indeed a self-interpreting animal. He is constantly interpreting himself, trying to understand who he is, what he's doing, and where he's going. We witness Dexter's changing self-interpretation, and through this interpretation his becoming human. In the earliest episodes, Dexter interprets himself as more of a monster than a human being. At one point he describes himself, only half in jest, as "the wooden boy" ("Popping Cherry," Season 1). But unlike Pinocchio, who dreamed of someday becoming a real boy, Dexter doesn't suggest any such hopes for himself. Yet as the series unfolds, his self-understanding is challenged by what Michael C. Hall calls Dexter's "percolating sense of his own humanity."[2] As his relations with others develop, Dexter encounters his humanity surging up—much to his surprise, and at times, perplexity. Dexter's humanity is highly problematic, but it's growing, and we see a vital sign of it in his desire to understand himself. Dexter's condition as a self-interpreting animal—which is to say, as a human being—is evident in three ways: in his self-evaluation, in the need for recognition, and in the narrative order of his life.

---

[1] Charles Taylor. *Sources of the Self: The Making of the Modern Identity* (Harvard University Press, 1989), pp. 34, 112.

[2] Interview with *Collider* <www.collider.com/2010/09/25/michael-c-hall-interview-dexter-season-5/>.

Dexter's Inescapable Framework

One way we interpret ourselves is by evaluating ourselves. We distinguish which actions, feelings, and ways of life are good or bad, higher or lower, noble or shameful, deep or superficial, more or less fulfilling. These distinctions reveal a sense of responsibility: I'm responsible for myself. To paraphrase Martin Heidegger, my being is an issue of concern for me.[3] It's somehow up to me what sort of being I am going to be. But who do I want to be? And who should I be? What is the meaning of my life? What sort of life, what activities, what relationships are worth pursuing? To be human is to be in the process of asking—and living out a response to—these questions. To be human is to interpret oneself and one's aspirations in this way.

Taylor says we can never ask these questions without bringing along our fundamental assumptions about what is good, worthwhile, and meaningful. We ask these questions within a "framework" of meaning and value. This framework gives me a conception of "the good"—that is, what is good for me individually and what is good for human beings in general.[4] These frameworks give us "a picture of what human beings are like," what is good for them.[5] They give us a picture of what the world is like, about the way things really are.

We inherit these frameworks from a variety of sources, like family, social practices, cultural traditions, art, religion, and philosophy. In Dexter's case, they come mostly from Harry, who gave Dexter the Code, but even more significantly embraced him as his son and showed him love. Of course, like Dexter we all have to take up these frameworks and make them our own: we critique them, reinterpret them, and sometimes reject aspects of them. But we can never build them from scratch, choosing whatever we happen to prefer. One's sense of the good, meaningful, and worthwhile runs much too deep for it to have arisen from arbitrary choice. In a certain sense, these frameworks are given to us, and we cannot simply revise them on a whim. They reach too deeply into our identities for that.

---

[3] *Being and Time* (Harper and Row, 1962), pp. 32, 236.

[4] Alasdair MacIntyre. *After Virtue* (University of Notre Dame Press, 1984), pp. 218–19.

[5] *Sources of the Self*, p. 39.

Because we have these frameworks, we never encounter the world as a bunch of cold hard facts. Instead, we encounter the world as already interpreted according to our sense of what matters, what is meaningful, what is worthwhile, and what is good. Even when we're unable to articulate this framework theoretically, it's still there. It's also true that different people often have different frameworks; but it's impossible for a human being to exist without one. As Taylor puts it, these frameworks are "inescapable."

Has Dexter Overcome Humanity?

Is Taylor right? Are these frameworks really inescapable? It might seem that Dexter is an exception—that he doesn't have real convictions and intuitions about the moral order of things. It might seem that Dexter has no real basis on which to evaluate himself or his actions; he is a sociopath with murderous impulses and an impaired sense of right and wrong. That's why Harry's Code is so important: it gives Dexter guidelines to avoid being caught and executed for his killings. The Code is a useful convention to protect Dexter, but it doesn't provide any deeper orientation regarding the moral order of things, such as why human life matters or why murder is actually wrong.

But that's a superficial understanding of the Code. However problematic the Code might be, it's nevertheless set within a framework of fundamental convictions and intuitions about good and evil. When Harry explains his plan for Dexter to kill people who deserve to be killed, he's clearly presupposing certain convictions about the moral order of things: there is good, and there is evil, and some people deserve to be killed. This background proves vital to Dexter's formation; without it, he would very likely have ended up like his estranged brother Brian, the Ice Truck Killer. Dexter clearly operates according to fundamental convictions about the higher and lower, better and worse. The Code is too abstract, too formal to have any real claim on Dexter unless it was rooted in some deeper, more fundamental intuitions about the nature of things: for example, life is worth living, innocence should be protected, and evil deserves to be punished. Dexter owes these intuitions to Harry's influence in his life, but they are too fundamental, too deeply rooted, to have arisen from the Code alone.

This is not to say that Harry, Dexter, or anyone else in the show gives an argument defending these fundamental convictions. But there is an implicit framework of meaning and value that forms the background of Dexter's actions, and this indicates something of his humanity—however damaged that humanity may be.

This humanity is not apparent to Dexter. At times he sees himself as having moved beyond humanity: "I'm neither man nor beast. I'm something new entirely, with my own set of rules. I'm Dexter" ("Let's Give the Boy a Hand," Season 1). And by the end of Season 2 it might seem that Dexter gives up evaluation altogether when he overcomes the binding authority of Harry's Code: "Am I good? Am I evil? I'm done asking those questions. I don't have the answers. Does anyone?" On this account, Dexter might seem to have escaped any framework of meaning and value; perhaps he has even moved beyond humanity, like Nietzsche's Overman (*Übermensch*), creating his own moral reality, beyond good and evil. But even if we take Dexter's self-interpretation as authoritative—and it's not always clear that we should—does this mean he has left all moral frameworks behind?

No, it doesn't. Dexter may feel justified in revising Harry's Code, making it his alone, but even his revision of the Code assumes certain fundamental convictions about reality, and it's impossible to create new convictions that have no reference to the way things are.[6] Although Dexter continues to show a startlingly clear conscience over his killings, this is because he believes that he's justified in killing these people, since they deserved to die. So in Season 4 his response is quite different when it turns out that Farrow, the thoroughly loathsome photographer whom Dexter killed, was not in fact a murderer. Following this mistake, Dexter finds himself burdened by his responsibility. He tries to shake this burden by reinforcing his sense of who he is ("I don't do 'should'ves.' That's not me. It's not me"). But he is "uncomfortable" nonetheless—not merely because he violated an abstract Code, but because Farrow, unlike Dexter's previous sixty-seven victims, didn't deserve to die ("Road Kill," Season 4).

None of this suggests that we should view Dexter as living a good life. Dexter's understanding of himself and his actions is highly problematic, and he has a very murky understanding of what is good and why. But it's clear that he interprets himself and

---

[6] Even Nietzsche's attempt to overcome humanity presupposes strong evaluations regarding what is "good," what matters, and is worth pursuing: the will to power, strength, creativity with new values, the joyful celebration of life.

his actions against a background of more fundamental convictions about the nature of reality, and this is a vital sign of his humanity. He's not merely an inhuman monster acting on animal impulses and following a formal code to avoid being caught. Dexter is severely damaged, but his humanity is still evident in the fact that he interprets and evaluates himself and his actions.

The Need for Recognition

You haven't got the first idea who you are, have you? Dexter, meet Dexter. I'm going to help the two of you get to know each other.

—LILA ("See-Through," Season 2)

Human beings are also relational animals, and our sense of who we are is inseparable from our relations with others. As Taylor argues, we do not interpret ourselves in isolation; instead, we work out our identities in dialogue—some overt, some internal—with others.[7] Most contemporary discussion of this idea derives from Georg Wilhelm Friedrich Hegel, who argued that identity is always mediated by others.[8] My sense of who I am is mediated and confirmed by those significant others whose opinion matters to me. There are endless ways that I can interpret myself, but unless others recognize me as I see myself, my sense of identity cannot be fully realized.

In order to understand ourselves, then, we need to be understood. This is a recurring theme for Dexter, who describes this need for recognition as a desire to be "seen" for who he really is. Yet genuine recognition seems almost impossible for Dexter, since it would reveal his identity as a serial killer. The young Dexter did, however, experience this recognition from Harry. Early in the first season he tells us that "Harry was the only one who saw me—really saw me." Harry recognized Dexter's dark impulses, showed

---

[7] Charles Taylor, *The Ethics of Authenticity* (Harvard University Press, 1991), p. 47.

[8] Hegel's description of mutual recognition is a lot of fun: "Each is for the other the middle term, through which each mediates itself with itself and unites with itself; and each is for itself, and for the other, an immediate being on its own account, which at the same time is such only through the mediation. They *recognize* themselves as *mutually recognizing* one another." *Phenomenology of Spirit* (Oxford University Press, 1977), p. 112.

him genuine love, and tried to help him. This recognition is crucial to Dexter's sense of identity.

Yet Dexter also admits that "Sometimes I'm not sure where Harry's vision of me ends and the real me begins" ("Let's Give the Boy a Hand," Season 1). Dexter's sense of himself is caught in a conflict of interpretations—between Harry's vision of who Dexter is, Dexter's sense of who his "real" self is, and the humanity that Dexter finds surging up within himself as his relationships develop. This tension is heightened by the fact that Harry wants Dexter to be human, yet has given him a Code that works against that possibility by limiting Dexter's human relationships. The Code focuses on Dexter fitting in, but these relations with others are meant to keep up appearances; he warns Dexter not to let other people get close. He tells Dexter that Deb will keep him "connected" ("Popping Cherry," Season 1), but even she can't see the "real" Dexter. The real Dexter can never come into the open, which is why Harry is always warning him not to become too involved with others. But the problem is that Harry's Code doesn't take seriously enough the possibility of Dexter becoming human, that he will desire to be "seen" by others. And so Dexter continues to think of himself as a master of disguise, wearing masks to protect his "true" identity.

Because of this very human desire for recognition, Dexter faces serious challenges when others promise to understand him for who he really is. When Brian reveals himself to Dexter as his long-lost brother and fellow serial killer, he holds out this promise of recognition: "You're not alone anymore, Dexter. You can be yourself, with me. Your real, genuine self." But in the end, Dexter has to kill him, the one person who could see him and "handle" his "truth" ("Born Free," Season 1).

In Season 2, however, Dexter finds a new possibility in Lila: "I thought I closed the door to anyone seeing me for who I am, but this woman sees me. She doesn't know it, but she's looking behind the mask and not turning away" ("The Dark Defender." Season 2). All of Dexter's previous relationships had been "built on not knowing," but Lila presents the possibility of "a life without secrets." She promises to help Dexter discover who he is—in Hegelian terms, to mediate his identity. She pushes Dexter to ask himself honestly who he is, what he needs, what he wants ("I thought she was going to give me answers. Instead I just got more questions"). A deep bond develops between them, but we know how that ends: Lila turns out to be a pyromaniac and killer, and Dexter kills her.

The same fate awaits Miguel Prado, who also sees Dexter and doesn't turn away. With Prado, however, Dexter doesn't find the recognition of a brother or a lover, but a friend. Aristotle famously describes the friend as "another self,"[9] and at first this is what Dexter finds, as Prado begins to share Dexter's taste for vigilante killing. But when Prado's killing turns vindictive and spurns the Code, Dexter has to take him out as well. In short, things don't turn out well for those who see Dexter's hidden side. Even Harry was ultimately unable to bear what he had helped Dexter become, and committed suicide. Dexter seems tragically unable to form relationships based on mutual honesty. Despite his desire to be seen, he remains an outsider, donning the appropriate mask for the occasion. All of these failed attempts at recognition feel like so many failed attempts at humanity.

Dexter is highly conscious of feeling like an outsider, looking in on human beings who seem so normal. He tries to act the way humans are supposed to act, but all the while insists that this is merely a mask. As the series progresses, however, we start to see a conflict between Dexter's familiar self-interpretation, and the humanity that is revealing itself. This conflict is particularly apparent in the way he responds to Rita's murder. Just before he discovers Rita's body at the end of Season 4, Dexter seems to have made a breakthrough in his humanity. He starts to see how his Dark Passenger is ruining his life. Harry objects, "It *is* your life." But Dexter replies "I don't want it to be. I don't want it." Dexter is beginning to glimpse the possibility of being rid of the Dark Passenger, of getting away from the old Dexter and embracing his family life. But this hope comes crashing down when he discovers Rita dead in their bathtub, a victim of the Trinity Killer: "I thought I could change what I am, keep my family safe. But it doesn't matter what I do, what I choose. I'm what's wrong. This is fate" ("The Getaway," Season 4). Dexter retreats into his old self-interpretation, seeing himself as a character marked by a tragic flaw.

After finding Rita dead, Dexter can't grasp the full significance of what has happened, and he doesn't know how to respond. He interprets his lack of emotional response in familiar terms: the real Dexter is the unfeeling outsider, wearing masks to appear human. As Rita lies in her coffin, Dexter confesses to her: "I'm a serial killer.

---

[9] *Nicomachean Ethics*, line 1169b7.

That's what I am. I know I led you to believe I'm a human being, but I'm not. It's a lie" ("My Bad," Season 5).

Should we take Dexter at his word here? What if the supposedly real "Dexter" is actually the mask? Blindsided by such a devastating loss, it's easier for Dexter to retreat from his humanity and the very real grief this loss entails. Dexter finally allows this grief to surface in the rest-stop bathroom, where he kills the man who crudely insults Dexter's dead wife. Facing Dexter in a broken mirror, Harry says to him: "That's the first human thing I've seen you do since she died, Dexter." Dexter sinks to his hands and knees, letting out a chilling shriek, finally able to respond to what happened. Now what is "human" is not the mask Dexter wears to fit in, but the honesty of his response. In that moment, what is most real is Dexter the human being.

We're not likely to see Dexter reconcile his conflicting identities, nor watch him find a healthy relationship based on mutual recognition. Those who can see and accept Dexter's homicidal activities are not the sort of people Dexter can really embrace. As he puts it, "the willful taking of life represents the ultimate disconnect from humanity. It leaves you an outsider, forever looking in, searching for company to keep" ("Popping Cherry," Season 1). And yet it's precisely in this unfulfilled desire for company, this need to be "seen," that we catch sight of Dexter's humanity.

A Story in Search of a Narrator

As human beings, our identities are always in transition; we're always changing, sometimes for the better, sometimes for the worse. But if I'm always changing, how can I be the same person at different points in my life? Am I the same person I was ten years ago? Can we say that Dexter is the same person he is in Season 5 as he was during Season 1, during his *Early Cuts*, his teenage years, or when he was a young child? Clearly Dexter has changed, grown, and developed in many ways. And yet he's still Dexter. How is this possible? What provides this continuity through time and change?

A number of contemporary philosophers, most notably Alasdair MacIntyre, Paul Ricoeur, and Charles Taylor, have argued that personal identity over time depends on narrative. Who we are changes over time, but our identities have a certain continuity because of the stories we tell about ourselves. I can tell who I am by giving an account of how I got here and where I am going, and I understand who others are through their stories. We interpret ourselves through self-narration. By telling our stories we make sense of our memories, experiences, goals, and hopes. Narrative brings our past, present, and future into a meaningful whole. Human existence is a story waiting to be told.

Now, Dexter Morgan's life is a great story, and we know who he is by following this story. As viewers and readers we're privy to his actions in the present as well as flashbacks that help us to piece together fragments from his past. As these details emerge, we're always implicitly sorting them out in the order of a plot. And as we follow Dexter's story, we're also anticipating what this means for his future. Our ability to watch and understand Dexter depends on its narrative ordering. The details are often sketchy and fragmentary, which is appropriate since Dexter only discovers the formative events of his identity in bits and pieces, as he discovered the truth about his mother, his brother, and Harry. This is also appropriate because Dexter's story is always subject to reinterpretation. This is true for everyone: self-interpretation is a work in progress. Narration is ongoing, subject to re-interpretation in light of new discoveries about the past, new experiences in the present, and new expectations for the future. Until we die, then, we can never conclude our stories with a tidy "The End."

In addition to having a great story, Dexter is also a great storyteller—in one sense, at least. As he explains at the scene of a multiple homicide, blood spatter tells a story, and it's his job to trace out the plot. Dexter's job is to tell stories written in blood, which is fitting since blood is central to his own story. He was "born in blood," having witnessed the gruesome murder of his mother when we was a child. He also keeps slides with blood samples from his victims, a token of his past, a reminder of who he really is. These slides are almost like notes—in point form—for the day Dexter tells his own story. But that's a story he is less eager to tell.

Dexter does let us in on much of his story. He tells us a lot in his voice-over narration, much like the tragic heroes of film noir. Yet noir protagonists typically tell us how they came to their present predicament; they narrate, in other words. Dexter's voice-overs, by contrast, are often less narration than commentary (often with razor-sharp irony). He interprets himself, his actions, his circumstances, but he also leaves us in the dark about certain things. In Season 4, for instance, he suddenly has a storage unit. Dexter has his reasons for not telling his full story—to us as viewers, or to anyone else in his world. Besides the obvious legal reasons, there's also the troubling fact that everyone who has "seen" Dexter has not fared well.

And yet we can't help but wonder if Dexter will ever tell his story, if he will give an account of himself. The possibility that he might, whether voluntarily or not, is part of the suspense of the show. But it's also a question inherent in Dexter's developing humanity, as part of the need for recognition. We need to tell our stories with others. The problem with solitary self-narration is that no one can challenge, correct, or supplement one's individual account of things. As Alasdair MacIntyre argues in *After Virtue*, our individual narratives always interlock with others, so we are accountable to others in the stories we tell about ourselves: "Asking you what you did and why, saying what I did and why, pondering the differences between your account of what I did and my account of what I did, and vice versa, these are essential conditions of all but the very simplest and barest of narratives."[10]

In addition to his desire to be seen by another, is it possible that Dexter will become aware of the need to be heard by another? He loves to reveal himself covertly, with comments whose double meaning is only apparent to us, his loyal viewers. Is it possible that these ironic comments indicate an unconscious desire to be open?

Dexter is torn between his desire to remain hidden and a desire to come into the open. Therein lies his power to fascinate. If Dexter were simply a sociopath trying to keep secrets, he wouldn't intrigue us like he does. He clearly has a human desire to understand and be understood. He is a self-interpreting animal. Does this mean Dexter is human? He is clearly not a healthy, flourishing human being. But if he were simply a monster with no humanity, or an outsider posing as a human (like the Terminator, or the alien in *Species*), he wouldn't be so conflicted, so marked by the desire to understand who he is, what he's doing, and where he's going.

This also leaves us fans of Dexter feeling torn. We want to see him disclose himself and become more fully human—and yet we don't want it, since we know this will spell the end of the conflicted humanity that makes Dexter such a fascinating character. In the meantime, we'll keep watching to see what happens.

---

[10] *After Virtue*, p. 218.

7
Is Dexter Morgan *Practically* Perfect in Every Way?

RICHARD GREENE

One of the first things we learn about Dexter Morgan is that he has virtually no emotions. He has compulsions, which are kind of like strong feelings—his Dark Passenger certainly exerts some sort of coercive power over him—but he lacks any real feelings beyond a penchant for things like coffee, doughnuts, and pulled-pork sandwiches.

Dexter doesn't feel love, empathy, friendship, guilt, remorse, compassion for others, or fear. This, of course, makes him extremely rational. Without pesky emotions getting in the way, Dexter is in the position of always doing the rational thing, given his particular set of desires.

This is exactly how Dexter is presented to us in both the series of books and the television show—a hyper-rational agent calculating the consequences of every action to perfection. Every detail and variable is taken into consideration and placed under the microscope that is his famously huge intellect. His plans rarely hit a snag, as reason tells him exactly what to expect. Dexter is neat, exacting, and meticulous.

Practical rationality is the area of philosophy that asks the question: what does reason dictate that we do in a particular situation? Dexter is presented as nearly always being practically rational. Even when it comes to things such as matters of the heart, he acts on reason. For example, his relationship with Rita Bennett begins because Dexter calculates that being in a relationship helps him hide his identity as a serial killer by appearing normal, and thus, making it easier to fit in. There are exceptions to this. For example, Dexter should not have prevented Trinity from falling off a roof in hopes of killing him himself later, but these lapses in judgment are few and far between.

This characterization pretty much fits Dexter perfectly until he meets Lumen Ann Pierce early in Season 5.

Groomin' Lumen

When we first encounter Lumen, Dexter has just killed Boyd Fowler, another serial killer who tortures his victims for some time before eventually disposing of them in metal drums, which then get thrown into a swamp. Unbeknownst to Dexter, Lumen—whom Fowler had held captive, tortured, and raped for some time—witnessed him kill Fowler. Immediately after the act is completed, Dexter hears Lumen sneaking away from her viewing position on the other side of a slightly ajar door. Dexter consequently finds himself in a tough predicament. Harry's Code—the set of rules by which Dexter qua serial killer operates—dictates that Dexter do whatever is necessary to ensure that he not get caught. Here the easiest and most efficient way of acting in accordance with this part of Harry's Code would be to simply kill her. On the other hand, Harry's Code requires Dexter to refrain from harming innocents. Lumen is clearly an innocent. In fact, she's a victim of both Fowler and the circumstance she presently finds herself in.

This would be an interesting place to raise questions of practical rationality. What does reason dictate that Dexter do? Is there any way to act in accordance with both tenets of the Code? We're not, however, going to address practical rationality here, as there are even more interesting questions ahead.

After ruminating on the situation for some time, Dexter, in a very uncharacteristic fashion, decides to take a leap of faith—he decides to trust Lumen not to turn him in or notify the authorities, thus satisfying the "harm no innocents" requirement. This is a bit of a departure from Harry's Code, as the Don't Get Caught requirement is routinely presented throughout the series as being of the utmost importance. Here we see Dexter opting for the moral requirement over the purely self-interested requirement. (Obviously, I'm not an ethical egoist.)

Given that Dexter lacks feelings such as guilt and remorse, it's curious that he chooses as he does. Even more curious is what follows. It turns out that Boyd Fowler was not acting alone. He was part of a ring of five or six friends that had been torturing, killing, raping, and disposing of women in the aforementioned manner for several decades. Lumen was to have been the fourteenth victim. Lumen decides to seek revenge on her captors. Dexter initially counsels her to let it go and move back to the Midwest. Eventually Dexter decides to assist Lumen in her efforts to kill each of the men involved in the ring. Later Lumen asks Dexter to train her to be a Dexter-like killer, and Dexter acquiesces. It is these two decisions—the decision to help Lumen avenge the crimes enacted upon her, and the decision to train Lumen to become a "professional" killer—that I'd like to consider from the perspective of practical rationality. Was it rational for Dexter to do these things?

Corrupting the Youth of Miami

It is often said that "the ends justify the means." Of course, this expression is likely as often denied as affirmed, but the ubiquity of the expression alone suggests that it is at least worth considering as a norm of practical rationality. So our first stab at determining whether it was rational for Dexter to help Lumen gain revenge and become a killer herself will involve examining the *consequences* of his doing so.

Generally speaking the consequences of Dexter's actions were good. Things worked out pretty well for Dexter and very well for Lumen. Neither Dexter nor Lumen were caught (although it was a bit "touch and go" toward the end), each of the perpetrators was killed and disposed of in a way that won't come back to haunt either Dexter or Lumen, our couple had a nice, albeit brief, romantic relationship, in which Dexter actually felt loved for who he was (as opposed to having to hide his true self in order to maintain a relationship), and Lumen appears to have exorcised the demons that being raped and tortured bestowed upon her.

Does the fact that Dexter's decisions led to good states of affairs make those decisions rational? Not by itself. To see why, suppose that one month Vince Masuka has enough cash to pay some but not all of his monthly bills. Also suppose that Masuka decides to spend what cash he has all in one evening at a local strip club, instead of paying those bills that he can pay. (Vince loves the ladies!) At this point I think it's fair to judge that Masuka has not acted rationally, and it doesn't alter our assessment of Masuka's rationality if we add to the story that on the way out of the strip club he found a bag with a large sum of money in it. Under such circumstances the right thing to conclude is that Masuka was lucky, not rational.

While merely focusing on the consequences alone is not sufficient for determining the rationality of an act, perhaps focusing on the clearly foreseeable consequences can salvage the strategy. Certainly Masuka could not have foreseen that he would find the bag of money and that his financial problems would be solved, but perhaps Dexter could have foreseen how things would likely go with Lumen upon deciding to assist her in exacting revenge. This, however, seems quite unlikely. A large part of what allows Dexter to keep from getting caught is his ability to control most or all of the variables when he goes on a kill. Prior to agreeing to assist Lumen he had plenty of reason to believe that she was somewhat erratic and in a highly emotional state a large percentage of the time (who wouldn't be after what she had just been through!)—she had been dishonest with him about her intentions to return to the Midwest, for example. Dexter had no reason to think that Lumen would allow him to follow Harry's Code while they attempted to exact revenge on her captors.

Moreover, Dexter could not have foreseen that his turning Lumen into a killer would go as well as it did. In Plato's dialogue *The Apology* Socrates is put on trial for corrupting the youth of Athens (among other things).[1] In his defense Socrates points out that anyone who corrupts the youth must do so either voluntarily or involuntarily. He provides the following argument for the position that, had he corrupted the youth of Athens, he would not have done so voluntarily. Wicked people harm their associates, where as good people benefit them. Everyone would rather be benefitted than harmed by his or her associates. Therefore, anyone who corrupts his or her associates runs the risk of being harmed by them. Since Socrates knows that the previous premise is true, he concludes: if he harms his associates, he does so involuntarily.

Dexter must also recognize that corrupting Lumen could put him at risk of being harmed by her, especially given that he would be the only one who could identify her as a murderer. So, rationally speaking, Dexter does not have reason to believe that helping Lumen would work out as well as it did. He had Socrates's reasons for thinking that it might not work out so well.

---

[1] Plato, *Apology*, lines 24b3–28a1.

In fact, Dexter's interactions with former District Attorney turned killer Miguel Prado, actually provide Dexter with a very good reason for thinking that things with Lumen might not go so well. While the circumstances surrounding Dexter's turning Lumen into a killer are somewhat different from the circumstances in which he helps Miguel become a killer—Miguel had something on Dexter, such that Dexter was sort of forced to help him—the relevant features are identical: in each case Dexter ended up training his protégé in the ways of Harry's Code. Miguel did not adhere to the code much at all and eventually became Dexter's adversary. Dexter's very life was at risk, along with his secrets and his identity.

Albert Eistein is reported to have said, "Insanity is doing the same thing over and over again and expecting different results." From this we can see that one hallmark of rationality is learning from past events. Were Dexter being rational in the case of Lumen he would have learned from the case of Miguel. Thus, the possibility of good foreseeable consequences serving as a ground of practical rationality, does not help Dexter in these cases. If Dexter's decisions to help Lumen and to assist her in becoming a killer are going to turn out to be rational, we're going to need to turn to different models of practical rationality.

The Homicidal Imperative?

A number of prominent moral theorists have argued that it is always rational to do the ethical thing and never rational to do otherwise. This is a point worth addressing because, if it is correct, then any further analysis of Dexter's decisions becomes unnecessary: to the extent that they involve unethical action, they would be irrational by definition.

Plato argues that to be ethical is, ultimately, a matter of being psychologically healthy (of having a well-ordered soul), which, in turn, gets defined as being rational (or, more precisely, having the rational or reasoning parts of the soul control the various other parts of the soul).[2] Kant argues that rational actions are those that are in accordance with maxims that can be universalized and, hence, are not contingent on one's personal desires or sentiments.[3] He further argues that, if an act is not contingent on one's desires

---

[2] Plato, *The Republic*, Books II–IV.
[3] Immanuel Kant, *Grounding for the Metaphysics of Morals*, sections 1–2.

yet one has a reason to perform that act, then one must be commanded by reason to perform that act. Thus, on Kant's view, moral acts are always, by definition, rational actions, and immoral actions are always, by definition, irrational.

Plato's view offers us no real guidance in answering the question of whether Dexter's helping Lumen is practically rational. It tells us that the moral thing to do is to act in accordance with reason or to do as reason dictates, but it does not further tell us what reason actually dictates in theses circumstances. At best it tells us that if Dexter is doing what reason requires, then he's doing the right thing.

Kant's position, on the other hand, is more helpful. Kant provides means by which we can determine the morality of specific actions. We can look to see if those actions can be universalized without contradiction. We can ask whether our action is the kind of thing we would want everyone doing. Also, we can examine to see whether particular actions are treating the humanity (that is, the rational capacity to set one's own goals) of persons as an end in itself. In other words, we can ask whether we are violating people's autonomy when we act.

Neither of Dexter's actions—helping Lumen exact revenge and training her to become a killer—will turn out to be moral on Kant's grounds. Consequently, neither action will turn out to be rational. We wouldn't want to live in a world where everyone was a killer (since we might end up getting killed) and we violate a person's autonomy in the worst way when we kill him or her. This assessment seems right: Dexter is helping Lumen become a killer, for Pete's sake. Even if her assailants deserve to die, the way Dexter and Lumen are going about it doesn't appear to be moral in any sense. So the strategy of attempting to get Dexter's actions to come out as rational by examining the morality of those actions appears doomed to fail.

Kickin' It New School

Let's look at some contemporary views of practical rationality. These days, theories of rationality tend to fall into one of two broad categories: instrumentality theories and maximizing theories. Instrumentality theories tend to focus on the means employed by agents as they attempt to meet various goals. Here, rationality (roughly) gets cashed out in terms of whether said means are effective or optimal for meeting said goals. Maximizing theories tend to focus on the goals of the agent themselves. Rationality (again, roughly) gets cashed out in terms of whether the goal itself is one that is rational to have, given the overall desire set of the particular agent.

Let's begin with a maximizing theory. Decision theory is a paradigmatic example of a maximizing theory. According to decision theorists, rationality involves determining by means of a mathematical calculation which of all available actions will bring about the best state of affairs and then acting on the basis of that calculation. The mathematical calculation is a function of the relevant probabilities of a particular outcome resulting from a given action and the value of that outcome. The product of a decision-based calculus is the endorsement of the particular action or strategy that produces the optimal state of affairs, given the agent's overall set of desires. Such an action or strategy is considered to be the rational strategy or course of action.

According to Decision Theory, Dexter's actions would be rational only if they brought about the best state of affairs, given his overall set of desires. It is not possible to know what all of Dexter's desires are, but we do know that he places great emphasis on Harry's Code. As we've seen, the desire to not get caught is very high up on Dexter's list. Moreover, we've already seen that the way things turned out for Dexter and Lumen was not foreseeable. Thus, it stands to reason that Dexter was not acting according to the dictates of Decision Theory, as his calculations would have suggested a very different course of action.

Now consider instrumentality theory. Were Dexter's means an effective or optimal way of meeting his goals? The consequences were good, and he was able to assist Lumen, but just because a strategy works out in a particular instance doesn't mean that it is an optimal strategy. Again, consider Masuka's strategy of paying his bills by getting plastered in a strip club. It worked out once, but would most likely not work out so well on other occasions. So to assess Dexter's means we have to consider their general likelihood of working out. Presumably Dexter's goals in this case are (roughly): 1. Don't violate Harry's Code; 2. Help Lumen exact revenge, and 3. Train Lumen to become a killer. Attempting to meet each of these goals simultaneously, in most cases, would not work out. Specifically #2 and #3 are largely antithetical to #1, for all the reasons we've already considered: Lumen is a bit of a loose cannon, corrupting her could yield very bad consequences for Dexter, Dexter is able to adhere to Harry's Code precisely because he is able to largely control all the relevant variables, and so on. It would appear, then, that neither of the most popular contemporary accounts of practical rationality render the verdict that Dexter's actions are rational, either.

I've Got No Strings . . .

One conclusion that we can draw is that no account of practical rationality is going to maintain that Dexter's interactions with Lumen were rational. We've not examined every possible theory of rationality, but the one's we have considered are pretty broad. They represent the most general strategies, and in each case his actions fail the rationality test.

Dexter's actions aren't rational in virtue of their good consequences; as the view that consequences determine rationality has been shown to be implausible in its most general form and inapplicable to Dexter in its most plausible form—when focus was placed on foreseeable consequences. His actions aren't rational in virtue of their being moral (because they simply aren't, in fact, moral). His actions aren't rational in virtue of their maximizing satisfaction of Dexter's desires, as his strongest desires involve things such as not getting caught, and a decision-theory calculus based on such desires would have had Dexter performing very different actions. Finally, Dexter's actions are not rational in virtue of their being optimal for meeting his goals, as they simply would not likely meet his goals in most cases.

Is this result bad for Dexter? Perhaps not. To the extent that Dexter has no real emotions, he is in some sense deficient. It's great to be very rational, but no one desires to be rational at the expense of not having the full range of human experiences. Acting in non-rational ways doesn't give one emotions, per se, but it may be a sign that Dexter is changing in a fundamental way. Maybe our little wooden boy is starting to become a real boy.

BODY PART II

The Cut of Dexter's Jib

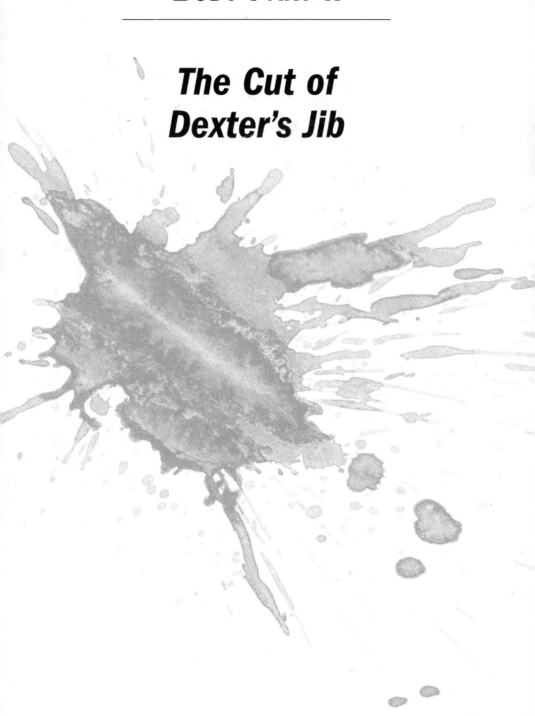

8

Dexter's Mirror

JERRY S. PIVEN

What drives Dexter? What makes him murder? Is Dexter a sociopath? Here we have a serial killer who shows no remorse and no empathy for the victims whom he wraps in plastic and murders ceremoniously. Dexter ritualizes death, sanctifies it, draws a blood sample from each murdered murderer and informs them that they are destined for death because of their own loathsome crimes.

Beyond guilt, Dexter seems to thrive on death. He relishes the ritual, craves it, and hungers for death when deprived of the opportunity. When life intervenes to thwart death, Dexter feels anxious, antsy, frustrated, and foggy, jonesing for murder. Beyond death, in life Dexter also displays the marked absence of empathy and human feeling that are so conspicuous among sociopathic killers.

We often hear that Dexter is a sociopath, or a psychopath, or an antisocial personality, or even a dissocial personality (different schools of psychology have a diversity of lexicons and definitions). It's also fashionable to explain the darkness of serial killers and sociopathy as the result of bad genes. So genes are invoked to explain why Dexter is such a fumbling brother, a total "tard" as his sister calls him, a person who lacks the usual desires and feelings, but can murder without that kind of torturous guilt that makes Shakespeare characters wring their hands and cry to the heavens. Surrounded by death, blood, anguish, laughter, and sexuality, Dexter is aloof and askew, and has to remind himself to act "normal" because it just isn't him.

The Seduction of Blood

But is *Dexter* merely a story about a person with defective genes or cognitive impairment? The show may indeed force us to question the extent to which people are the product of their genes. It certainly revisits the issue of whether we have free will, and how much our genes, or wiring, determine our behavior regardless of environment or upbringing. However, *Dexter* is also a dark reflection on the human capacity to murder, and with each episode we reach down deeper into the soul of a serial killer to find not genetic dispositions, but the all too human suffering and despair that inhabits and moves us.

The possible genetic origins of sociopathy notwithstanding, Dexter is more complicated than a simplistic diagnosis, and he is certainly written as a more intriguing character. What's so fascinating and relevant about *Dexter* is that it explores what kinds of suffering can make people vengeful, violent, and capable of murder, while they have no genuine understanding of why they are truly motivated to kill.

But is Dexter even a sociopath? Dexter *does* care about others, such as his sister Deb, his paramour Rita, and her kids. Dexter is eerily devoted to his father. This is not the callousness or calculation of a sociopath, but that of a vulnerable boy who seeks the love of his father and is afraid of disappointing him. Dexter's sensitivity to his father's wishes transcends death. As an adolescent Dexter exhibits remorse before his father, and peers anxiously into his eyes for approval. Even as a fully-actualized adult serial killer, Dexter's need to please his father is so intense that he yearns for the sanction of a specter, a ghost who becomes his conscience.

Dexter hardly lacks empathy. The son is still haunted by the admonishment and love of a ghost. In death Harry is Dexter's super-ego, like the spirit of Hamlet's father stalking the son who has strayed from his almost blunted purpose. Dexter even feels a measure of empathy for the family-abusing serial killer Trinity, and *his* pitiable family.

That's a significant clue. Dexter despises injustice and victimization so much that he's driven to exterminate murderers, and to inform them that they have so victimized others that they deserve to die. For a person so out of tune with others, Dexter isn't bereft of empathy. He's so empathic about innocent suffering that he needs to punish predators and make them languish in terror before their imminent dismemberment. Dexter's suffering when he witnesses persecution actually raises an important psychological and philosophical question about morality and our own needs to punish: how much of our convictions of right, wrong, justice, and punishment are related to an inner anxiety about innocence and victimization?

Truly, most of us aren't serial killers, but *Dexter* is a fantasy about the demons that lurk within not only mass murderers, but perhaps us as well. The fantasy of the vigilante or angel of death is one that resonates with us, as viewers and voyeurs, as those who participate vicariously in punishing the wicked, as we identify with the rage and violence of the killer even if we would never allow ourselves the exquisite pleasure of torturing and vivisecting someone who really deserves it. We can luxuriate in vicarious bloodshed but find murder terrifying and loathsome, until we hear that some vile enemy despises everything we stand for, and then it's permissible (or our patriotic, solemn duty) to massacre them. There's a fabulous episode of *Futurama* where a conscripted soldier asks what they are dying for, and the smug yutz of a commander tells them "They stand for everything you don't stand for. Plus they said you guys look like dorks!"

That's facile, to be sure, but some odd 14,600 wars in human history, the propaganda, rhetoric, and clichés of warfare, the ongoing senseless massacres, the ease with which people can come to stereotype and despise "them" as despicable, demonstrate how susceptible we are to falling into rife hatred of people we don't even know. As much as Dexter is the case of a unique killer so vastly different from ourselves, the irony is that it's easy to get ordinary civilized people who deplore murder to accept the slaughter of countless innocent civilians, if they are demonized as evil.

This is why the philosopher Hannah Arendt explored "the banality of evil," the way ordinary human beings can perpetrate acts of immense cruelty or injustice so long as the society deems such behavior acceptable. The banality of evil illustrates how such ordinary citizens can participate in Nazi genocide, or for that matter, be so terrified by vague images of inhuman enemies that we can believe that torture camps and mass exterminations are a good thing. This is why thinkers from Plato to Ernest Becker could say that most of the evil and bloodshed in history is actually intended to eradicate evil, to do the right thing. That's a very dark secret about *our* humanity. We are not mass murderers, and yet when socially sanctioned, so many of us can become vicious killers and blot out conscious empathy for innocent victims.

And this is the genius of *Dexter*: it explores that part of us that can be seduced into murder, the part that becomes outraged by injustice and victimization but can so easily slip into punishing and victimizing others. It explores our needs to slake our thirst for blood. And the show does not merely pretend that malice is aberrant genes or even human nature (whatever that is); we are given clues that tell us what experiences guide us toward slaughter. Dexter's experiences are horribly atypical, yet they illustrate the human wounds and abscesses that enable us to resonate with his story, with messages of death, the seductions of murder, and the narrative ploys we use to make murder seem righteous.

The Void, Dread, and Murder

The very first episode gives us clues about Dexter's yearning for slaughter. There are breadcrumbs from the opening moments that lead us to the profound psychological crises of murderers, the trauma and cataclysms that massacre their souls and set them upon quests to kill. One of these clues is the cavernous void inside Dexter. He repeatedly says that he feels empty inside. Not just unemotional, but empty. There's something missing, a hollow that he feels, as though something had been surgically removed, as if he should be filled with something and is ever feeling that space inside him. From Episode 1, Dexter tells us about the void within himself, a void that we gradually come to understand when we learn the tragedy of his own life.

Now some might say that we all feel unfulfilled, or empty, and one of the brilliant ironies of the show is that while Dexter wears a mask to hide the real killer inside, and to appear "normal," there is also the suspicion that we all somehow pretend. Normalcy is masks. We pretend to be what we are not, whether that means conforming to our peers, lying so as not to appear weird or pervy, or keeping so many feelings inside.

Dexter can pretend so that he is not revealed as a serial killer, but that wouldn't explain his emotional void, his inner emptiness. People wear masks and keep secrets, but we also hide feelings from ourselves to protect our fragile egos and ward off the excruciating pain of vulnerability and rejection. We sometimes succumb to the drive to what psychologists Bollas and Hantman call "normopathy," a pathological striving to submerge oneself in normality and acceptable virtues, a timorous obedience that squashes any inkling of independent thought, or deep emotions such as anger toward the friends who reject anything slightly different, or empathy toward those who languish.

Michael Eigen writes of the "psychic deadness" we sometimes feel, the way we numb and excise our own feelings so we can avoid shame, anguish, vulnerability, neediness, desire, and rage. Existentialist philosophers even talk about the excruciating void that we mask every day, even from ourselves, so as to deny the intense pain and despair within. We flee from terror and despair into social conformity and emotional deadness, so Kierkegaard and Heidegger say. We live inauthentically in the face of death and flee from life, obliterating consciousness as we strive for oblivion. We commit what Firestone calls acts of "microsuicide" to kill off our feelings, stifle our yearnings, and close ourselves off from the pain of loss, love, betrayal, and death. So what of Dexter's void? Consider the possibility that Dexter is vacant because he is frozen, deadened, and withdrawn from something cataclysmic inside.

Some Buddhist philosophers also speak of the void, "sunyata," emptiness. Actually this emptiness can be a good thing, when one comes to realize how false the masks are, how destructive desires can be, and is enlightened of the burden of feeling the need to be something, or someone. The Buddhists realize that all our desires and attachments cause us (and others) pain, and so being nothing, letting go, being empty, is seen as a positive state. But the feeling of that void in the self is what causes us to cling to the desires of the ego, to be ambitious, to feel like we want to be someone special and more important than others. We are so anxious and empty that we do outrageous things to be unique individuals, put our names in lights, buy the coolest toys and cars, and show it all off.

While we can dissociate or close ourselves off from deep feelings, that inner void and deadness can drive us relentlessly, so that we take our pain and frustrations out on others, become callous and inhumane, greedy and acquisitive, desperately seeking social status, fame, or possessions to fill in that void that remains deadened to those vulnerable needs we just can't let ourselves experience. That callousness can be emotional flatness, or mere insensitivity, or it can merge into degrees of intolerance, cruelty, spite, and contempt for anything needy, emotional, or weak. In *The Insanity of Normality* Arno Gruen writes of those who have numbed and deadened their feelings, but contain such utter abjection and rage within that they can inflict brutal suffering on others unfeelingly. This should seem eerily familiar to fans of *Dexter*. His void is an enigma, and a conspicuous mystery of the show is how a person who seems so numb and unemotional can crave acts of horrid gore.

Some Buddhists believe that this emptiness and insecurity is so painful that it causes us to compete with others, desire to dominate and hurt others, even destroy them. One screams "I am not nothing! You are nothing! And I will destroy you to prove it!" A Zen master friend of mine named David Loy wrote a beautiful article about terrorist violence, saying that there is a "god-shaped hole" some people suffer because modernity challenges our beliefs and makes it difficult to have faith. This actually assumes that there is a void without God, and indeed the infamous philosopher Pascal wrote that the vastness and emptiness of infinity drove him desperately toward faith, and further, that we would all become as passionately religious if we ever allowed us to really feel that horror and infinity closing in around us, the emptiness of life, and the cold inevitability of death. If God fills that void, so Zen master Loy asserts, other faiths, ways of life, and defeats in life engender doubt, dissolve the blissful presence of God within, leave a painful void, and thus arouse rage. This void motivates terrorist vengeance against those with a different religion, a belief in God that makes them question their own. They fill their void with murder, just as Dexter fills his.

But what does that teach us about Dexter? If we all feel an inner void, as some Buddhists say, do we conclude with Pascal and Zen master Loy that we must fill this void with God or murder, or else dissolve into a quivering puddle of existential misery and terror? Let us grant that if we do experience an existential vacuum, or Buddhistic void, maybe we aren't all equally vacuous or empty inside. *Dexter* shows us that however empty and unfulfilled some people feel, obviously not all are so profoundly empty that they crave terrorist pyrotechnics or ritual death. As empty and frustrated as we may be, and as much as we may want to strangle someone sometimes, most of us don't feel antsy if we don't get our weekly fix of bloodshed (real bloodshed that we personally inflict, as opposed to our favorite shows or the nightly news).

Thus Dexter shows us something fascinating: His void reminds us of ours; the masks and conformity of daily life enable us to empathize with a serial killer, to experience his needs and desperation, as well as his struggle to feel. And yet as much as we empathize, we are not Dexter. So we identify with him, and like him personally, want him to kill his evil and deserving victims, and are further drawn into his story. We're exposed to our own void, our masks, our desperation, and our own desire to kill, and we feel a similarity even when we are so vastly different. Withal, we still want to know what makes Dexter need to kill.

Dexter's Ritual Transcendence of Death

And so the show shows us. Dexter is not empty and unempathic because of a genetic condition, or even some God-craving terrorist void. It's something far less abstract, and more vicious. We find out that his mother was murdered before his very eyes. Dexter saw her slaughtered before him, and lay crying in a pool of her blood. This was the psychological devastation that (virtually) obliterated the capacity to feel. Dexter needed to forget, and blot out vulnerability, and pain, and rage, to survive. That void is a gap in memory, and an emptiness of being eviscerated emotionally. Where the mother, and love, and joy once were, now there is blood, rage, and emptiness. But the excruciating pain of that loss and the feelings of anguish, helplessness, vulnerability, and rage were too overwhelming to endure, and Dexter must feel (almost) nothing.

Like so many dark emotions we cannot consciously endure, however, the abject helplessness and seething rage take on a life of their own. That dark void of infinite rage and vengeance grips Dexter and possesses him to murder, even as he is consciously emotionless. Like so many murderers, and others who have suffered catastrophic, traumatic losses, Dexter is compelled to revisit symbolically the scenario that destroyed him.

Each murder is a compulsive attempt to restage death as its master, to recreate helplessness and terror as the angel of death instead of his victim, to inflict overwhelming terror and helplessness on the victimizer and then murder him. Every murder is an act of recreation and magical undoing, and every slain murderer is a symbolic substitute for the one who slaughtered Dexter's mother and left the child bereft of love, in a pool of blood. Where he was drowned in a sea of blood and terror before, now he inflicts terror and diminishes the oceanic blood to a drop on a slide he can imprison, own, control, and possess. Each uncontrolled and remorseless murderer

is demeaned, reduced to an inhuman globule helplessly splayed
and squashed by transparent glass. The ritual recreates and avenges
death, masters it, and punishes the doppelgangers symbolizing the
murderer who ravaged him. Each slaughter ritualizes the transformation from wretched helplessness to utter control over blood and
death.

Here we enter into the psychology of ritualized and compulsive
behaviors, where the compulsion to repeat, master, avenge, and
transmogrify trauma can be seen in rituals as ordinary as obsessive
compulsive tendencies, in violence, even in sexual scenarios that
restage painful and humiliating experiences. In many spheres of
life we unconsciously revisit and recreate the circumstances that
once terrorized us. Dexter's ritualization is a parable for the mas-
tery of tragic violence, but many of us are also compelled to repeat
the same banal mistakes, find the same kind of dysfunctional
lovers, and master archaic experiences that wounded us. Most of
the time we have no idea that we have recreated the situation and
wonder how the same absurd things have befallen us again and
again.

Some scholars believe that certain religious rituals are also ways
of transforming the dread of helplessness and death into magical
control, order, and life. There are so many kinds of religious ritual,
but let us pause for a moment and consider some of the myriad
human and animal sacrifices, rituals of appeasing nature, warding
off death and disaster, even communing with God, and at least
inquire to what degree human beings have been so terrified of devastation that magical, ritual means of control have become sacred
acts. The sheer proliferation of religious rituals throughout history
that have tried to ward off cataclysmic disaster, evil, contagion,
plague, and death through sacrifice and ritual murder (even of
humans) suggests that Pascal may have been on to something, that
we live in such dread of death that we turn desperately to religion.
Like so many other behaviors, and like Dexter's own benighted rituals, there may be more purpose to such acts than we know, or
would be willing to believe unless we had the courage to look
deeply into the eyes of our own dark passengers.

Dexter's transcendence of death is emblematic of a far darker
mode of ritualization, however: the way some people can trans-
form misery, abjection, and humiliation into triumphant conquest
through ceremonial violence. As Walter Davis explains in his
provocative book *Death's Dream Kingdom*, acts of torture and ter-

rorism are not only ideological, political, or strategic events. They are also ritualized forms of death transcendence. The torturer derives sadistic pleasure from humiliating and rendering victims helpless, forcing them to suffer, and inflicting terror. The recent scandal over the torture camp in Abu Ghraib in Iraq revealed photos of torturers smiling happily while holding their unclothed prostrate victims on dog leashes and piled naked in pyramids. That's a far cry from retrieving actionable information.

And again, as much as we may interpret terrorism and martyrdom operations as political and strategic acts, there is also a psychological dimension that transmogrifies the wounded victim of injustice to a heroic angel of death who wreaks vengeance on his (perceived) victimizer. I would argue, along with *Dexter*, that in their own ways these acts recapitulate our own unknown, dark pasts and emotional wounds, inflicting our own miseries and nightmares on others, even if we would rather protest that wicked desires and fears do not exist within us.

Thus *Dexter* has provided us with fascinating clues to our protagonist's need to murder, and when we're closed into that dark, suffocating, claustrophobic container where his mother was slaughtered, we are forced to empathize with his tragic loss, and become conscious not only of what drives him, but makes us desire vengeance. If he describes the shadowed impulse to murder as his Dark Passenger, we too become empathic travelers who begin to feel those desires with him. And so, perhaps we have a radical insight into both the way we deaden or excise feelings to survive, and the shadowy remembrance of loss, horror, vulnerability, and violation, that motivate some of us to seek out vengeance and death.

Perhaps the supreme insight and sinister lesson, however, is that just as Dexter feels that void and isn't aware of what drives him, we too may not realize just how much our own fear, dread, and vulnerability may render us susceptible to both psychic deadness, and then, the capacity for murder. Perhaps Heidegger and Kierkegaard were right when they asserted that we are so afraid of nonexistence and death that we immerse ourselves in oblivion, close ourselves off to the void of horror and despair within. Ernest Becker even writes that the mainspring of human activity is an attempt to deny and overcome our grotesque fate, that the fear of death haunts us like nothing else. We don't need to watch our loved ones slaughtered before our eyes to feel such terror and rage that we are driven to emotional deadness and ritual slaughter, and yet, even we are so utterly horrified by death that we can become numb, closed off, and easily seduced into murder.

Worse, over the past few decades experimental work in Terror Management has shown that if we are stimulated by the fear of death and given messages of dire threat, that we will become more militant in defense of our world views and even support policies that we would otherwise find reprehensible. In other words, beyond the operation of rationality and our conscious values, we will become more aggressive and supportive of violent acts that we would usually find disgusting. Terror Management psychologists continue to find that our dread of death motivates our attachment to worldviews that salve that dread, and that we will respond like monsters when that fear is reawoken by reminders of death. Zen master Loy was right: there may be a void within that is filled with religion (or *other* death-denying) unguent, and so many of us will respond to threats to that death-containing belief system with violence. Yes we are not terrorists, or Dexter, but we too are vulnerable and terrified within. Yet another irony: we don't have to be as wounded as Dexter to murder. That dread of death, that human void filled in with death-denying belief, can make slaughter so utterly banal if we are scared enough, and we will kill with impunity if guided into it with the right rhetoric, the right justifications or excuses that make carnage seem right. That brings us back to Dexter's father, Harry . . .

All for Love

It is Harry who channels Dexter's violent impulses toward remorseless predators who victimize the innocent but manage to escape the punishment they deserve. This actually has sinister implications that relate to both Dexter's moral code and the way our own "rational" moral and ideological tenets are so tethered to our own dimly-conceived needs for love and acceptance. For Dexter begins murdering people not only to channel that helplessness and rage, but to satisfy Harry. The boy who looks timidly and longingly into his father's eyes does his bidding to make father happy. Dexter is inflicting his own rage on victims, but when he murders criminals, envisions his father, has imaginary conversations, and follows the Code, he is fulfilling his father's wishes as well.

Harry looks like a father deeply concerned with the safety of his son (and perhaps he is) but he is also expressing his own desire to kill murderers who escaped the system. As viewers we may interpret that intense gaze as paternal concern, but that look is also a manipulative, imprisoning stare that encumbers Dexter with the burden of doing his father's bidding. It is the look directed deeply into the eyes of someone who will be bent to one's will. And indeed, that will so manipulates and coerces Dexter that even as an adult, he is ghosted and plagued by Harry, who condemns him beyond death when he deviates from the Code. Were this merely parental concern Dexter wouldn't be stalked and harassed like a visitation from the ghost of Hamlet's father or a Dickensian character pleading with a spirit to haunt him no longer. There would be no guilt, no conflict, no painful struggle that strangles and condemns Dexter every time he desires autonomy, sees a glimmer of happiness, and departs from his dead father's commandments.

The sinister political implication is that while we may suffer a cavernous void within, plagued by the fear of death and nothingness, wounded from our own personal failings and losses, leaders can manipulate these fears, inform us of dire threats, and goad us into murdering to satisfy their wishes and purposes. The power of charismatic leaders resides not in their magical abilities, but in our disposition to depend on them, trust them, yearn for their protection. We look to them for safety and salvation, and this is why psychologists studying groups continually emphasize how susceptible we are to manipulation by leaders. We become dependent children psychologically regressed so that we no longer see leaders for whom they are, and we are easily seduced by their deceptions and fearmongering.

Dexter is an intriguing parable about the way we may murder from our own inner voids, our own wounds, and Dark Passengers. *Dexter* further illumines how we can be goaded to murder out of a desire to please someone else, how our own pain and terror can be manipulated so that we fulfill their wishes, and feel as if we're being good sons and daughters when we murder evil. I encourage readers to read transcripts of political speeches telling citizens that their loyal patriotic duty is to kill the evildoers, or for that matter, to read the speeches of Osama bin Laden to see just how much his followers are guilted into slaughter, for it is the duty of every Muslim (he says) to obey and kill infidels. Anything else, any independent thought or refusal, is betrayal, selfishness, cowardice, and commiseration with evil. We too have been manipulated into slaughter, and seduced by messages that make carnage a sacred and patriotic imperative in the war against terror and evil.

Dexter's genius is in depicting the story of us, the inner void and dread that make us lash out and want to kill, and the vulnerability that makes us yearn so deeply for love, that we will kill to attain it. This is why Ruth Stein could call her recent book (in my opinion the most insightful on the psychology of terrorism) *For Love of the Father*. But it isn't only those fanatics over there. We too suffer our own inner dread. We don't just kill out of hatred, but for *love*. Now that is sinister.

9

A Very Special Kind
of Monster

AARON C. ANDERSON

Season 4 of Dexter opens with a cruel bang: a long, intimate, and graphic murder. Called "Living the Dream," the first episode finds Dexter trying to fit into the suburban "dream" and the Trinity Killer ritually re-enacting the nightmares of his childhood. We see Trinity brutally murder Lisa Bell and we see Dexter stalk and kill Benny Gomez. This is one of the only times we see Dexter dismembering a victim, albeit in a few quick cuts (and in "Remains to Be Seen" we briefly see Gomez's dismembered body stuffed into a heavy bag).

"Living the Dream" opens by playing with our expectations and showing some of Dexter's dark humor. We see Dexter driving home, speaking, through voice-over, of being called by a "primal sacred need." While Dexter's "need" is sleep at this point, the Trinity Killer desires something else entirely.

Dexter's arrival home is crosscut with an image of a nude Trinity Killer setting up his own version of a kill room in his soon-to-be victim's house: towels on the floor, a half-filled bathtub. Lisa Bell comes home, enters her bathroom and sees Trinity in her bathroom mirror. He chokes her unconscious and we see a long shot of Trinity's fully nude body from behind, violently choking his victim.

The show crosscuts to Dexter's child, Harrison, crying, then cuts back to Trinity and his victim. The camera pans up across their bodies revealing Trinity seated behind his victim in the bathtub. She is crying, begging for her life, over a foreboding score. As weekly viewers of Dexter know, this scene is far from Dexter's "clean," detached killings. This is not "taking out the garbage." This is intimate, violating, and abject.

We see a close-up of the victim's face, still in a choke-hold. We are forced to see her in close-up, to witness her struggling. While she struggles, the camera pans up to a close-up of Trinity who looks rather indifferent in the face of the violence he inflicts. The camera punches out to an overhead shot. Trinity keeps his hold on his victim as she pleads. Trinity hushes her, choking her and she loses consciousness. Trinity, in a sense, re-assuring her, but also speaking of Vera's death says, "It's already over."

The scene already feels extremely long. It's difficult to watch and only gets worse as Trinity grabs an open straight razor. An overhead shot shows him bringing the blade underwater. An extreme close-up shows Lisa Bell's leg as the razor penetrates her skin and cuts her femoral artery. Blood begins to flood the bathtub and spill over as Trinity's victim struggles. Finally, Trinity grabs a hand mirror showing us the face of this vicious murderer, as he kills, in close-up.

Trinity's slow, meditated movements contrast sharply with the movements of his struggling, dying victim. We see her face in the hand mirror, crying, dying. She stops struggling, becomes a corpse, her body penetrated by a blade. The "border" of the skin destroyed and the body deprived of life and meaning. An overhead shot cranes back and we see Trinity and his latest victim, in the blood-and-water-filled tub. Trinity holds her and his ritual nears its end. Cut to black.

While this cross-cut scene lasts just over three minutes it provides a stark contrast to normally quick kills we see come at the hands of Dexter. In these scenes the camera tends to cut away quickly after Dexter inflicts the death blow. Within moments, Dexter disposes of the body. The shock of being forced to witness the brutal murder of Lisa Bell, can, in many ways, be likened to the feeling of "abjection" that philosopher Julia Kristeva writes of in her book *Powers of Horror*: we want to, need to, turn away from this violence and the corpse that it leaves behind but we are, in a sense, being forced to watch.[1]

Corpses and Nothingness

In *Powers of Horror*, Kristeva draws on a huge body of philosophical and psychological work to provide a sweeping, lyrical account

---

[1] Julia Kristeva, *Powers of Horror: An Essay in Abjection* (Columbia University Press, 1982), p. 2.

of fear of the self's destruction. She introduces the terms "abject" and "abjection" to describe the psychological foundations of this fear, coming from those things that threaten us and our understandings of our selves with destruction. This "sensation" of "abjection" is a defense against these frightening, "loathsome," and "separate," things and the knowledge of meaninglessness that they bring.

The sensation of abjection is like the "gagging sensation" that one has when something disgusting is seen, thought about, tasted, etc. It is similar to the experience of encountering a loathed "item of food, a piece of filth, waste, or dung." As Kristeva describes it, abjection appears as "the spasms and vomiting that protect me. The repugnance, the retching that thrusts me to the side and turns me away from defilement, sewage, and muck."

Far from mere "lack of cleanliness or health," Kristeva notes, the abject "disturbs identity, system, order." It "does not respect borders, positions, rules. The in-between, the ambiguous, the composite." It is the "traitor, the liar, the criminal with a good conscience, the shameless rapist, the killer who claims he is a savior" as well as crime in general that "draws attention to the fragility of the law." However, "premeditated crime, cunning murder, hypocritical revenge are even more [abject] because they heighten the display of such fragility." They "confront us . . . with those fragile states where man strays on the territories of animal."

One of the most striking causes of abjection is the corpse. According to Kristeva, the corpse confronts us with our own deaths, our own meaninglessness. Seeing a corpse pushes Kristeva to "the border of my condition as a living being." The corpse is "the most sickening of wastes," it is "a border that has encroached upon everything." Kristeva writes: "The corpse, seen without God and outside of science, is the utmost of abjection. It is death infecting life. Abject. It is something rejected from which one does not part, from which one does not protect oneself as from an object. Imaginary uncanniness and real threat, it beckons to us and ends up engulfing us" (pp. 3–4).

Violence and the Return of the Abject

In the flashbacks and fantasy sequences of the vicious killing of Dexter's mother, Laura Moser, Dexter faces the abject at a formative age. He also seems to face the abject when he discovers

Rita's corpse at the end of Season 4 ("The Getaway"). Dexter, however, also kills, creates corpses, destroys meaning, and does not experience abjection, nor do his killings seem to cause abjection in the audience.

Experiencing abjection might be the "normal" reaction to these horrific killings and dismemberments. Dexter has, however, encountered the abject once, at the scene of his mother's murder, and he continually re-experiences parts of this through flashbacks and fantasy sequences. Without using Kristeva's terminology, Dexter has a fantasy conversation with Harry while searching for the remains of Benny Gomez that touches on this very issue ("Remains to Be Seen," Season 4). Harry asks Dexter when was the last time his "memory was a blank," to which Dexter replies that it was at his mother's murder scene. The reason? In Dexter's words: "Because not remembering saved me."

In other words, the experience of witnessing his mother's murder and seeing his mother's corpse forced Dexter to confront the abject and his only defense against the abject was to turn away, to forget, to allow meaning to be destroyed. Dexter faced the abject as a child and does not face it again, except in flashback or fantasy, even at his own crime scenes and even as he dismembers his victims. However, the abject, for Dexter and the audience, returns with a new nastiness at the site of Rita's murder in the final episode of Season 4 ("The Getaway").

So, for instance, we see the Skinner literally take skin off of Anton's body and we see the partially-skinned corpses of his other victims. This is a literal sort of breaking the boundary between inside and outside that skin creates for the body. But we always need to remember that Dexter does this as well, in a sense, when he literally butchers his victims after killing them, although prior to Season 5 we rarely get glimpses of this. We are repulsed when we get quick cuts of the Skinner's victims and this repulsion shares something with the sensation of abjection, in some ways defending against the knowledge that our bodies can be cut, broken, opened up, killed, dismembered, and emptied of meaning.

The abject follows Dexter as well as the detectives of Miami Metro wherever they go. It follows us, as well. We're regularly given glimpses of the abject through flashes of murder victims and crime scene photos. We see corpses, whether missing skin and laying out in the sun or butchered into doll-like pieces or in blood-filled bathtubs or having leaped off of ledges. Yet when Dexter kills, prior to the more graphic killings at Dexter's hands in Season 5, we rarely see corpses, only neatly wrapped black garbage bags (at least until we see the remains of the Bay Harbor Butcher's victims and again later when Dexter deals with the remains of Benny Gomez).

In contrast, with the Ice Truck Killer, we see the corpses, drained of blood, posed. With the Skinner, we see victims murdered, their skin cut off, and decomposing. With Trinity, we see the killing and the bloody aftermath.

Taking Out the (Six) Garbage (Bags)

While those that Dexter stalks and kills are active, aggressive monsters, tormenting society and somehow getting away with it, it seems there is no more active "monster" than Dexter himself. In this, he seems to embody a part of ourselves that, as a society, we may partially repress: the revenge-minded vigilante. Think of the newspaper headline asking if the Bay Harbor Butcher is Miami's "Friend" or "Foe" ("The Dark Defender," Season 2).

Dexter's kills are clean and clinical but monstrous nonetheless. He stabs his victims in the chest, or, if appropriate, finds some other sort of object with which to break their bodies open, in a form of what might be called "poetic justice." We do see blood—sometimes more, sometimes less—but we do not see the dismemberments and other violations of the body that follow—at least not until Season 5. With a few exceptions, the first four seasons of Dexter repeatedly refuse to show us what happens in between the kill and the disposal of the evidence.

Dexter uses kill rooms, portable, covered in plastic sheeting, and always designed to "avoid a crime scene." The bodies of victims laid out, immobilized by plastic wrap. When he cleans them up, his actions are "automatic." They are a ritual. In this, Dexter truly is a monster. But he's also someone who can use rituals to avoid the abjection that his kills might and should inspire. They also allow him to avoid the abjection he experienced as a young child who witnessed his mother's murder and was forced to lie in her blood for days.

When he disposes of his victims, we see nondescript black garbage bags that, from the outside, can no longer be identified as human. The evidence is disposed of and Dexter relaxes. With a few exceptions, we do not see crime scenes or crime scene photos from

Dexter's premeditated kills. Although these killings are "abject," in Kristeva's terminology, the evidence is quickly done away with and the audience is spared the abjection that might come with watching, in gruesome detail, Dexter killing and dismembering one of his victims.

This manipulation of our experience of the abject is showcased when Dexter kills Trinity ("The Getaway," Season 4). This kill scene contrasts with the Trinity killings that we have witnessed—or seen the aftermaths of—over the course of Season 4. This scene also provides flashes of Dexter's "conscience," even if it is one only acquired through training. While images of Trinity's victims line the wall, Dexter's killing of Trinity actually seems more motivated by a sort of revenge for Trinity's family as, in a flash of conscience, Dexter reminds Arthur: "You destroyed your own family."

The depiction of the kill is brief. Dexter turns on the model train at Arthur's request. "Venus" by Johnny Tillotson kicks on the turntable. Arthur mumbles lyrics. Dexter dons a splash-guard mask. We see a close-up of a hammer and recognize that this will not be a knife-kill but rather one of "poetic justice" sort.

Next, a close-up of Dexter's face and the camera pans to the hammer in Dexter's hand hovering above Arthur's head. Dexter flips the hammer over as we saw Trinity do earlier in the season. We then see Arthur's shoulders and face, in a sort of ecstasy, with the hammer's shadow over him. A couple of quick cuts, a loud splat sound effect, and a cut to black. Short of the taking of the blood sample, we never see Arthur's skin penetrated. We don't see his skin, his "boundary," broken by the hammer, although we did, earlier in the season, through surveillance cameras, see Arthur break someone else's body in a similar way. With the exception of briefly witnessing a crime, we never see the abject. We do not have to experience abjection.

The camera fades in to Dexter's boat, the *Slice of Life*. The sky is blood red. Dexter dumps black garbage bags over the side of his boat and we hear a musical score of relief and resolution. The season is over and our hero has prevailed—and all this without subjecting his audience to the abject. He has tracked and killed his "prey," dismembered him, and "taken out the garbage," without exposing us to too much of the violence. We see no corpse. We see no butchering. We only see the six garbage bags that, according to Dexter, it takes to hold a body.

Kicking the Dark Passenger

Following his last encounter with Trinity, Dexter heads home, making voice-over plans to change his life, to make his "getaway" from the Dark Passenger. The music of resolution from the previous scene in which Dexter disposes of Trinity continues as Dexter walks into the house that he shares with Rita and their children. He focuses on the images of his wedding and his family that cover the wall. The upbeat music drops out when Dexter gets a message from Rita saying that she had to return home for her ID. He calls Rita back and becomes distressed when her phone rings right there, inside the house.

Against the noises of a child crying, Dexter runs in slow motion toward the sound. As he dims on the bathroom light, foreboding music comes up. We see Dexter's reaction to the murder scene before we actually see it. It's a reaction packed with fear and meaninglessness. Then we see what Dexter sees: his son, Harrison, in a pool of blood on the floor of the bathroom. A close-up shows Dexter's shocked face. Cutting back and forth between Dexter and his son we see Dexter experiencing abjection for perhaps the first time since his mother's murder.

The camera punches in closer to Dexter's son, the image blurs, and a flashback takes over the screen, familiar flashbacks of Dexter as a child, the blood spatter of chainsaws across his body, "born in blood," at his mother's murder scene. This is the beginning of a sort of dissolution of the self for Dexter. Meaning begins to collapse. To survive, he experiences abjection, violently turning away from the knowledge of dissolution of the self that Rita's corpse confronts him with.

The sounds of children crying now become odd and hallucinatory as the flashback sounds of Dexter as a child and his own child meld together. Dexter gets down on his knees to help his son and glances over to see Rita's corpse in the bathtub, here eyes open, lifeless, in a tub filled with blood. An overhead camera follows Dexter as he moves to the side of the tub where we only see her arm, her shoulder, her head. The rest is a very deep blood red running over the sides of the tub.

Dexter checks Rita's pulse and we see his reaction of shock, disbelief, abjection. This is something that must be turned away from, not seen. In an extreme close-up, Dexter closes Rita's eyes with his fingers. But we see it all—an extreme close-up of Rita's bloody hand, her wedding ring resting on the lip of the bathtub.

Rita's corpse is abject in a way that we aren't used to seeing. We don't see this with Dexter's killings, the show's "regular" killings. Though we do not see Rita's murder, we do see her corpse, the abject evidence of an abject crime. It forces us to see the abject, forces us to experience abjection, and the apprehend the knowledge that this brings for both us and Dexter. For Dexter, this may be only the second time in his life that he experiences abjection, the first being his mother's murder.

Up to this point in his life, however, Dexter has a problem with abjection: he says he can't feel anything. This problem is intricately related to his ongoing "identity crisis," a conflict between the self and an "other" that is both outside the self and a part of the self. In Dexter's understanding of himself, this may be the "Dark Passenger," or memories and fantasies of Harry Morgan. But it also boils down to a more profound and existential crisis. Not only the "Dark Passenger" versus "Dexter Morgan," or employee of the Miami Metro Police Department versus criminal, good versus bad, virtuous versus evil, or human versus animal. Dexter is all of these things at once. So it is a not a matter of being one or another, it is a matter of that which is inside of him but also threatens to "annihilate" him—and controlling it through the ritual of the Code.

Rule Number One

Harry's Code begins, "Don't get caught." It seems this rule even holds up when it comes to Dexter's relationship to us, his audience. Our experience of Dexter Morgan is, before the candidly vicious nature of Season 5, dictated by the avoidance of showing us the abject results of his kills—as well as dark humor when we do occasionally see these things. In a sense then, we don't "catch" Dexter at his most vicious. We aren't forced to experience anything like abjection in order to cope with the knowledge that Dexter's killings could bring.

Instead, when we do see dismembered body parts of Dexter's victims, as we do with Benny Gomez, we only get glimpses of them and Dexter uses dark humor to soften us up, to re-assure us, to put us on Dexter's side. As Dexter kills and disposes of his victims' corpses, our horror is put to rest, at least partially, by avoiding images of the abject. By not having to see dismembered bodies, we are not forced to confront the abject, to feel abjection. We may feel conflicted about Dexter's actions, but we are allowed to feel this way because we are not forced to watch him at his most ruthless. We can safely identify with, and perhaps empathize with, a vicious serial killer from the comfort of our living rooms. There is also Dexter's soothing voice-over, always filled with dark humor, bringing us over to his side of every story and episode. Even when we are finally threatened with the experience of abjection, as we are with Rita's murder, we still experience it frame-by-frame with Dexter, our very special monster.[2]

---

[2] Crucial thanks: to my doctoral committee for helping me flesh out some of these ideas in conversation and in writing and always pressing me to go further (Don Wayne, Denise Ferreira da Silva, William Arctander O'Brien, and Yingjin Zhang), to my advisor Alain J.-J. Cohen for his support and guidance through some truly disturbing material, and to Justine Lopez for unwavering intellectual and emotional support (and willingly watching and re-watching and re-watching *Dexter* with me in preparation for this article), and to Richard Greene for his inexhaustible patience as an editor. Any mistakes or omissions are my own.

10
The Sublime Dexter

PATRICIA BRACE

In *Dexter by Design,* the fourth book in Jeff Lindsay's *Dexter* series, Dexter and his new bride Rita honeymoon in Paris. They visit the Galerie Réalité to view a performance piece titled "Jennifer's Leg." This gruesome work consists of a series of video monitors showing a young woman, clearly in agony, de-fleshing her own *still attached* leg down to the bone from knee to ankle, then a sculptural display of the amputated leg itself and finally, the artist enters the room on crutches, her stump bandaged, and declares her missing limb "Sexy."

While Dexter has a fellow flesh artist's interest in the de-fleshing saw technique, he wonders what makes the rest of the audience, including gentle Rita, continue to move from monitor to monitor as the images grow more and more horrific. For that matter, why even create such a work? What aesthetic purpose can something like this fulfill?

Eighteenth-century English philosopher Edmund Burke is well known for his writings on beauty and its juxtaposition to what he called "the sublime." In his *Philosophical Enquiry into the Origin of Our Ideas of the Sublime and Beautiful,*[1] Burke explains that art works which induce a violently emotional state, such as terror, are sublime. Most people can readily understand how one may derive pleasure from the perception of beautiful things, but Burke argues that the horrible, excessive, and dark may also provide pleasure for the perceiver. They may not be beautiful but they may be sublime.

---

[1] *On the Sublime and Beautiful.* The Harvard Classics (Collier, 1909–14; 1965 reprint), p. 36.

Astonishment, horror, and then pleasure are common reactions to first contact with the Dexter novels or the *Dexter* TV show. Though critically praised and a winner of multiple writing, design, and acting awards (most recently garnering both a Golden Globe and SAG Best Actor statue for its star, Michael C. Hall) *Dexter's* violent and gore dripping scenes of murderous excess combined with its moral ambiguity are disturbing to critics and regular viewers alike.

The protagonist of these tales is a cold-blooded serial killer, but since he follows his adoptive father Harry's Code and only kills *other* killers, he is set as our hero. But, as Dexter's unapologetically murderous brother Brian "The Ice Truck Killer" Moser tells him, "You can't be a killer and a hero—it doesn't work that way!"(Season 1, "Born Free"). The tension created by the fine line Dexter walks between his secret murderous vigilantism and his other "legitimate" life, created through his relationships with his foster-sister Deb, girlfriend Rita and her children, and his co-workers, heightens the sense of terror, pushing the viewer deeper and deeper into the sublime. As we watch, wondering if he will finally get caught this time, our fear for the hero is necessarily ambiguous. He is a criminal so we should root for his downfall and yell at the screen to warn his next victim or point out a clue to Sergeant Doakes or Lieutenant LaGuerta so they can apprehend him. But we don't. Instead we cheer him on.

The Power of the Sublime

Burke's concept of the sublime explains our ability to feel more alive by experiencing strong emotional reactions to the world we perceive around us. Humans, Burke explained, go through life in three states: indifference, pleasure, and pain. While many believe that the absence of or relief from pain and deprivation is the motivating force behind human action, Burke insisted instead that feelings such as fear, terror, and astonishment are much more powerful and effective. We seek out things which provoke, reinforce and sustain these stronger emotions. As Burke put it,

> Whatever is fitted in any sort to excite the ideas of pain and danger, that is to say, whatever is in any sort terrible, or is conversant about terrible objects, or operates in a manner analogous to terror, is a source of the *sublime*; that is, it is productive of the strongest emotion which the mind is capable of feeling. (p. 35)

In Season 2's first episode, "It's Alive," we see a teenage Dexter lean over the edge of a very tall building, almost to the point of falling—just so he can feel his heart race in terror. Numbed from his childhood trauma, he only feels alive when experiencing the sublime.

Like Dexter, we may seek out these kinds of experiences to feel more alive. The observation and experience of sublime works of art also provoke these emotions. We derive pleasure as we identify and sympathize with characters in the works, and, as Burke states, "It is by this principle chiefly that . . . arts . . . are often capable of grafting a delight on wretchedness, misery, and death itself" (p. 40).

People slow down to look at traffic accidents or experience satisfaction at the misfortune of others—what the Germans call "Schadenfreude." Burke seemed aware of this phenomenon, but cautioned, "I am convinced we have a degree of delight . . . in the real misfortunes and pains of others . . . This is not an unmixed delight, but blended with no small uneasiness" (pp. 40–41). We understand that someone is suffering, and hopefully our moral compass draws us forward to offer aid and assistance, but there is also a thrill at the *observation* of tragic events and their aftermath. As Burke continues, "When danger or pain press too nearly, they are incapable of giving any delight, and are simply terrible; but at certain distances, . . . they are, delightful, as we every day experience" (p. 36).

Most people not living in New York City or Washington DC experienced this while glued to their television sets after 9/11, by definition an example of the Burkean sublime. Of course a fictional depiction of an extreme series of events can provoke this same response. Andrew Frost, in his review of the film *2012*, cites Burke when discussing why audiences delight in apocalyptic disaster epics. But Frost somberly reminds us, "The problem with our collective imagination is that the end of the world isn't something that we'll get to watch from a comfortable chair in an air-conditioned cinema. It's something that we'd be a part of."[2] That may be the best reason for the unease—we watch the spectacle unfold, then wonder how we would react when faced with the situation in the real world.

If feelings of fear, terror, and unease are our goal, then the most effective way of achieving them, outside of the observation of real

---

[2] Andrew Frost, "It's the End of the World but Not as We Know It," *Sydney Morning Herald* (4th December, 2009).

events, is through the viewing of the performance of a theatrical tragedy. According to Burke, our full identification with the protagonist is the key: "The nearer it approaches the reality, and the farther it removes us from all idea of fiction, the more perfect is its power" (p. 42). We need to believe in the reality of the action; say to ourselves, "That could really happen" or "That must happen all the time," to remain engaged in the narrative and most fully experience the sublime. Most of us are familiar with popular police procedurals from *Dragnet* to *CSI*. When watching a show like *Dexter*, then, there's already some familiarity with what it takes to catch a killer, making Dexter's career choice even more titillating. Adopted and raised by a policeman, schooled in forensic science as a blood-spatter expert, working with his detective sister, Debra, and socializing almost exclusively with other cops in the Homicide Division of Miami Metro, Dexter is quite literally surrounded by the enemy. However, because of Harry's Code, Dexter is also a decidedly moral monster, with strict rules on who deserves his particular brand of justice. He's terrifying, but only if you're guilty of some heinous crime, usually murder. Knowing how he got to be this moral monster only helps us identify with him all the more.

The Passions Aroused by the Sublime

Of the "passions caused by the great and sublime in nature," Burke lists pain, danger, fear, astonishment, and horror, and their sources the uncontrolled excess of things like power, strength, infinity and vastness. Another powerful passion, terror, with "death as its king," is caused by the perception of color, light, sound and smells. Pain is an emissary of death, for "what generally makes pain itself . . . more painful, is, that it is considered as *an emissary of this king of terrors*." And like the pain he inflicts, Dexter may also be seen as an emissary of death. As Burke tells us: except for *strong red*, mostly dark colors like black and purple are the only sublime ones; "excessive *loudness* alone is sufficient to overpower the soul, to suspend its action, and to fill it with terror. . . ," and that ". . . no *smells or tastes* can produce a grand sensation, except excessive bitters, and intolerable stenches."

A seminal incident in Dexter's life, full of all of these passions, put him on the road to the sublime, and allows us to understand the root of his compulsion to kill, that thing which he refers to as his "Dark Passenger." In the Season 1 episode, "Truth Be Told,"

Dexter calls the memory of his mother's murder "The Dark Passenger," but in the books, it is personified as a living entity, "IT," existing not only in Dexter, but in his serial killer targets and even in Rita's abused children Astor and Cody. The introduction to *Dexter in the Dark*, "In the Beginning," traces its existence back to before the primordial ooze: "IT had been there first and, seemingly, forever, except for the vague and disturbing memory of falling."

Dexter Morgan was born Dexter Moser, son of police confidential informant Laura Moser, and brother to Brian. In 1973, when Dexter was three and his brother was five, the drug dealers on whom she had been informing locked them with their mother in a shipping container. While the boys watched, the dealers used a chainsaw to kill and dismember Laura, then left them locked in the container, where they remained, sitting in two inches of blood, undiscovered for two days. To live through their mother's horrible death and the terror it incited within them, their minds had to create some kind of coping mechanism. In a sense, they fought their fear of death by becoming its agents. The trauma of that event created in them what Burke would call a passion for survival: "The passions therefore which are conversant about the *preservation of the individual* turn chiefly on *pain* and *danger,* and they are the most powerful of all the passions" (p. 35). In Dexter's case, his need to inflict pain and death on others was recognized and channeled by his adoptive father, Harry Morgan, into a Code that would allow him to kill evil-doers and survive. For Brian, without Harry's guiding hand, the compulsion to kill led to him becoming a remorseless serial killer who enjoyed inflicting horror and pain on his victims by slowing dismembering them over several days while they were still alive.[3] They never knew when the final cut would come, ending their lives, which made the anticipation all the more terrible. As Burke reminds us, ". . . because there are very few pains, however exquisite, which are not preferred to death: nay, what generally makes pain itself, if I may say so, more painful, is, that it is considered as *an emissary of this king of terrors.*"

When Brian comes back into Dexter's life more than thirty years later, he wants to reconnect with his baby brother, and so sets up a series of puzzles for Dexter to solve using the dismembered body

---

[3] Known in the television show as the "Ice Truck Killer," because he preserved the dismembered body parts in a portable freezer truck. In the books he is the "Tamiami Slasher."

parts he has gleaned from his victims, and from which he has removed all the blood. To an ordinary person, this appears sick and not a little twisted, but for our hero, it is astonishing and gives him great pleasure. Brian understands Dexter, and, it seems, may have read his Burke: "The passion caused by the great and sublime in nature, when those causes operate most powerfully, is *astonishment*; and astonishment is that state of the soul, in which all its motions are suspended, *with some degree of horror.* Astonishment, as I have said, is the effect of the sublime in its highest degree; the inferior effects are *admiration, reverence, and respect.*" And that is exactly how Dexter reacts to the Ice Truck Killer. As Brian's ever more personal clues hidden in horribly inventive murders draw Dexter's thrilled admiration, they also unlock his buried memories of his mother's gruesome end. Brian's killings set up a competition—a sort of serial killer sibling rivalry—in which both technique and artistry draw the brothers closer together. Even something as simple as Rudy/Brian helping Dexter pack up their biological father's house is wrought with his desire to have Dexter as his partner in slaughter. Watch as they use all the same tools as for murder: duct tape, rope, black plastic bags, and a very sharp box cutter ("Father Knows Best," Season 1).

One incident in particular triggers both a physical and emotional terror in Dexter by making use of color, light and darkness, sound and smell. In Season 1's "Seeing Red," Brian stages a motel room to resemble the cargo container by dousing it with the thirty-five quarts of blood he had saved from bleeding his previous victims.[4] As a blood spatter analyst, Dexter is dressed in a white hazmat suit and sent in first. The dark, relatively small space has deep red blood pooled at least two inches deep on the floor, flung on every wall, piece of furniture and the ceiling, the radio blaring and a stench so foul later analysts entering will wear face masks. He takes two steps into the room and totally freaks out, having a flashback of a small boy covered in blood, then falling head first into the pooled blood in a faint. Remember, this is the usually fearless man who matter-of-factly stabs and then dismembers his victims for easy disposal. Now, as he says in voice-over, "The boy in the blood scares me and I want him to go away." That Dexter's

---

[4] In Season 3 Dexter tells Miguel Prado, "There are six quarts of blood in the human body; this is not going to be pretty" ("The Damage a Man Can Do"). The Ice Truck Killer has bled five victims dry at this point, so 6 x 5 = 35.

white suit resembles one of his own spatter pattern tests is not lost on us—Brian is pushing Dexter to remember and testing him by using the perception of the senses as triggers.[5]

When he later returns to the room, he remembers his mother as she was about to be killed, telling him to close his eyes, as if the darkness could save him. Dexter has retreated into that darkness, which Burke recognizes as one of the most powerful indicators of the sublime. The following episode, "Truth Be Told," opens with Dexter's vision of a Hell, a long dark blood red corridor with flashing police lights and weird strobing sound, a terror scene much like what Burke describes as the effects of the *intermittent:* "But light now appearing and now leaving us, and so off and on, is even more terrible than total darkness; and a sort of uncertain sounds are, when the necessary dispositions concur, more alarming than a total silence" (pp. 70–71). The cargo container scene as a point of extreme sensory horror is invoked throughout the series, but never more devastatingly than when it is intercut with the shocking season four finale, "The Getaway," when Dexter finds his infant son Harrison covered in Rita's blood as she lies, murdered, in their bathroom tub. He had just been so hopeful that he could finally leave his need behind and have a normal life, but instead he came full circle. We despaired along with him as he says in voice over, "Born in blood. Both of us. Harry was right. I'm what's wrong. This is fate." This is the sublime.

Look for Something Bludgeony

A second source of passion which can arouse the sublime is uncontrolled excess of power. As Burke says, "I know of nothing sublime, which is not some modification of *power*" (p. 55).

In the first season Dexter finds himself in a power struggle for the affections of Rita and her children when their father, Paul Bennett, is released from prison. A former drug addict, Paul beat Rita and the kids, and was arrested by Debra, reporting to the domestic abuse call made by little Astor. Debra then introduced them to Dexter. Still, Bennett claims to love his children and tries

---

[5] Another instance of using the blood-spatter imagery to a frightening foreshadowing effect is in the Season 3 finale, "Do You Take Dexter Morgan," when blood from Dexter's broken wrist drips onto Rita's white wedding dress. We see that this marriage will literally be the (very bloody) death of her.

to worm his way back into their affections. At different points he threatens both Rita and Dexter when they try to limit his access to the children, culminating in his drunken attempt to rape Rita (which she quite effectively stops by bludgeoning him with a baseball bat kept under her bed).

Blocked by Harry's code from unleashing his dark monster to murder Paul, who is not a killer, Dexter reaches a breaking point when Paul files charges against Rita for defending herself, a power play to gain custody of Astor and Cody. In "Seeing Red," while they are quietly talking in the kitchen, Paul taunts Dexter, saying, "If you or that skinny bitch try to screw with what's mine I swear to God I don't care who I have to hurt"—and *wham!*—our hero cracks Paul over the head with a cast iron skillet.[6] The sudden unexpectedness of the violence makes it shocking and powerful. In one eloquent, violent act, Dexter totally reversed the power dynamic from Paul to himself. Burke understood how suddenness could be sublime, "In everything sudden and unexpected, we are apt to start; that is we have a perception of danger, and our nature rouses us to guard against it." (p. 70). For the viewer, who has been primed to dislike him since the first mention of his name, there is pleasure in seeing Paul drop to the floor like a stone. There is also pleasure in his frame up, subsequent arrest, and prison sentence because it removes him from Rita and the kids' lives. Yet there's also a deep ambiguity—Dexter uses the very type of violence that we condemn Paul for committing—in the storyline's symmetry.

In the third season, Dexter struggles for power with his "frenemy" Machiavellian Assistant District Attorney Miguel Prado. As an effect of his need to kill, and subsequent need for secrecy in keeping with Harry's Code, Dexter avoids any truly honest relationships. He cares for the two women in his life, his foster sister Debra and his girlfriend and wife Rita, but chooses to keep his true nature hidden from both of them. On those few occasions where he has given up some of his carefully controlled power by trusting someone enough to reveal his true face, such as his brother Brian in Season 1, his lover Lila in Season 2, and his buddy Miguel in Season 3, it hasn't gone well (he was forced to kill all three) mostly

---

[6] The subsequent "Oh crap," look on Dexter's face as he realizes that there will be a consequence for this is priceless. That in a previous episode Paul had been looking for that very skillet to worm his way back into the household by cooking the kids' breakfast is also a neat irony.

because those in whom he chose to confide refused to even attempt to rein in their own darkness.

Prado is already a powerful man in the Miami Cuban community when Dexter meets him, the kind of man others call "patrón" and "jefe." The words translate as "boss" and "chief" and imply deference and respect for a powerful man. Prado has what Burke calls "*natural* power," the power "which arises from institution in kings and commanders" and "has the same connection with terror. Sovereigns are frequently addressed with the title of *dread majesty*" (p. 57). Prado clearly likes to be the one in control (defense attorney Ellen Wolfe provides evidence that he has used his office to bend the law to his liking on many occasions and his behavior has prompted an ethics investigation) and to provoke fear. In "Our Father" when their lives become entangled by the death of Miguel's brother, Oscar (unknown to Miguel, Dexter accidently did the deed) the two men bond. When Miguel witnesses the aftermath of a kill in "Finding Freebo," instead of turning Dex in, he praises him. Astonished at the possibility of a someone who knows the real monster inside of him and still wants to be his friend, Dexter warms to the role: "It destroyed my brother, consumed Lila, but not Miguel Prado—somehow he looks at me and he's proud" ("Turning Biminese," Season 3).

Using his justice system connections, Prado points Dexter towards people he says deserve death, but unbeknownst to Dex, he is actually using our hero as his own personal vendetta machine, removing anyone who is a threat to his power. In "The Damage a Man Can Do," a flattered Dexter acquiesces to Miguel's desire to learn the Dark Defender business first hand and they perform a joint kill on a bookie's enforcer who bludgeons people to death.[7] When later that night, Prado, drunk with the power of holding life and death in his hands, breaks Harry's Code by killing an innocent, his enemy Ellen Wolf, Miguel's ecstatic response to his action, "I feel real for the first time in my life," shows an understanding of

---

[7] In an example of the show's often flippant use of language for dark humor, while Dexter and Miguel search their potential victim's house for evidence of crime, Dexter says, "We know he bludgeons people to death so look for something—bludgeony." They find a baseball bat with blood on it, a possible call back to Rita's use of a similar bat to ward off her ex-husband's attempted rape of her in Season 1. Trinity is also a bludgeon killer in Season 4, preferring a claw hammer as his weapon of choice.

the *effect* of the sublime ("About Last Night"). But since he has used his strength for selfish ends, he doesn't truly reach it. There can be no sublime in this, as Burke states, "Whenever *strength* is only useful, and employed for our benefit or our pleasure, *then it is never sublime*" (p. 56).

When he discovers that Miguel has brutally murdered Wolf, Dexter has to figure out a way to deal with him. It speaks to Miguel's power that Dexter's first inclination, to send him in pieces on a one-way trip down the Gulf Stream, is initially vetoed because of Prado's standing in the legal and Cuban immigrant communities. Harry taught Dexter self-preservation and disappearing someone so high-profile is dangerous, even if Prado did flout the Code. Miguel abused Dexter's trust, friendship, and mission by employing Dexter's strength and abilities for his own selfish ends.

With Harry's help, Dexter channeled his desire to kill to more socially (if not legally) acceptable targets, but as he says in the first Dexter novel, *Darkly Dreaming Dexter,* he is still not really in control of "the growing Need, rising in me like a great wave that roars up and over the beach and does not recede, only swells more with every tick of the bright night's clock."[8] That fits Burke's definition of the sublime. Dexter has an overwhelming internal compulsion to kill—whereas Miguel kills to gain more personal power. Dexter realizes this truth in "Go Your Own Way," when they have a confrontation on the roof of the police station over Miguel's series of betrayals. Prado's statement, "I'll do what I want, when I want to whomever I want—count on it," shows his selfish disregard for anyone who gets in his way. He plots to kill LaGuerta, a trusted friend, when she suspects him in the Wolf murder, and sets Dexter up to be killed by the latest Miami serial killer, "the Skinner" (they do seem to attract a lot of them in the series, despite Florida's death penalty). In a bit of poetic justice, Prado's murderous plans actually help Dexter do away with him. He traps Miguel in LaGuerta's house when the A.D.A. comes to kill her, and then uses the Skinner's M.O. to hide his kill in plain sight as just another serial killer victim. Yes, Miguel's death kept Dexter safe, but Dexter's assertion of power over his former friend was not merely for selfish need. Prado was killing innocent people, and just as he did with his brother, Brian, Dexter had to follow the Code and take him out.

---

[8] Jeff Lindsay, *Darkly Dreaming Dexter* (Vintage, 2004), p. 4.

Dexter's Aesthetics

Season 2 villainess, modern artist Lila Tournay, asks Dexter for one of the blood spatter test analyses she watches him create and later we see it hung on the wall of her studio. At a dinner party she declares him to be an artist ("Dex, Lies, and Videotape," Season 2) and even directs their lovemaking as if it was a painting ("That Night a Forest Grew," Season 2).

The similarity of Dexter's spatters to the Abstract Expressionist painter Jackson Pollock's paintings has been noted by many critics. Pollock's technique of seemingly randomly flung gouts of paint was actually carefully controlled for color choice, application tools and methods. Dexter's own "paintings" are a reverse engineering of a crime scene, attempting to map out the criminal's actions and as such are also created under carefully controlled circumstances. He displays them like art on the walls of his office and they are also used in many of the promotional materials for the show and on the cover design for the hardback edition of *Dexter by Design* which shows Dexter standing in front of a red splattered white canvas with an artist's palette all in red and a bloody butcher knife. In this book, Dexter recognizes the parallel between his hidden calling and the works he sees in the Paris museums: "Art is, after all, all about making patterns in order to create a meaningful impact on the senses. And isn't this just exactly what Dexter does? Of course in my case 'impact' is a little more literal, but still—I can appreciate other media" (p. 5). Dexter's *true* art, however, cannot be so publically displayed.

Dexter takes the same care and precision in the preparation and clean-up for his art—his killings—as he does in his crime scene analysis. The extensive research to determine guilt, the creation of a kill room, the stalking and capture of the subject and the dismemberment and disposal of the body are all vital parts of his ritual process (paralleled in the show's Emmy winning opening credits and cleverly spoofed in the first episode of Season 4 when sleep-deprived new father Dexter finds baby puke on his white t-shirt and breaks his shoelace). For Dexter there is beauty and symmetry in the fulfillment of both Harry's Code and the bloodthirsty needs of his Dark Passenger. Within the context of the narrative, the only audience for almost all of his true art process is the victim.

As Burke explained, art works that induce a violently emotional state, such as terror, can be sublime. For the person strapped nude to Dexter's table with saran wrap, the aesthetic experience is short-lived, but undeniably intense. The reader or viewer of the *Dexter* series can experience the sublime anew with every novel and episode. Just like Rita in Paris viewing "Jennifer's Leg," that is why we keep coming back—we find pleasure in the fear, terror, and astonishment we feel following Dexter's adventures, with "not an unmixed delight, but blended with no small uneasiness" (pp. 40–41).

11

Dexter's Specimens

JASON DAVIS

Specimen / ˈspɛsəmən / *noun* 1. a part or an individual taken as exemplifying a whole mass or number; a typical animal, plant, mineral, part, etc. 2. *Medicine* a sample of a substance to be examined or tested for a specific purpose. 3. *Colloquial* a person as a specified kind, or in some respect a peculiar kind, of human being; he's a poor specimen.[1]

In *Dexter* specimens come in threes. The most recognizable are the measured amounts of crime matter taken from the murder scenes that are bagged, tagged, and tested as lab samples.

Then there are Dexter's after-work *re-enactments* of specimen taking. These specimens are one part in Dexter's quarantine ritual of latex gloves, laboratory aprons, pipettes, and face shields, all clinical barriers and surfaces needed for traceless murders.

The third type of specimen inhabiting the world of *Dexter* is the walking, talking, life-taking kind—the varieties of serial killers we encounter in each episode, Dexter included. As much as Dexter, or rather Michael C. Hall, is a fine male specimen for some of us *Dexter* watchers, Dexter's also typical of what we know about serial killers. The traits and behaviors Dexter typifies and shares with other killers in the series are also what define his questionable moral difference from them—Dexter's victim types are killers. But as much as *Dexter* presents us with examples of what we recognize and know about serial killing, there are unfamiliar "specimens" too.

---

[1] *The Macquarie Dictionary*,
<www.credoreference.com/entry/macqdict/specimen>.

Try Our New Dahmerland Section at
Specimens 'R' Us

We're consumers of serial killers, both in popular culture and popular science. Dexter is also a consumer of serial killers. From syringe to specimen slide to Hefty bag; each capture and murder satisfies Dexter's urge to kill, until the next time. He doesn't "feed" on them literally, but he is like a consumer satisfying his unquestioned needs with things whose origins aren't reflected on. Dexter isn't concerned about what makes killers the way they are, only that they're available and free range. That's the point of looking at *Dexter* in terms of specimens. What's presented to us about serial killers and serial killing—their behavior, their victim types, their psychological profiles—are consistent with what we know. *Dexter* draws on our shared ideas and understandings of serial killing. If we recognize these specimens, then what's taking place is a form of identity thinking.

'Identity thinking' is Theodor Adorno's name for how knowledge about a particular thing, say a novel about a serial killer who works as a blood-spatter analyst, involves making that individual thing into a case or example or specimen of something already known, such as an established genre. Likewise, an act of murder as a particular event can be identified as a specimen of individual psychology or as an example of how social beliefs sanction hate crimes. In each case, identification of a particular thing as belonging to a larger group or category involves fitting it within a concept.

> Regardless of whether I understand the thing as an instantiation of a Platonic form or an example of a scientific class, what matters is that the object is no longer a unique and strange thing but is rather a member of a category that makes sense to me. This process . . . causes a belief that concepts fully capture the objects to which they refer.[2]

This isn't to argue against concepts because of the way they reduce things to likeness as a member of a category. Placing things within concepts is necessary for developing our understanding of the world. What Adorno reminds us is that over-reliance on con-

---

    [2] Nick Smith, "The Splinter in Your Ear: Noise as the Semblance of Critique," *Culture, Theory, and Critique* 46:1 (2005), p. 45.

cepts and categories involved in identity thinking runs the risk of making the material world fit an accepted abstract idea of it. When something particular is overlooked what could be seen or known differently is lost.

Attention to the difference between concept and thing is one way of getting further into the world of *Dexter*. For one thing, focusing on the particular means thinking with what resists, or is considered insignificant, or what remains invisible to understanding. In a way, Adorno's philosophical approach sounds like forensic detection and homicide police work. After all, how does something become evidence against the background of the everyday? Or what patterns can be found within the chaotic "noise" of the spatter, pools, and trails of human blood at a crime scene? But Adorno would want us to think beyond the concepts that keep explanations and popular cultural portrayals of serial killing focused on the individuality and individualizing acts of the killer. What can something seemingly marginal in connection to the world of Dexter—specimen slides, nonhuman animals, and friendless women—tell us about the world of serial killing?

Counting Specimen Slides

The owner of the specimen collection of "trophies" we see in nearly every episode of *Dexter* is more than a "very neat monster." It belongs to a minimalist serial killer. A minimalist serial murderer is what you get when a killer son follows his police father's survival code to remain traceless. Focused and controlled satisfaction of his urges keeps the murderous double-life of Dexter and his criminal, yet acceptable killing for viewers, appealingly Dahmer-Lite. And yet, might there be more to the prized specimen slide collection of the blood-obsessed Dexter than the risky breaking of Harry's Code and the product placement of an LG Air Conditioner?

As a discrete catalogue of nameless "trophies," Dexter's specimen collection is an eerie window into serial killing in *Dexter*. The glass-on-glass sound of the warm blood being tapped out and the dull arrhythmic tinkle they produce when Dexter runs his finger across them in their wooden case make them delicate keepsakes of anonymous deaths. They're also clinical and impersonal mementos, but each addition "speaks" of a haunting repetition. Each slide Dexter adds isn't just the recording of another death. Each one of those numberless thumb-print-sized mementos is also a token for those that were killed by the killers added to Dexter's collection. And these slides also remind us that this specimen-making is underway with no date for completeness or closure. It's an open set. The slides are a reminder that the world of *Dexter* is made up only of individuals: those who are innocent, and those who do the evil others only dream of.

Dexter, Specimen Maker

Identity thinking is very much at work in Dexter's killing. Dexter acknowledges his victims' self-defining compulsion to kill as something he unmistakably shares with them as a fate "gifted" beyond their control. But he also defines himself as completely *other* to them in terms of who they kill. Dexter, the "lab rat," is a specimen maker in the sense that what he kills are but *examples* of serial killers. They are specimens in the sense that Dexter has no interest in what distinctly makes them kill. Dexter isn't interested in how his victims reflect their difference from the others. And he isn't remotely concerned with how his victims reflect or are shaped by a society that may give their murderous actions justified possibilities, even sanctions.

The therapist Emmett Meridian ("Shrink Wrap," Season 1) is compelled to make his professionally successful women patients dependent on him to the point that he can rationalize for them their suicides as meaningful acts of escape from the suffering he sustains in them. It's only enough for Dexter, and presumably the creators of the series, that Meridian has induced women to kill themselves before and will do it again. But there is no exploration or even teasing out further why a man wants control over the life and death of publicly powerful women. It's only enough for Dexter to determine that Meridian *can* be killed, rather than glimpse how the self-defining need to make women suffer connects to more wider social truths about the lives of women in a male dominated society.

To ask just who or what Dexter is killing is to think about more than just who and what Dexter is dissociating himself from when he kills serial killers. That Dexter is working with a "concept" of the "serial killer" when he knows their "types," their "thinking" is to suggest Dexter is living the life of the unexamined serial killer. Or more slyly, we could say Dexter is a consumer who understands not what he consumes. He is the subject distinctly different from his object. He is a subject who doesn't want to know what makes his object the object that it is. The "social stuff" that maketh the serial killer outside of gothic family origins and forensic facts has no place in Dexter's individual-based concepts of the serial killer.

Buddy's Bones

Remember the very first flashback of Harry's intimate father-son talk with Dexter about Buddy, their neighbor's missing dog? ("Dexter," Season 1) For anyone familiar with the biographic popularization of "real world" serial killers, it's a scene that plays out an understanding of what the abuse, torture, and killing of defenceless animals is a "rehearsal" of. Young Dex's rationale for the one-off killing of the barking Buddy—concern for his mother's sleepless recovery from illness—is challenged by Harry's discovery of Buddy's bones in a hidden growing grave of animal remains. And the flashback connects a cop father's strong instincts about his son with what Dexter sees in the violent pornographic appetites of the rapist killer, Jamie Jaworski; that their "needs are evolving." With a remembered story about an unseen dog, the beginnings of Dexter are established. And Buddy's bones sink back into the hidden graves of personal history.

But the short back-story that's Buddy can tell us something more than passing behavioral information about young Dexter. I say "behavioral information" because as clinical as that sounds, it does bring out that what we learn is specimen-like. What we get is an example or token of what's already known about serial killers. It's an added dimension of authenticity. And if you already knew this connection, it fits with the idea or concept—the behavioral history—we have of serial killers. Saying this detail is a specimen isn't to dispute the "real world" connection of the criminological linking of animal killing with violence towards humans. It's to have both the accepted and minor status of this detail open up other ways of understanding the relationship of nonhuman animals to identity thinking, especially identity thinking about serial killers. And that involves looking more at how nonhuman animals become part of the meaning making of human actions and human identity.

Born Free of All That's Human

Nonhuman animals appear throughout *Dexter*, mostly as a way of expressing human likeness to predatory animals. Think of Brian leading Dexter ("Let's Give the Boy a Hand," Season 1) to the amputated body of Tony Tucci like the offering up of injured prey to a feline cub by a lion parent keen to awaken a suppressed taste for innocent humans. Or the opening scenes of "Crocodile" where Dexter is immersed in water with unblinking eyes above the water-line like the reptile of the episode title. Then there's Brian's calling to Dexter's real nature—images of lions taking down their hunt and feeding on a bloodied carcass—to be "Born free of all that's human" ("Born Free," Season 1).

Brian's carnivore references suggest the natural order of things between predators and prey against the "civilizing" influences of Harry's Code directing Dexter's compulsion to kill. Even Dexter refers to Brian as a predatory animal when he tells him "You need to be put down," a euphemism for putting to death aggressive, injured or diseased nonhuman animals. This likeness to nonhuman animals as a way of justifying violence in *Dexter* echoes Adorno's arguments about the role of making human others into animals as a form identity thinking.[3] Human-on-human violence involves pro-jecting the nonhuman onto the human, a perception that separates a human self off from a nonhuman other. What's been done to nonhuman animals can, for that very reason, be justifiably done to humans.

It's this criminological linking of animal abuse and killing to human violent behaviour that is behind current developments in US law enforcement and prosecution measures involving animal cruelty taskforces and Humane Society investigators targeting human abuse and cruelty of nonhuman animals. As Alisa Mullins points out in her PETA report quoting L.A. mayor Antonio Villaraigosa on the need for such laws, "When we protect animals, we are protecting ourselves, we are protecting our communities."[4]

The recognition of the rights of nonhuman animals now plays a role in the future prevention of human violence against humans, even for identifying violent tendencies that are still to "evolve." This is one way in which forms of identity thinking involving human relationships with nonhuman animals have been changing. But this

---

[3] Theodor. W. Adorno, *Minima Moralia: Reflections on a Damaged Life* (Verso, 2005), p. 105.

[4] Alisa Mullins. "What Serial Shooters and Steve Green Have in Common," *American Chronicle* (September 1st, 2006), <www.americanchronicle.com/articles/printFriendly/13067>.

raises another question: is the legal recognition of nonhuman animals and their suffering in relation to the human world of criminal violence another historical episode of *speciesism*? Does this rethinking of nonhuman animal suffering in relation to human violence privilege some animals over others?

Asking this question isn't to deny the moral good involved in greater protection of nonhuman animals for the wider social benefit of humans. Rather, it's to think more about the relationship of the violent treatment of nonhuman animals and the relationship of that violence to human identity thinking. The nonhuman animals we encounter in *Dexter* are not on any Miami menu. So what about the non-criminal putting to death of nonhuman animals? What connection could there be between the identity thinking shaping the violence committed by humans against humans and the noncriminal killing of animals that is part of our everyday consumption of them?

Pulled Pork Sandwiches and the Sexual Politics of Meat

Something of how the threading of human identity, violence, and the consumption of nonhuman animals begins to appear in *Dexter* when we look at Carol J. Adams's *The Sexual Politics of Meat*.[5] Even the cover of the book prompts visual associations of how meat eating and identity thinking are at work in the first season of *Dexter*. The image of the woman's naked sectioned body corresponding in location and name to the meat cuts of butchery is eerily like the Ice Truck Killer's victims, especially the scenes where Brian adds the cutting lines to the naked body of Monique, the amputee escort worker. Adams's book looks at the historical and cultural justification of a society based on the eating of meat and how this connects to the oppression and domination of women. Looking at the cover image—an ad urging us to "Break the Dull Beef Habit" with the choicest cuts of the Cattle Queen—it's almost as if it were a how-to guide for the Ice Truck Killer. And that's the point of Adams's feminist study.

Dexter draws on wider cultural associations about how the bodies of women and nonhuman animals are interchangeable as objects for a meat-eating, male dominated society. After all, the

---

[5] Carol J. Adams, *The Sexual Politics of Meat: A Feminist-Vegetarian Critical Theory* (Continuum, 2010).

image above is what brings out a connection between the blood-drained parts of women's bodies, paper wrapped and string-tied like parcels from the local butcher, to the porterhouse steaks Brian/Rudy shares with Dexter as part of their brotherly bonding. And you need only think of what the second corpse of the Ice Truck killer awakens in Dexter on his date with Rita. Dexter's admiration for the artistic "cuts" of meat performed by his brother is re-enacted on her as an unconscious sexual pass ("Dexter," Season 1). So how does *Dexter* consume this other species shared between men?

You Kidnapped a Cop This Time, You Know? Not Some Invisible Hooker

Deb's defiant reminder of who she is to Rudy/Brian speaks clearly of the differences between herself and the women sex workers who were his victims ("Born Free," Season 1). It tells us what cops and society won't tolerate in terms of *which* women suffer at the hands of men. Deb's defiance also reminds us of the working-class differences between them. Deb has worked her way up to detective, while Rudy/Brian's victims have been street working prostitutes, or in the case of Monique, the amputee sex-worker, working for a "legitimate escort service." Although unspoken by Deb, the racial differences between herself and these women as well as Monique's disability are also telling reminders of what women experience in the world of *Dexter*. Deb's calling out who she is and who she isn't is one of the few scenes in *Dexter* where differences *between* women are acknowledged. And it's one place to begin looking at identity thinking and how women characters *are made to exist* differently from men.

As much as Deb is the Ice Truck Killer's last female kidnap victim, she isn't the "Final Girl" in the way women are in slasher horror films of the 1980s and their twenty-first century remakes.[6] Tough Deb survives her lover and would-be killer, but she isn't "transformed from terrified screamer to active heroine."[7] And it isn't just the case that Dexter saves her. Deb is after all given a sacrificial role in the bonding between Dex and Biney. Deb is the final

---

[6] Carol J. Clover, *Men, Women, and Chainsaws: Gender in the Modern Horror Film* (Princeton University Press 1992), pp. 21–65.

[7] Barry Keith Grant, "Screams on Screens: Paradigms of Horror," *Loading: Journal of the Canadian Game Studies Association* 4:6 (2010), p. 10.

girl in piecing together the reunion of blood brothers, but this should make us think more about what the "gifts" of bloodless pieces of girls left by Brian for Dexter to puzzle over tell us about women in *Dexter*. As recreations of Brian and Dexter's murdered mother, they're offerings to Dexter to take up innocent women as the proper objects he has been substituting with his more deserving, and mostly male, victims.

In *Dexter*, women are important for male bonding as well as boundary making between men. Think of Detective McNamara's use of James Doakes as "bait" as payback for Doakes's secret affair with McNamara's murdered sister ("Let's Give the Boy a Hand," Season 1). And Dexter's initial interactions with Paul, Rita's violent ex-husband, are dominated by Paul's sexual jealousy towards Dexter, tensions hinting at Paul's still-lingering sexual ownership of Rita. But Deb provides us with another clue as to what women share in *Dexter* that makes them even more secondary to men. Deb is after all the girlfriendless "final girl."

Designing Women in *Dexter*

Until Season 3, when Rita is befriended by Sylvia Prado and Maria LaGuerta develops her friendship with Ellen Wolf, the women of *Dexter* exist very much *without* female support or companionship. Deb, Rita, and Maria don't have any female friends. By the second season, women experience each other as competitive, even threatening presences. Think of Lila Tournay's attempt to come between Dexter and Rita. Driven to possess Dexter, Lila is likewise without connections to other women. Christine Hill is devoted to her father the Trinity Killer, but she's like Deb, without attachment to other women. What makes this strange absence in each of their lives so much stranger is how this shared trait contrasts with what the men of *Dexter* experience.

In *Dexter* father-to-son (Harry and Dexter), brother-to-brother (Dexter and Brian), friendship or brotherly surrogate (Dexter and Miguel) bondings are the strongest, most meaningful emotional relationships the adult male characters experience. That's not to say that these relationships aren't what men should be experiencing in *Dexter*. But compared to the strong ties, sexual and non-sexual, that men experience with both sexes, the women of *Dexter*, cut off from other women, seem like they're living half-lives. It's as if the secret men's business of killing is more defining of the types of relationships men can have while women seem secondary in their relationship to men. It isn't just that women are kept out of this male bonding. It's as if they're designed not to have the types of relationships the adult male characters have. *Dexter* is a very masculine world and we can say that *homosocially* it's a very male dominated one. This means that nonsexual ties and attachments such as friendships are more available to, and become more meaningful for, the adult male characters than the female characters.

Homosocially Yours, Dexter

Individually, all of the women of *Dexter* are strikingly different in their personalities, but their absence of meaningful involvement with other women brings out their sameness as something like a *specimen class*. What they share makes them belong to a kind or type of "woman". Saying the women of *Dexter* are specimen-like sounds absurd—they're human characters, not objects like glass slides or concepts we use to make sense of serial killing. But the point is to look harder at what is missing from the identity thinking at work here, even in the creation of fictional characters.

What if there is something about the differences between women's lives in *Dexter* that we're not seeing because of their sameness? And what if those differences lead us to think differently about how we understand serial killing? The sameness of the female characters has to do with how the world of *Dexter* not only makes women secondary to men. It also makes the women of *Dexter* separate from, even indifferent to, other women. And the type or kind of woman that the women of *Dexter* represent is also an example of the concept of "woman" that feminist philosophers have been challenging.

Seeing how women are depicted in Dexter in this way provides a way of understanding how identity thinking has contributed to feminist questioning of women's experiences. For feminist philosophers of sexual and racial identity such as Drucilla Cornell, Judith Butler, and Reneé Heberle, philosophical thinking about women's differences from each other has provided possibilities for giving voice to women's experience of suffering outside of the concept of "woman." This concept has been defined by forms of feminism that haven't included experiences of sexual and racial differences, disability, and economic class other than those shaping the identities of able-bodied, straight, white, middle-class women. Added to this is the need to question how women's differences, especially class and racial differences, have been publicly recognized when women have been victims of multiple murderers.

Deb's defiance about being an invisible or forgotten victim like the sex workers of the show is a comment on *Dexter* itself. *Dexter* is premised on the forgetting of the history of feminist-led women's rights campaigns aimed at raising public consciousness about women as victims of violence. Take Back the Night demonstrations have been a political tool for organizing and mobilizing women's efforts to reclaim public spaces after sunset as part of women's social and legal right to safety and protection outside of the home.[8] These political movements have also challenged and escalated attention about the racial and class-bias against institutional failures of the police, the courts, and the media to respond to the plight of sex workers and non-white women targeted by serial murders. Deb as the "final girl" was destined to survive as "dearly damaged Debra," dutiful daughter of Harry Morgan. Deb survives not because she isn't an "invisible hooker." It was her sisterhood to Dexter that both endangered and saved her. What is celebrated in the ending of Season 1 isn't the lone survivor of a serial killer who targeted women. In the daylight celebration of Dexter, sex workers become more invisible. After all, it was Dexter who took back the night.

Specimen Watching

Dexter is a world of everyday surfaces with shadowed depths beneath. The closeness of the ordinarily domestic to the dangerous is after all what makes the double-lives its characters lead, especially Dexter and his prey, doubly intriguing. And within this serial world we consume we do encounter some connections to the real world of serial killers. What we get are examples that add touches of authenticity, but which we don't think long enough about, much less think they can tell us anything more about the reality they're from. But specimens, as well as those things we don't think of as specimens, can tell us different stories about the "real world" of serial killing than what *Dexter* thinks we know. The "supporting" roles

---

[8] Philip Jenkin, *Using Murder: The Social Construction of Serial Homicide* (Aldine de Gruyter, 1994), pp. 146, 165; Laura Lederer, *Take Back the Night: Women on Pornography* (Morrow 1980).

specimen slides, animals, and women play in *Dexter* as part of the everyday world of the Dark Passenger also have double-lives. They can make us think a bit differently about serial murder than what surfaces through the secret men's business of killing.

Watch *Dexter* for more specimens. They're there, between the obvious crime-scenes of a killer on repeat.

BODY PART III

What Would Dexter Do?

12
Pathetic Rule Follower or Vigilante Hero?

M. CARMELA EPRIGHT and SARAH E. WORTH

"Kids. I could never do that. . . . I have standards" ("Dexter," Season 1). Dexter Morgan, blood-spatter expert, psychopath, and vigilante serial killer does have *some* standards. He is an avowed killer who thoroughly enjoys his work—but he follows a seemingly strict moral Code. One of the many things that makes Dexter so interesting is his adherence to these rules, which gives him the *appearance* of being moral, even though most people would never consider a murderer a pillar of moral virtue.

At the beginning of the series his rules are known as the "Code of Harry," and they were taught to young Dexter by his adopted father as a way of controlling his murderous impulses and channeling his blood lust into killing the "really bad people out there" ("Crocodile," Season 1). At first Dexter follows the Code almost mechanically (maniacally?); he never kills anyone who doesn't fit Harry's Code. Later in the series Dexter adapts the Code for his own purposes but never rejects the notion that one must be governed by a set of rules.

But Dexter's Code and his struggle to adhere to it demonstrates many of the problems that come with a rule-based approach to ethics. The moral Code he chooses, like other rule-based theories, seems moral on its face, but this doesn't make the actions that follow from it—in Dexter's case, cold-blooded murder—justifiable. We think that genuine morality requires more than just adherence to rules—it depends on things like empathy, concern for others, and doing, well, *moral* acts. Dexter may be a good rule follower, but he should not be considered moral in any sense of the word.

What Is a Moral Code?

There are several ethical theories based on following rules. Many would cite the Ten Commandments as their first guide to ethical behavior as it is a convenient and succinct set of rules about what to do and what not to do. The Golden Rule works too as a relatively straightforward rule that can be applied widely (although it has some serious limits when it is applied by serial killers or masochists—using your own self as a standard can be tricky!).

In philosophy, rule-based moral theories include Immanuel Kant's "categorical imperative": "Act only according to that maxim whereby you can at the same time will that it should become a universal law" (or, in normal language, act according to rules that can and should be adopted by everyone); and various forms of the "principle of utility" as offered by such thinkers as Jeremy Bentham and John Stuart Mill. These are rules like "Maximize pleasure and minimize the pain for everyone involved" and "Do that which results in the greatest good for the greatest number of people."[1]

Although it's more complicated than this, the assumption is that if you properly interpret and act upon any given moral rule then it follows that your actions will be moral—even if the outcome might seem morally questionable. Some of these rules are based on the likely consequences of either acting or not acting in a particular way; others are based upon intentions. All of them assume that moral people are reasonable and rational and that they can calmly look at extremely difficult questions abstractly and act not on their desires and emotions but according to a careful application of rules. Yeah, right . . . I can make life's most difficult decisions by making a list of pros and cons, weighing and measuring each with absolute precision, and naturally, the most rational outcome for as many people as possible will result. Or, I can in all cases stick to a list of predetermined rules—regardless of the context or consequences.

As you can imagine, there are many problems with these sorts of "rule-based" theories—first it's often difficult to establish whether the rules in question are "right" or "moral." How do we know that the *source* of the rules (the Bible, one's father, Kant's or Mill's interminable texts) provides the right principles? Furthermore, following the rules may lead you to do things that seem wrong or even

---

[1] Carmela Epright hates it when people describe utilitarianism this way, but her hatred doesn't stop anyone from doing it.

ridiculously wrong. For example, a consistent Kantian would never lie—not even to the Nazis who are questioning him or her about the Jews who are currently hiding in his or her basement. A consistent utilitarian might, if the stakes were high enough and there were no other options, agree that some people not only *should* be tortured but that they *must* be tortured if lots of other people would benefit significantly. In Dexter's world, the rules allow him to kill those who deserve to be killed but this doesn't make doing so right or moral.

The original set of rules that Dexter follows, the "Code of Harry," includes "don't get caught," "always be sure that your victims are guilty" (Dexter takes this to mean guilty of murder, but Harry never actually says this), and "control your urges, do not let them control you." The strictness of the code forces him to struggle with the thought of killing Sergeant Doakes since, while he doesn't fit the code, he knows so much about Dexter's second profession that Doakes is capable of destroying him. Dexter lucks into an answer to this dilemma that doesn't violate Harry's Code when Lila kills Doakes to protect Dexter. Sadly this doesn't solve all of his problems; he still needs to kill Lila (who clearly needs to be killed, if anyone does, as she is just *so* evil!); eventually he succumbs to this temptation, but only because she comes to meet the criteria (minimally)—precisely because she did his dirty work by killing Doakes.

Harry's faults lead Dexter to question and eventually to rewrite the Code. When he learns of Harry's indiscretions (having an affair with Dexter's biological mother Laura Moser) and outright deceptions (lying about Dexter's biological father, destroying evidence in his mother's chainsaw murder case) Dexter rejects Harry as his "God" (a convenient external dictator of morality) and freely *chooses* to act according to the Code—rather than following it robotically as he does in the first season. At the end of season two he says: "The Code is mine now and mine alone, so too are the relationships that I cultivate. My father might not approve, but I am no longer his disciple. I am a master now. An idea, transcended into life" ("The British Invasion," Season 2).

His revised Code permits him to perform actions that would have been disallowed under the strict terms of Harry's rules. After becoming his own man with his own rules, he kills Oscar Prado in self defense with no preparation; he wrongly condemns Freebo for killing Teegan (a murder that he did not commit, although he was guilty of others); and he kills Nathan Marten, a pedophile who was guilty of stalking Rita's daughter Astor, but not of murder (which had been his strictest criteria in Season 1). By Season 3, Dexter has moved away from the strict rule-based Code of Harry and makes rules that fit his needs. He becomes less careful, he does less research, he misguidedly teaches Miguel his Code, and (in Season 4) he even mistakenly murders a photographer who was not guilty. Whereas in the early seasons Dexter's killings were primarily a means of controlling his Dark Passenger, as the plot develops, killing isn't just about channeling his urges anymore. It becomes a way for Dexter to control his own world. So, he needs his own Code.

Weird but Likeable Psychopath?

Dexter's audience is led (at least early on) to believe that he has antisocial personality disorder[2] (also known as being a psychopath or a sociopath). People who have antisocial personality demonstrate a "pervasive pattern of disregard for and violation of the rights of others." They are incapable of really caring much about what others think, want, or need. Dexter meets a number of criteria for this diagnosis, including:

- A "failure to conform to social norms with respect to lawful behaviors"—he is, after all, a cold-blooded murder.

- "Deceitfulness"—he manages to keep up relationships and appearances as a blood-splatter expert and works closely with the police while he slaughters people in his spare time.

- A "lack of remorse"—he joyfully searches for new victims and feels no apparent guilt about the people that he dismembers and disposes of in the dark depths of the Gulf Stream.

In the early seasons, Dexter does not and cannot feel empathy for others—sometimes despite his best efforts and strong desires to do so. He doesn't understand normal human emotions, such as love,

---

[2] Antisocial personality disorder is the clinical diagnosis outlined in the American Psychiatric Association's Diagnostic and Statistical Manuel IV-TR, Section 301.7.

even though he wishes he did. He says at one point "I don't have feelings about anything, but if I did, I'd have them for Deb" ("Dexter," Season 1). He's clearly attached in some meaningful way to Rita and her kids, but has no idea how to talk to them intimately and no conception of their emotional needs. In another example he confesses to being puzzled by grief; he says, "Most people have a hard time dealing with *death*—but I'm not most people. It's the *grief* that makes me uncomfortable. Not because I'm a killer. Really. I just don't understand all that emotion, which makes it hard to fake" ("Popping Cherry," Season 1).

He is, however, an *odd* psychopath. He doesn't demonstrate "impulsivity or failure to plan ahead," as demonstrated by the fact that he refers to himself as "a very neat monster" (his apartment and office are perhaps compulsively cleaned) and he meticulously follows prescribed rituals—preparation, cleanliness, organization, attention to detail, always bringing the right tools when killing his victims. Furthermore, he scrupulously follows most social norms (aside from those that forbid stalking and killing others) and even demonstrates concern for others when driving. He says on his way to work one day "the only problem with eating and driving—which I love to do—is that it makes it impossible to maintain the ten o'clock–two o'clock hand position. It's a matter of public safety" ("Dexter," Season 1). Obviously, he loves following rules despite his sociopathic tendencies.

In the later seasons Dexter seems to develop something like empathetic responses, his care and concern for Rita and the kids deepens—enough for him to claim that he would rather that they "learn the truth" than lose them. He's also genuinely concerned when he rushes to Debra's side following her shooting, claiming "if anything happens to Deb . . . I would be . . . lost." It remains to be seen whether he will continue to meet the requirements for anti-social personality disorder in Season 6 and beyond, and if he doesn't how it will impact his role as a serial murderer.

If Dexter is indeed a sociopath (whether sociopaths are made or born is a question we will leave to the psychologists and screenwriters), Harry's training and channeling of Dexter's murderous impulses doesn't merely make sense; it's an absolute necessity for him—at least to prevent him from receiving the death penalty, which was Harry's biggest concern. But what does it mean in terms of morality? Dexter has the trappings of a moral life—he follows (at least a few) moral rules, he has developed what appear to be ethical principles; he doesn't kill innocents, he doesn't drive recklessly, and he tries, despite his limitations, to respond to the emotional needs of others. He attempts to be a good citizen in the ways he sees as most effective. Besides, he rids the world of the truly bad people who society is better off without anyway; he distributes vigilante justice. How immoral could he be?

Emotions, and Rules, and Morality (Oh My!)

While Dexter can follow rules, he has trouble creating any that take into account things beyond his own psychopathic desires. This is because he lacks what some thinkers hold to be the central tools of a moral life, namely, emotions. Neuroscientist Jonah Lehrer says psychopaths are particularly dangerous because "they have damaged emotional brains," because they are "missing the emotions that guide moral decisions in the first place. There's a dangerous void where their feelings are supposed to be." [3] Dexter's disorder does not prevent him from making reasoned judgments, from learning and following rules, it only prevents him from having appropriate and unrehearsed emotional responses. Lehrer says, "The madman is not the man who has lost his reason. The madman is the man who has lost everything except his reason;" in particular he is the person who has lost the ability to empathize, as has Dexter.

From the standpoint of traditional, rule-based moral theory, the fact that sociopaths operate strictly in accord with reason yet come to such appalling moral conclusions makes little sense. As Lehrer points out "The luminaries of the Enlightenment, such as Leibnitz and Descartes tried to construct a moral system entirely free of feelings. Immanuel Kant argued that doing the right thing was merely a consequence of acting rationally—no more no less. Immorality, he said, was a result of illogic." Lehrer quotes Kant when he claims that "the oftener and more steadfastly we reflect on our moral decisions the more moral those decisions become" as we impose reason onto our responses.[4] Kant, the quintessential stuck-in-his-head philosopher, thinks that the essence of *morality* consists in following reason and shunning emotion. But this doesn't seem right. With

---

[3] Jonah Lehrer, *How We Decide* (Houghton Mifflin, 2009), pp. 171–75.

[4] *How We Decide*, p. 172. Immanuel Kant, *Groundwork of the Metaphysics of Morals* (Cambridge University Press, 1998), p. 57.

respect to their total incapacity for emotion, *Star Trek*'s Spock and Dexter would get along famously, yet they hardly make similar moral judgments.

If Lehrer and current neuroscience is to be believed, ethical decisions are more like aesthetic judgments (that rely on emotion) than purely rationally based judgments; we respond to moral questions *emotionally* first and foremost. Rational judgments come *after* the emotional assessment has already been made. According to Lehrer,

> Kant and his followers thought the rational brain acted like a scientist: we used reason to arrive at an accurate view of the world. This meant that morality was based on objective values; moral judgments described moral facts. But the mind doesn't work this way. . . . When it comes to making ethical decisions, human rationality isn't a scientist, it's a lawyer. This inner attorney gathers bits of evidence, post hoc justifications, and pithy rhetoric in order to make the automatic reaction seem reasonable. (p. 172)

According to Lehrer, most of the major players in the history of philosophy are completely wrong about the role of emotions in our moral life. As it turns out, emotions are *essential* to being moral. They don't work *against* moral decision-making. Who knew? Certainly not philosophers who, since Plato, have denied that emotions could do anything but distract us from The Truth.

Good? Evil? Icky? Sticky?

From the perspective of this new neuroscience, attempting to base morality on reason is pure folly—it would require us to conclude that a perfectly logical and consistent sociopath like Dexter is moral, a claim that not even Dexter would make. For his part, he just throws up his hands at the question "Am I evil, am I good? I'm done asking those questions. I don't have the answers. Does Anyone?" ("The British Invasion," Season 2). Although we do not claim to have all of the answers to Dexter's questions, we'll try to make some sense out of our visceral, emotional hesitation to see Dexter as moral because he follows moral rules.

One reason that we hesitate to call Dexter moral is that his ethical responses are so immature, particularly before he revises Harry's Code, but even with his modified list of rules. In response to interviews with children and adults about moral decision-making, social psychologist Lawrence Kohlberg developed what he referred to as the Three Levels and Six Stages of Moral Development.[5] The lowest, "pre-conventional" level is broken into two categories. The first of these, the "punishment and obedience orientation" is generally exhibited by ten-year-olds. This stage is typified by moral reasoning that is motivated by fear of physical punishment or desire for a reward. Children who reason in this way are usually trying to get cookies and avoid being put into "time out." Dexter is trying to avoid a lethal injection and satisfy his murderous desires. The stakes are a bit higher for him, but he is still less morally developed than a fifth-grader. He progresses a bit by revising the Code, but still doesn't escape what Kohlberg refers to as "pre-conventional" reasoning. Indeed he barely crosses into the second stage of pre-conventional thinking—"the instrumentalist relativist orientation" (who talks like this?).

In this stage, eleven- to twelve-year-olds think in terms of satisfying their own needs, which occasionally requires satisfying the needs of others. Dexter demonstrates some form of this reasoning through most of his relationships—Rita is a cover for normalcy, and to obtain this he has to give her, among other things, sex (much to his hesitation, especially in Season 1, and again in Season 4 when he would much prefer sleep to a romp with Rita and her basket of sex toys). His relationship with Miguel, although in some respects based on a real desire for friendship, is similarly instrumental. He wants Miguel to like him, so he is willing to let him in on some aspects of his ritual (he keeps some from him too, as exemplified by the fact that he never tells him how he disposes of his bodies). As Kohlberg notes, this stage is filled with "you scratch my back, I'll scratch yours" reasoning, which seems to be as far as Dexter has advanced.

Dexter's moral reasoning never really crosses into the third or "conventional level"—where most people who don't spend their days obsessing about moral theory bottom out. Although he does care about social approval (Kohlberg's Stage Three) for pragmatic reasons, he doesn't seek the approval of society in making moral judgments, such as whether or not it's a good idea to wrap people

---

[5] *The Philosophy of Moral Development: Moral Stages and the Idea of Justice* (Harper and Row, 1981).

in hefty bags and throw their dissected bodies off the side of his boat. He doesn't think that it's necessary to adopt the rules of the social body, such as laws or church doctrines (Kohlberg's Stage Four) because of a reasoned understanding and respect for the authority of those rules.

Kohlberg's highest level of moral reasoning is defined not by rule following, but by an understanding of universality and genuine respect for others. Here moral actors develop principles based on the long-term needs of others, and recognize the inherent worth of persons. Rules, to the extent that they are followed, are adhered to because they have validity outside of the scope of an individual's needs and speak to the greater concerns of humanity. Highfalutin? Yes. Consistent with anything that Dexter does? No. So despite his best efforts to "do good" Dexter really fails miserably on the morality scale (this one at least).

Someone more morally mature than a fifth-grader might also respect rules, but would not follow them so blindly in the way Dexter does. He follows Harry's rules early on as an externally imposed structure so he knows how to most productively channel his urge to destroy life. Without those rules Dexter would likely kill arbitrarily and would likely get caught. But even after the beginning of the Season 3 when he claims he owns that Code, that he has internalized it, he is still merely following a set of rules. He doesn't ever shift to a greater sense of justice that needs to be served. He could have matured into someone who sees the real benefits of ridding his community of the really bad people, but he doesn't kill for his community. He doesn't do it for justice. Dexter kills merely to pacify the Dark Passenger. More morally developed people can move beyond rule-following because they can see the bigger picture of the consequences of their actions.

Vigilante Hero?

If we're right that your average elementary school student reasons with more moral sophistication than Dexter, then he really is *just* a pathetic rule follower. But is he *also* a vigilante hero? In all but three cases—his murder of photographer Jonathon Farrow (who he mistakenly thought to have committed several murders that were actually committed by his assistant), his mercy killing of Camilla Figg, and a murder committed in the heat of passion in Season 5—every one of his murders dispensed vigilante justice by eliminating the worst of all possible criminals (assuming here that pedophiles rank near murderers on the "bad people" scale). So you might argue that he is actually doing good, that he is a righter of moral wrongs.

Can you be a pathetic rule follower *and* a vigilante hero? Could he really be doing some *good* in the Miami-Dade area? He's ridding the community of some seriously evil people who for one reason or another the justice system has failed to put away (usually due to some pesky rule designed to protect the innocent from the abuses of authority). It would be easy to contend that any community would better off with a "Bay Harbor Butcher" who protects innocent citizens by taking out the evil ones.

Although we tend to think of the vigilante heroes as idealizations of days past, and they are very popular as fictional characters, there are (at least) two charges against real men who also saw Dexter as a vigilante hero and idol. Mark Twitchell committed a murder in 2008 after luring his victim to his home by posing as a woman on-line who was looking for married men to have affairs with. Twitchell had just completed a manuscript for a Dexter movie when he committed his crime and he claimed Dexter's kind of justice to be an inspiration. In 2009 Andrew Conley, only seventeen years old at the time, killed his ten-year-old brother, and also claimed to be inspired by Dexter (more that he had killing tendencies than that he was seeking justice). He even used black Hefty bags to dispose of his brother's body.

While taking the law into your own hands, especially when the law is limited and imperfect, seems exciting and morally praiseworthy, the real Dexter-inspired murders bring gravity to this moral analysis. As much as we might idolize these renegade heroes, the reality is that most of us don't *really* want to live in a community where a psychopath—with a Dark Passenger—delivers the justice. As Dexter says, "when it comes to my brand of justice, I don't have to compromise" ("Turning Biminese," Season 3). And his brand of justice is somewhat arbitrary (or at least subject to mistakes) and is particularly brutal. This works great for fiction and drama, but the reality of it is that he can't be considered a hero in this light at all.

In the final analysis, poor Dexter remains a pathetic rule-follower and not really much of a hero, even though he is really good looking, which can sometimes distract us from a realistic moral evaluation. The plot is hugely successful not because he is somehow seen as moral (as appealing as that might be) but because of the idea of a serial killer who only kills other killers and the kind of justice that idolizes. Dexter isn't moral though, and he doesn't kill for moral reasons. He is a selfish killer who kills in a somewhat controlled (read "rule governed") way to indulge his own needs. We don't think this can be construed in any way, shape or form as moral.

Don't get us wrong here, though. Dexter himself is one of the most intriguing characters to hit the screen, but that's largely because his character is well developed (along with lots of the other characters on the show) and the idea of a killer who only kills other killers seems intuitively curious to lots of viewers. He doesn't kill because he's moral, he kills because he's an addict. He doesn't use the Code to be just in any way whatsoever, he uses the Code so he doesn't get caught. The lesson here might be, however, that *merely* following a set of rules or a "Code" doesn't constitute morality. Merely following rules will *never* make any action good, and it doesn't justify what Dexter does.

13

Deontology in Dahmerland

SARA WALLER and SEAN McALEER

Is Dexter a good citizen of Miami? He doesn't want people to know what he really does; rather, he tries to avoid showing society what his talents are. He does not expect that the sandy beaches will make him mentally well, or that the bright sunlight will light the way for his Dark Passenger. But he loves his city—because it's "Dahmerland" with "a solve rate for murders at about twenty percent."

He's not interested in Miami for its justice, but rather for its injustice. Indeed, the longer Miami remains a murderous city, the longer he can practice his craft, because he must follow the rule of only killing other killers—those who haven't been brought to justice by other means. So, is Dexter a bad guy who does good things in Miami, or a good guy who does bad things in Miami?

Before we look at what kind of moral theory applies to Dexter, we have to ask whether morality applies to Dexter at all. Is Dexter moral—or is he just amoral?

Why Might Dexter Be Amoral?

When someone or something is amoral, that means that they are neither moral nor immoral, but rather, not able to be placed on a moral scale. For example, someone who cannot be responsible for his or her actions is amoral, because he or she is not making choices that we can praise or blame, or consider to be right or wrong. This is why we have an insanity defense; if someone doesn't understand the consequences of his actions or what he is doing, perhaps because he has mental deficits, then we say that he is not to blame for his actions. He may have done something we don't like, but we still consider him to be (in a sense) innocent because he did not choose his actions and did not intend their consequences, so he's not responsible for them.

New research has shown that sociopaths may well be amoral, that is, their brains simply do not connect emotional responses to their desires, thoughts, or actions. They don't realize how painful and terrifying their urges to kill are, and so they don't have enough information about their own urges to make deliberate, responsible decisions about acting on them; they don't understand what morality is, so they don't understand the difference between right and wrong. We see this sort of aspect of sociopathy in Dexter, who says at a funeral, "Most people have a hard time dealing with death, but I'm not most people. It's the grief that makes me uncomfortable . . . I just don't understand the emotion, which makes it tough to fake. In those cases, shades come in handy" ("Popping Cherry," Season 1). Dexter doesn't feel what other people feel, and so when he chooses, he chooses without evaluating all the information available.

Secondly, Dexter may be amoral because he sometimes believes that he can't control his urges to kill. He believes he has a Dark Passenger inside him, something that forces his behaviors, something over which he has no control. As Dexter says to Lila, "I never expected to get better" ("The Dark Defender," Season 2) and Harry, his step-father, seems to feel the same way, remarking to Dexter that Dexter has "a Dark Passenger that's always got one hand on the steering wheel" ("Remains to be Seen," Season 4). If we can't make choices because our mental faculties are somehow stunted, or if we're compelled to act and have no control over which choice is made, then we're not responsible for our actions.

So, if we are to argue that Dexter is, in fact, a moral being, then we must first show that Dexter does have access to some emotions and the information that they bring us. After all, no one has a perfect understanding of the world, or perfect access to every detail of every choice, and yet, we do consider most people, most of the time, to be responsible for their actions. If Dexter is missing a little information, about as much as any other person might be missing as he or she makes choices, then he is on par with every other human in terms of responsibility. Similarly, we must show that

---

[1] "Inside the Mind of a Psychopath," *Scientific American Mind* (September 2010).

Dexter, though he suffers from a compulsion to kill, can and does control when he kills. Such control would make his actions not compulsory, and therefore subject to moral evaluation.

Does Dexter have access to emotions, or is he as empty as a box of doughnuts? As much as he protests that he has no feelings, his actions in the show tell a different story. When push comes to shove, he does not kill his sister. He knocks out Rita's treacherous husband Paul and frames him because he is upset at seeing Rita suffer. He may feel uncomfortable at funerals, but even then he's experiencing emotional discomfort. In numerous episodes, he actively misses his step-father Harry. He feels very strongly, while practicing what he wants to say to his mother's vicious killer, "I feel like . . .I am not the person I'm supposed to be . . . I hide . . . unable to reach out to people close to me, afraid . . . I'll hurt them" ("The Dark Defender," Season 2). Perhaps even more poignantly, in Season 5, he sobs over the body of a man he killed in a bathroom after realizing that a good murder won't make him feel better about Rita's death. Dexter may have deficits in his emotional life, but he has emotions. His brain is not radically different from the normal, responsible, human brain.

Does Dexter have control over his actions? The very fact that Harry trained him and developed a code for him reveals that Dexter is not an out of control killing machine. He deliberates and chooses who to kill, and when. As Harry Morgan says in the very first episode: "Okay, so we can't stop this. But maybe we can do something . . . to channel it; use it for good." Dexter has urges just as we all do, and he controls them, according to his judgment and through reflection, just as we all do. His Dark Passenger is merely his version of all of our socially unacceptable, immoral, desires and urges. It's the thing in all of us that causes us to create moral systems. Dexter is a moral being. Which then leads us to the question: What kind of moral being is he?

The Three Moral Theories

One helpful way to organize the three main moral theories we will discuss is to see them in terms of three moral concepts—goodness, rightness, and virtue. Each theory takes one of these to be basic—to explain the others but not in turn to be explained by them.

Consequentialist theories take goodness to be basic, defining rightness and virtue in terms of goodness: the right action to perform is the action that produces the best (or a good enough) outcome. Consequentialists might disagree about how to define goodness and how much goodness an action must produce to be morally right or required, but they agree that an action's rightness depends upon the goodness of its outcomes, and they agree that a virtuous person is someone with a reliable disposition to produce good outcomes. John Stuart Mill's Utilitarianism is the best-known version of consequentialism; it holds that an action is right if and only if it maximizes total happiness (for every being concerned, considered equally).

Deontologists, by contrast, take rightness to be basic. Certain actions are right (or wrong) in themselves, without regard to their consequences, or right because they accord with a correct moral rule. These rules would not in turn be justified by one of the other key moral concepts. Kant's deontology is the best known version of this theory, and it emphasizes actions done out of respect for a set of moral laws.

There are utilitarians who believe we should adopt rules which will maximize human happiness, rather than looking at each action in isolation. We call these utilitarians *rule-utilitarians*. A rule-utilitarian looks like a deontologist because she holds that actions are right if they accord with the valid moral rules, but since she thinks that what validates a moral rule is that following it produces the best outcomes, she has made rightness depend indirectly on goodness, so she's not a deontologist (even though she looks like one at first).

A virtue ethicist takes virtue to be basic. For example, a virtue ethicist might hold that an action is right in a particular situation if and only if a fully virtuous person would perform the action in those circumstances, and that a good state of affairs is one that a virtuous person would choose or value. Aristotle is the best-known proponent of this view, and he emphasizes personal excellence through practicing moderate actions that lead to happiness, or the good life.

Dexter's Deadly Virtues

Followers of Aristotle, known as *virtue ethicists* think that the virtues are basic: virtue ethicists define right conduct in terms of the virtues, holding that an action is right if and only if a virtuous person would perform it in the circumstances.

Now, if these virtue ethicists defined the virtuous person as someone who does what is right, their theory would be hopelessly circular. But virtue ethicists avoid this by giving rich accounts of the various character virtues that don't appeal to the notion of right conduct. Aristotle thought the virtues were intrinsically connected to eudaimonia or happiness in that you can't be happy or flourish as a human being without being virtuous and exercising the virtues. This is an interesting and surprising claim, since so many people think that being virtuous is at odds with happiness. It may seem more plausible if we think of what a virtue is. Our English word 'virtue' translates the Greek word areté, which could as easily be translated as 'excellence', for the virtues are excellences of various kinds. A virtue is the state or condition a thing must possess to perform its function or task well—and thus to be good.

To take a prosaic example, think of Dexter's favorite knife. Its purpose or function is to cut, and a knife cuts well (and is a good knife) when it is sharp. Hence sharpness is the virtue or excellence of a knife, and its vice—the state that prevents it from performing its function well—is dullness. Human beings are more complicated than knives—even more complicated than the most multi-functional Swiss Army Knife—but, like knives, Aristotle thinks we have a function, grounded in our being rational animals. Our function might be called rational agency, the capacity to act based on reasons (as opposed to having our actions caused by desire or instinct or design).

The character virtues, states like temperance, courage, generosity, proper pride, are those states that enable us to act well or rationally—and thus to be good, just as a knife that possesses the virtue of sharpness performs its function well and is a good knife. Since happiness is the human good, the good all human beings seek, we are happy when we reason well, expressing our rational agency toward such social ends as justice, equality, fairness in government, magnanimity, and temperance.

Aristotle thought that the virtues of character (which are often called the moral virtues) have a distinctive structure: each virtue is a mean between extremes of excess and deficiency. Take courage, for example, the virtue that concerns how we act in situations that typically arouse fear. A coward feels more fear than a situation warrants and thus doesn't act well, while a rash or foolhardy person feels less fear than a situation warrants and thus doesn't act well, since she takes too many risks.

Is Dexter a virtue ethicist? Does he think that his actions are right because they are what a virtuous person would do in the circumstances? Aristotle thought that character virtues are means between extremes, but he also thought that some activities and feelings simply cannot express mean states: envy is an example of a feeling that can't be a mean; adultery and murder are examples of actions that can't express a mean state. There's no such thing as committing adultery with the right woman, at the right time, in the right way. It's simply impossible to commit adultery correctly. The same goes for murder.

Thus it would be a deep mistake to think of Dexter as a virtue ethicist. While Dexter is a skillful killer, he hardly seems to be virtuous. What's the difference? Virtues strongly resemble skills, and we often find Aristotle and his teacher Plato drawing an analogy between virtues and skills. But skills have narrower scope than virtues, and they do not seem subject to moral evaluation. Skills can be put to moral or immoral uses, but in themselves they are not moral or immoral. A skillful violinist—a virtuoso—is a better violinist than an unskilled violinist, but she is not thereby a better person.

Aristotle's claim that the virtues are necessary for happiness might be controversial, but the claim that the virtues are necessary for moral goodness will seem a platitude. An upshot of this is that possessing and exercising the virtues can't make one morally worse. So the skills possessed by a terrorist aren't really virtues, though they look like virtues, since—assuming terrorists are morally bad—these skills make him a better terrorist and thus a worse person. A skillful killer is good at being a killer. Much of Harry's Code concerns skills that anyone striving to be a good—meaning efficient—serial killer would want to master, such as avoiding detection, being careful to clean up and not leave evidence, not making things personal, or being able to fake emotions so as to appear normal. Fostering these traits will make one a good killer, but being a good killer does not make one a good person—just the opposite, usually.

But if we attend to some of the other elements of Harry's Code, we may be less certain that it's a mistake to think of Dexter in virtue-ethical terms, for some parts of the Code have a moral dimension, for instance: Don't kill innocent people, and be sure that your potential victim is not innocent and is likely to kill again. As Dexter internalizes these rules, he develops reliable dispositions not to kill innocent people, and to kill only non-innocents who are likely to kill again. Though it sounds a bit weird to say it, these dispositions are moral virtues. Most of us don't have to work at developing these virtues as Dexter does, but that doesn't mean that they're not genuinely virtues. So while it's true that there is no mean and thus no virtue with respect to murder, since Dexter kills only killers who have escaped justice and who will kill again, he is not murdering innocent victims.

While he certainly strives to be excellent, he strives to be excellent at anti-social, anti-humanistic ends. He does not strive to be an excellent murderer for the sake of honing his character, or to increase justice, equality, or fairness within the city of Miami. Though he may make Miami a safer, better place to live, Dexter ultimately is acting on his urges rather than on higher, more contemplative Aristotelian ends. He's not trying to improve himself through practice, nor attempting to flourish as a human being. Indeed, he often finds his neat, but monstrous, tendencies to be at odds with flourishing in the rest of his life. Rather, he strives to be excellent in order to follow Harry's Code—to not get caught. His practice of his craft is the result and continuing cause of his perpetual feelings of hollowness rather than inner fulfillment. Dexter does not do things "at the right time, for the right reason" as Aristotle would wish, but rather, he does things that might seem to be right for all the dark, wrong reasons we can imagine.

The Dark Defender and the Needs of the Many

Dexter is perhaps most plausibly seen as a utilitarian when he finds himself identified with "The Dark Defender" in Season 2. This super-hero sacrifices himself, and his very guilty, evil victims, to bring happiness to the world and protect the many from the few. Utilitarians, being consequentialists, define what's right in terms of what's good. And being hedonists, they hold that pleasure, and only pleasure, is intrinsically good (and pain and only pain is intrinsically bad). Thus, for a utilitarian, right conduct is what maximizes pleasure and minimizes pain for the greatest number of people. It's not the agent's own happiness that is the utilitarian standard, but the greatest happiness of all involved.

For utilitarians, the end justifies the means—literally. The end, total happiness, will justify actions such as killing so long as the killing is a means to more happiness than any available alternative. If Dexter's killing brings about the best balance of pleasure over pain, then his actions would be permissible (and, indeed, required) by utilitarianism. While this approach appears promising as a way of understanding Dexter's actions, the appearance is misleading: Dexter is not a utilitarian.

For starters, Dexter does not reason as a utilitarian would, he does not ask himself whether killing will maximize total happiness and then kill if—and only if—it will. But this objection might not be decisive, since many utilitarians think their theory is about what justifies actions rather than a theory about how people do or even should deliberate about what to do: Dexter need not think about whether his actions promote the greatest total happiness; what matters is whether his actions have the desired effect. Still, there is something unsettling about a moral theory telling us that, though our actions will be assessed according to that moral theory, we need not—and perhaps even should not—use that theory in deliberating.

For Dexter, actions are not required because they promote the greatest good, they are required because the rules—Harry's Code—require them. Even if a killing would not maximize total happiness, it would still be required, if Harry's Code requires it. Since what is required does not depend upon how an action contributes to human well-being, Dexter can't be seen as a utilitarian.

Not so fast, the utilitarian says, for we should distinguish between act- and rule-utilitarianism. According to act-utilitarianism an act is right if and only if it maximizes total happiness—this is the theory as we've been discussing it. According to rule-utilitarianism, on the other hand, an action is right if and only if it follows the correct moral rules—and the correct moral rules are those would maximize total happiness if they were generally followed.

Suppose that a doctor kills a patient to harvest her organs and distribute them to half a dozen other patients. Many people would find the doctor's action profoundly immoral, even if it would maximize total happiness. The rule-utilitarian shares this moral judgment, but can't shake his deep sense that moral rightness makes sense only if it is connected with human well-being. So he reasons that a moral rule prohibiting harvesting the organs of unwilling "donors" would produce more happiness than a rule allowing it, since the members of a society allowing involuntary organ harvesting would be forever on their guard, terrified that they might be treated as organ-fields, afraid to go to the doctor and consequently living with more pain than they otherwise would. So involuntary organ-harvesting is wrong because it violates a moral rule.

What makes this theory a utilitarian theory is its justification for the rules—that following them would maximize total happiness. Contrast the rule-utilitarian view with a justification of the moral rules that appealed to God's will. Both the rule-utilitarian and the divine command theorist think that killing the unwilling donor violates a moral rule. They might even agree on which rules are morally valid, but they offer very different justifications for why the valid rules are valid.

What justifies the rules that make up Harry's Code? Are they valid because Harry, a sort of god-like figure, says they are? Or are they valid because Dexter's following them will have better overall consequences than his following any other rules? Consider the rule of certainty: Be sure. Dexter must be sure not only that his potential victim is not innocent, but also that he will kill again. Without the second part, Dexter might appear to be merely doling out justice to those who have escaped it. In fact, though, he kills not to balance the books, so to speak, but to prevent the killing from causing more harm—just the sort of reasoning that a utilitarian embraces. However, the purpose behind the rules is far more clearly understood by Harry than it is by Dexter, who in Season 2 struggles with the rules, their meaning, and the real nature of their creator while he attempts to be "in recovery."

Dexter confronts himself and his actions in the therapy of Narcotics Anonymous, and realizes for the first time that murdering other killers can be construed as good, even as a utilitarian public service, rather than simply as a permissible outlet for his personal urges. And we come to understand that Harry made his "rules" as a frustrated police officer who does want killers to come to justice when they are lost in the system. During this time, Dexter discovers, and struggles with, Harry's hidden side (a liar, and someone who had an affair with Dexter's mother and police informant Laura Moser) and wonders why he is following rules made by someone who did not follow a clear moral code himself.

Working with the devilish Lila in his recovery program, Dexter re-thinks his moral code. He sees means and ends up close through his own personal lens. Lila lies, cheats and steals, and does so for reasons she suggests are good ones. For Lila, the end of art is so important that stealing is a morally acceptable means to accomplish it. The pleasure of eating at a fine restaurant justifies lying. Dexter slowly realizes that Harry's utilitarian commitments resulted in his mother's brutal death.

For Dexter, the broader end of justice can never completely justify the unwanted consequence of the murder of Laura Moser and the further consequences for himself and his brother. He enjoys being "The Dark Defender" with its utilitarian overtones, but ultimately, he kills killers because it is right in itself, that is, because it matches Harry's Code (now modified and divorced from Harry himself), and not because of the good results such vigilantism may or may not have. He kills because, as Dexter tells us in Season 5, "Some people don't deserve to live." He would kill even if he were not "The Dark Defender," because Harry's Code is more important to him than serving society.

Dexter's Dark Deontology

As we've said earlier, deontological ethics claims that certain actions are right (or wrong) in themselves, without regard to their consequences. Right actions are right because they accord with a correct moral rule.

A classic deontological theorist is Immanuel Kant, who argued that moral laws derive from the way human minds are hardwired: our rational faculties are structured in such a way that we understand morality only according to certain principles and within certain boundaries. He called these principles and boundaries the conditions for the possibility of morality. We cannot experience something as moral without it being universalizable.

So, for Kant, good actions are those that are universalizable, and evil actions are those that somehow contradict a rule that is necessary for everyone to follow. For example, Kant tells us that lying is wrong, not because it has bad consequences, but because if everyone lied, then the liar herself would not be able to communicate a lie. In other words, liars succeed in lying only because they assume that everyone else tells the truth; they take advantage of the universal rule of truth-telling and make themselves the exception. Hypocrisy, for Kant, is a perfect example of true evil. Ultimately, what we understand to be moral are laws that apply to everyone, without exception.

So we know immediately that Dexter is not a perfect Kantian deontologist, because he must lie and mislead everyone around him in order to succeed in his task. However, this does not mean that he is not a deontologist at all. Dexter follows a set of rules that have much in common with Kant's system: Harry's Code.

Don't kill innocents (that would be mere murder; instead, always kill for a good purpose)

Be Sure (that they have killed, and that they are likely to kill again)

Don't get caught

Be careful in the act and in the cleanup

Never make things personal

Blend in (fake emotion to appear normal)

You Control Your Urges—They Do Not Control You

Kant would easily agree with universalizing the rule to not kill innocent people. Indeed, Kant suggests both that we must protect the innocent and that we ought to execute those who have killed others; he is one of the traditional champions of the rightness of capital punishment. Kant reasoned that if someone decides that he can kill another person and does so, then he has chosen to create a rule that can be universalized, that is, a rule that can be applied to him. So a man who murders must consent to being murdered himself, because he has made murder a possibility that applies to everyone, including himself. Therefore, we're obligated to murder the murderers, out of respect for their rationality. Murderers assert that anyone can be killed, therefore they themselves can be killed.

In this way, Dexter, as the serial killer who only kills serial killers, is very like a Kantian Deontologist. He is dedicated to being anything but a mere murderer: he researches his victims, he is sure that they are guilty, he strives to make it right when he does kill an innocent, and he avoids at all costs being like those who prey on the innocent. As Dexter tells the child murderer in the very first episode, he has standards.

Indeed the only reason that Dexter lies is because he follows the rule "Don't get caught." This rule in turn entails the rules of carefulness, of not making his kills personal (that might affect his judgment), and blending in and faking emotion. In other words,

Dexter only misleads others as much as he has to in order to achieve his first imperative, to always kill for a good purpose. Not getting caught is a condition for the possibility of continuing to murder only other murderers, which is Dexter's reason for all his actions.

Another important aspect of Deontology is the notion that a truly moral person acts out of respect for the moral law, and not merely in accord with the law. That is, moral people do good things because they want to be moral, and not simply because they enjoy them, or it suits them. A truly moral person will tell the truth out of a feeling of duty and respect for goodness, and not because the truth suits her or pleases her. Dexter fits very well with this important Deontological tenet. He does enjoy killing, but he does not always enjoy it. He was very sad to kill his brother, and also sad to euthanize Camilla at her request.

Likewise, he does not always kill out of a compulsion or need to kill—it is a choice for him at all times, as illustrated in Season 2 (Episode 6, "Dex, Lies, and Videotape"), when he does not need to kill the man who is posing as the "Bay Harbor Butcher" but simply does it out of respect for Harry's principles. The clincher here is that while Dexter has urges to kill, he channels them according to Harry's Code, and out of duty toward that Code.

Indeed, such control over our urges is the condition for the possibility of all of morality, for all of us. In order for there to be moral rules, we must have urges that are somehow destructive, evil, or immoral. These urges cause us to develop a moral system to follow. The urges that we need to channel or control are conditions for the possibility of morality. As moral beings, we don't ask "Shall we act?" but rather "How shall we act?"

If we desire to act at all, we need a Moral Code to act by. It is this desire that is the condition for the possibility of the Moral Code. Without dark desires, there would be no deontology to light our way. Dexter does often think "I really need to kill somebody" (Season 2, "It's Alive"). But we all need to do something; action is a necessary component of human existence. And those needs are the origin, the purpose, of the moral rules.

14

Best of Luck, Dexter!

DANIEL P. MALLOY

> Lucky. I am lucky. What do I know about abuse? Without the Code of Harry, I'm sure I would have committed a senseless murder in my youth. Just to watch the blood flow.
>
> —DEXTER ("Popping Cherry," Season 1)

Any fan of Dexter has to admit that the show depends a great deal on lucky chances to get its protagonist out of some of sticky situations. Instances are numerous—such as Dexter's forgetting where he left a body, or having a body that's been disposed turn up. But that seems forgivable because the show's very premise depends on a lucky chance—Dexter was fortunate enough to be adopted by a cop who, instead of getting him psychiatric care, taught him how to kill without getting caught.

Luck is a tricky prospect for philosophers. It raises a variety of difficult questions, most of them having to do with probabilities and inductive logic. However, there is a philosophical problem raised by luck that does not require any abstract equations: the problem of moral luck.

First introduced by Bernard Williams and Thomas Nagel in a pair of essays in the late 1970s, the problem of moral luck is a new formulation of a problem that philosophers have been struggling with since Aristotle (384–322 B.C.E.). The problem asks, Is a person responsible for things in his or her life that are the result of good or bad luck? There are several different aspects of this problem played out in Dexter.

Dexter never chose to be a psychopath. He never chose to be adopted by Harry Morgan. Arguably, he didn't choose to learn the

Code of Harry. All of these things played important roles in making Dexter the "neat monster" that fans of the show love. So, given that Dexter didn't choose these influences, they were imparted to him by luck. This is *constitutive* luck—are we responsible for the types of people we are, given that we didn't choose the influences that made us the way we are?

A further problem connected to luck and morality is about the kinds of choices we're asked to make. Most of us have never had to choose between an adopted sister and a blood brother—much less a situation where the choice between the two will mean the death of one or the other ("Born Free," Season 1). But Dexter has. Is he responsible for the outcome? This is the problem of *situational* luck—we don't know what we would do in a particular situation until that situation presents itself. If the opportunity to make the choice between a morally wrong and a morally right action never presents itself, then a person can lead a life of perfect virtue without being especially good.

Finally, and perhaps most centrally, there is the problem of *resultant* luck. This is what first raised the issue in Bernard Williams's "Moral Luck." When we act, we cannot be sure of the outcome of our actions. That's simply a fact of life. So, given that fact, can we be held responsible for those outcomes? When Dexter teaches Harry's Code to Miguel, he has no way of knowing that his friend will use it to settle a personal vendetta. So, is he responsible in any way for the subsequent murder of Ellen Wolf? [1]

While the problem of moral luck is indeed a problem, its consequences are not as radical as some have claimed. Moral luck does not eliminate moral responsibility. Dexter's bouts of good and bad fortune throughout the series may mitigate his responsibility for his actions and their consequences, but they cannot eliminate it. In the end, Dexter is answerable for his crimes.

Picking Up the Dark Passenger

The first problem we face in dealing with moral luck is the problem of origins. None of us chose to be here. We didn't choose to be born into a particular family, nor did we choose to grow up a

---

[1] These distinctions were first put forth in Thomas Nagel, "Moral Luck," *Proceedings of the Aristotelian Society, Supplemental Volumes* 50 (1976).

certain way. Given the amount of influence these and other factors beyond our control have on who we eventually become, it seems that we may not be responsible for the end result of that process. By this logic, Dexter is no more responsible for being the monster that he is than a rose is for the color of its petals.

We can see the role of constitutive luck played out in the show in two ways. First, let's examine what we might call Dexter's bad constitutive luck. In the Season 1, it's strongly implied that what made Dexter (and his brother, whom we'll get to later) into an unfeeling psychopath was a particularly traumatic event in early childhood. Dexter and Brian witnessed the brutal murder of their mother. As Dexter puts it when reading the newspaper coverage of the slaying, "If I did have emotions, I'd have to feel this" ("Truth Be Told," Season 1). No one could claim that Dexter was responsible for his mother's death, or for having witnessed it, or for having been left with the dismembered corpses for two days. Nor could anyone blame Dexter for shutting down emotionally in response to those events. Shutting down was a survival tactic, pure and simple. So, Dexter is in no way responsible for becoming the psychopath that we all know and love (however much that disturbs us).

On the other side of the coin, Dexter was lucky enough to have been found and adopted by Harry Morgan, super-cop. This is lucky for Dexter in two ways. First, the Morgans are a decent family and provide him with a good home life. This may seem trite, but its value can't be overestimated. His relationship with his adoptive sister, though strained at times, is generally good. The Morgans take good care of young Dexter, as he himself is the first to admit. He says "Harry and Doris Morgan did a wonderful job raising me" ("Dexter," Season 1). Remember also that Dexter fakes his way through all of his relationships—it would prove difficult to do that without the model provided by the Morgans.

Dexter's adoption is fortunate also because Harry soon recognizes what Dexter is. Being a super-cop, Harry knows killers. Realizing that his adopted son is a killer, Harry faces a choice. He can either get Dexter psychiatric help, which will probably mean having him committed to a facility for the better part of his life, or he can teach Dexter to survive and to channel his dark urges in socially useful directions. Harry, of course, chooses the second alternative—good thing for us fans! This is the origin of Harry's Code. It keeps Dexter alive, out of prison, and focused on killing only those who deserve it—other killers.

To get a clearer idea of just how lucky Dexter is in all of this, give a second's thought to what might have become of Dexter without Harry's influence. Not much imagination is needed to see where this would go: you only have to think of Dexter's long lost brother, Brian Moser. Brian saw what Dexter saw. He reacted the same way Dexter reacted. He became what Dexter became. But he also became something worse. He became what Dexter later calls "an unchecked version of myself" ("I Had a Dream," Season 3). Brian, the Ice Truck Killer, kills solely to satisfy his urges. And, of course, he winds up dead. He probably would have met that fate a bit sooner if Dexter hadn't been so intrigued by him. I guess Dexter's good fortune in being trained by Harry wound up being a lucky stroke for Brian as well. For a while at least Dexter's curiosity led him to stall the investigation, thus leaving Brian free to keep killing.

Parallel cases, like those of Dexter and Brian, are important to our thinking about moral luck. Beginning from the same place, Dexter and Brian go in widely diverging directions because of something neither of them can control: the benevolence of Harry Morgan. Dexter becomes a hero—of sorts—thanks to something he had no say in. Brian, on the other hand, becomes just another serial killer.

These competing influences in Dexter's development shape the kind of person he becomes. Harry's benevolent influence is felt throughout the show—long after his death, Dexter still consults the memory of his adoptive father before every major decision. However, this shows only how Dexter came to have the options he has. It does not remove his ability to make choices. That is, whatever events made Dexter a psychopathic expert in the art of human dissection, they did not make him kill. Dexter still had a choice. His urges, his Dark Passenger, give him an ever-present motive to kill, but only his choice creates the intention to kill. Dexter is not responsible for his urges, nor is he responsible for the Code of Harry, but he is responsible for each and every time he gives in to those urges, for each and every time he uses the Code of Harry to choose his victim, to stalk and ambush him or her, and to get rid of the body afterwards. Dexter could have chosen never to take a human life, to satisfy his urges by hunting, or to avoid killing altogether—but that would not have made for a compelling show.

Better You than Me, Dex!

But there's more involved in Dexter's decisions to kill than just his constitution—he also has to have the opportunity to kill. Put Dexter on an uninhabited desert island before he gets the chance to kill anyone and he might just live a life of perfect virtue. Miami, however, provides Dexter with plenty of opportunities—even with his commitment to follow the Code of Harry. This points us to situational luck: that we are not always responsible for the kinds of decisions we are asked to make. Suppose someone close to you has committed a crime and you find out about it. You now face a moral decision: do you turn this person in or not? The point is that you did not choose to be in this situation, but you will be held responsible for whatever you do in it, whether good or bad.

The obvious parallel to this scenario would be when and if Debra discovers Dexter's unusual hobby. As that hasn't happened yet, let's turn to a couple of situations Dexter finds himself in where he has to make a choice, but he didn't choose the situation itself. To make things simpler, we'll focus on two situations where Dexter has to choose between two people: one innocent, the other a killer.

In the first situation, at the end of the first season, Dexter has to choose between the lives of his long lost brother and his adoptive sister. Dexter did not choose to be in the situation—given his druthers Dexter would have preferred to have both of them in his life in some capacity. He wants to keep Brian so that he can have someone with whom to share his Dark Passenger, but he needs Deb to maintain whatever link he has to the rest of humanity. In the end, of course, Dexter makes the "right" choice—he saves Debra and kills Brian. But the choice was difficult, as any interesting moral choice is going to be. The choice also helps the show. We see Dexter at the end of the first season as a monster, but he's our monster. That's why the discovery of his dumping ground causes us discomfort. We know he's a monster, we know he should be stopped, but we also know that even in the face of tremendous temptation, Dexter will follow the Code of Harry, which means he's only dangerous to killers.

At least, that's the theory. The closing episodes of the second season show that Dexter's threat isn't quite so clear cut. Once again Dexter has to choose between an innocent person and a killer. But this time the case is complicated because the killer is Dexter himself. As Agent Lundy and the Bay Harbor Butcher Task Force close in, Dexter finds himself forced to kidnap Detective Sergeant Doakes. The interesting decision occurs later, when the task force begins to focus on Doakes as a suspect, and Dexter begins contemplating turning himself in. He can't kill Doakes—that's against the Code. At the same time, turning himself in goes against the Code—the whole point of the Code is to prevent his getting caught. But, with the task force focused on Doakes, Dexter sees a way out: frame Doakes. This, of course, is what Dexter chooses to do. It means walking a fine line. On the one hand, it most likely means Doakes's death—the number of bodies attributed to the Bay Harbor Butcher would probably merit a death sentence, regardless of Doakes's record of service. On the other hand, Dexter isn't killing Doakes himself.

We might say Dexter makes the best of a bad situation. But while he's certainly doing the best thing for himself, given his dedication to the Code, we can hardly say that he's doing the right thing. Framing an innocent person for the murder of thirty or more people hardly seems like the right thing to do, under any circumstances. But regardless (for the moment) of the morality of his actions, the fact is that this situation was not of Dexter's choosing. His whole life is geared around not getting caught, not having his murders discovered at all, much less finding himself confronted with super agent Frank Lundy.

Clearly there are differences between these two situations. In one Dexter has to choose between himself and someone else; in the other between two people who are important to him. The first situation is something designed for him by Brian—all of the Ice Truck Killer's moves in season one were dedicated toward bringing Dexter to this point, this choice. The second situation, on the other hand, is something that results partially from Dexter's willful actions. Dexter didn't accidentally kidnap Doakes. Still, both situations are beyond Dexter's control, and they both confront him with difficult choices.

So, is Dexter responsible for these situations? No, it would hardly be fair to say that he is. However, that does not relieve him of responsibility for what he does in them. Dexter is still capable of opting to do the right thing or the wrong thing in any given situation. While he's not responsible for being in these situations, just as he's not responsible for having his Dark Passenger, Dexter is nevertheless responsible for what he does in these situations—or, more specifically, for what he intends to do.

Teaching the Code of Harry

When Dexter locked up Doakes, he had no way of predicting that Lila would burn down the shack. So, is Dexter responsible for Doakes's death? Doakes wouldn't have died if Dex hadn't kidnapped him. This is the problem of resultant luck, and it is the aspect of the problem of moral luck that got the ball rolling, as it were. In Bernard Williams's original essay "Moral Luck," this is the only aspect of the problem that interests him. And it has largely dominated the argument since then. We can easily see why: few people would argue that a person can be held responsible for their upbringing or the kinds of situations they find themselves in, but the consequences of our choices seem to be the best way we have of deciding the morality or immorality of those choices. But this presumes that we have a level of control over the consequences of our actions—which is not always the case. Dexter had no control over Lila. Or, to take another example from the show, when he chooses not to kill the Trinity Killer when he has the chance, he has no way of predicting the chain of events that will lead to Rita's death.

But let's follow our pattern and look at a couple of parallel cases specifically when someone teaches the Code of Harry to someone else. First, of course, Harry teaches the Code to young Dexter. Then, in the third season, Dexter teaches the Code to Miguel. In each case, the teacher has no idea how this will end up—the consequences are unknown.

In the first case, Harry teaches his Code to Dexter. There are a couple of questions we have to ask here. First, why did Harry do it? Second, what were the consequences, and how much chance did Harry have of predicting them? As to the first, we run into a bit of a problem trying to answer it. Unlike with Dexter, we don't have direct access to Harry's thoughts. We only know what he says. According to his testimony, he teaches Dexter the Code for two reasons. First, it will keep Dexter alive. The Code instructs him how to cover his crimes and to blend in, so that the people around him do not become suspicious (except for Doakes, of course). Second, it will channel Dexter's urges in a useful direction. In a sense, Harry understands that Dexter is a monster—part of the purpose of the Code is to prevent him from becoming a complete monster, in the style of Brian Moser or Arthur Mitchell.

What were the consequences of Harry's actions? Well, Dexter became a very good little monster. Sure, he's killed lots and lots of people. But, with two notable exceptions, those people were all guilty of fairly heinous crimes. So, it seems in this case Harry is justified by the consequences of his actions. But the fact is that he had no control over how Dexter applied the Code. For all he knew, in training Dexter as well as he did, Harry may have just been creating a more perfect monster. Had Dexter not taken the moral portion of Harry's Code to heart, it would have made him simply the most prolific monster in history. Harry got lucky, and is only justified because he got lucky.

By contrast, think about Dexter's attempt to pass on the Code to Miguel. First, we have to admit that Dexter's motives weren't quite as noble as Harry's. Harry was trying to save his adoptive son—Dexter was just lonely. He taught the Code to Miguel because he wanted, as he always seems to want, someone with whom he could share those parts of himself that aren't fit for public viewing. Even Harry, who trained him, couldn't handle that side of Dexter ("There's Something about Harry," Season 3). But, it seemed, Miguel could. So, Dexter taught him to kill because he wanted a friend. Not a terrible motive, admittedly, but also not an especially noble one. There is a difference between the understandable and the justifiable.

Also unlike Harry's choice, Dexter's didn't have great consequences. Miguel decided he could kill whomever he wanted, including defense attorney Ellen Wolf. We could certainly argue that Dexter isn't responsible for this—we can't be held completely responsible for the actions of other people. But Dexter did give Miguel the tools, not knowing how he would use them. If I give a child a loaded gun, then I am at least partly responsible for whatever he does with it. In the same way, Dexter is at least partly responsible for Ellen Wolf's death. He acknowledges this, in a way, when he kills Miguel. If there's anything Dexter's good at, it's cleaning up his messes.

In each of these cases we have the same action—teaching someone how to kill another person and get away with it. In each case the rightness or wrongness of the action depends largely on the consequences that follow from it. And, in each case, those consequences are out of the control of the person who took the initial action. So, how do we determine responsibility in cases like this? Is it fair to say that Harry was right and Dexter was wrong because Dexter follows the whole Code and Miguel chose to ignore the moral aspect of it?

I don't think so. At the same time, I do think it's fair to say that Harry was right and Dexter was wrong, but to see why, we don't need to rely on the consequences of their actions. Rather, we have to look at how their actions differed. There's a variety of ways that we can distinguish Harry's choice from Dexter's, but the most important difference is found in their intentions. Harry was acting from good, selfless intentions. He wanted to help his son and turn his darkness into something good. Dexter, on the other hand, was acting from selfish intentions. He wanted a friend.

. . . And No More Fucking Remorse

Still, there's a problem with our discussions of resultant luck so far. In each case, we were asking about the responsibility that one person has for another person's actions. While we do influence those around us, and may encourage or discourage certain courses of action, rarely can one person be held responsible for what another person does. Supposing, for instance, that Miguel had gotten caught; Dexter might have faced some punishment, but the murder of Ellen Wolf would have landed squarely on Miguel's shoulders. So, in order to fully flesh out the problem of resultant moral luck, we really have to look at something Dexter did himself.

The best example from the show of one of Dexter's actions having moral consequences different from those he intends occurs in the Season 4 episode "Slack Tide." In this unusual, though not entirely unexpected, turn of events, Dex gets sloppy and kills an innocent man, photographer Jonathan Farrow. It's only revealed at the close of the episode that Farrow was in fact innocent, and so the next episode, "Road Kill" is left to show us how Dexter deals with this error. It is intriguing because Dexter, for the first time ever, experiences remorse. However, being a psychopath, it's a little different from what you or I might call remorse. Dexter is quite insistent in his internal monologue that Farrow's murder was a mistake—the kind of blunder anyone might make.

Remorse, or more accurately agent-regret, is an important concept in thinking about resultant luck. The distinction between remorse and agent-regret is fairly simple. Remorse is the bad feeling that we have done something wrong. Agent-regret is the wish that we could undo some action we have taken. The two are often connected, as in Dexter's case, but need not be. I can feel regret

about some action I've taken without being remorseful about it—
I regret having dinner one night when I got food poisoning, but I
don't feel remorseful about it. There's nothing morally wrong with
having dinner. But the consequences of that particular dinner were
unpleasant, and I'd rather have avoided them. Dexter, in looking
on Farrow's murder afterward, feels both remorse and agent-regret.
Oddly, we might claim that he feels the one because of the other.
Because he's remorseful, an unpleasant feeling, he has the desire
to erase his earlier action—agent-regret.

But, as Dexter mentions several times, it was a mistake. He did-
n't mean to kill an innocent man. He meant to kill a murderer, as
usual. In this one case, Dexter was negligent. Usually, as he
proudly proclaimed to Doakes, his code "requires a higher standard of proof than your city's laws" ("There's Something about
Harry," Season 2). Indeed, just a few episodes before "Slack Tide,"
we get a reminder of just how painstaking Dexter can be when he
finds the evidence against Officer Kruger—searching her house,
finding the remains of a glove in her trash compactor, testing it for
DNA, and so on. But, in the case of Farrow, he slipped. He was
just so sure. But that certainty makes no difference. Dexter was
wrong, and he has to live with that.

This example from Dexter is similar to one of the more famous
examples used in discussing moral luck: the example of the reckless drivers. Take two reckless drivers. Both start from the same
point and are heading to the same place. One makes it there
safely; the other strikes and kills a pedestrian. The second driver
had no control over the movements of the pedestrian, and so he
is now a killer because of something he had no control over.
Similarly, Dexter has now killed an innocent man because of
something he had no control over: in this one case, the most obvious suspect happened to be the wrong one. He's no more responsible for that fact than the second reckless driver is for the
pedestrian's movements.

But, both—indeed all three (because we can include the first
reckless driver in this as well)—are responsible for their parts in
what happened. The reckless driver who killed the pedestrian isn't
responsible for the pedestrian's movements, but he is responsible
for driving recklessly. Once he's made that choice, he must accept
responsibility for whatever outcomes follow. In just the same way,
Dexter chose to kill Farrow—he has to accept that he has killed an
innocent man.

Where the Bodies Lie

So while the problem of moral luck presents a quandary, it is not unsolvable. Regardless of our background, circumstances, or even the outcomes of our actions, there's still one key element of moral assessment that we can always be held accountable for: our intentions. Dexter's a killer not because of his childhood or the wealth of opportunities to kill surrounding him, but because he chose to be one. In the end, he can still be held accountable for that.

An interesting illustration of moral luck, applicable to Dexter, comes from philosopher David Lewis. In his article "The Punishment that Leaves Something to Chance," Lewis argues that we should treat attempted murderers the same way that we treat successful murderers.[2] To assign an attempted murderer a lesser sentence is to ignore his intentions. This person intended to take the life of another. He's being rewarded with a lesser sentence for being incompetent, or for his intended victim's stroke of good fortune. The attempted murderer has performed precisely the same action as the successful murderer. The only difference between the two crimes is likewise the point in the two crimes that relies on luck. Remove that from consideration, and they are identical actions, and therefore should be treated in identical ways.

What does this mean for Dexter? First and foremost, it means that he's guilty. He is responsible for all of his crimes, regardless of any mitigating factors. To return to Farrow, we shouldn't be surprised that Dex killed an innocent man—we should be surprised that it didn't happen earlier. Every action is, more or less, a roll of the dice. But we still choose where and when and how we throw those dice.

What does it mean for us? Mainly that we have to rethink how we approach responsibility. Our focus must be on intention. That raises difficulties of its own—we cannot know what other people are thinking, as a general rule. We can, however, get a fairly good idea based on other actions. One of the reasons Dexter makes such a good example is because we have direct access to his thought processes. We are not so fortunate in real life. But we can generally predict a person's intentions from his or her behavior patterns or character. It's that, rather than the outcomes of our actions, that we can be held accountable for, and that Dexter will one day have to answer for.

---

[2] David Lewis, "The Punishment that Leaves Something to Chance," *Philosophy and Public Affairs* 18:,1 (Winter, 1989).

15

Why Kill or Not Kill?
That Is the Question

SULTAN AHMED

I shot a man in Reno just to watch him die.

—Johnny Cash, "Folsom Prison Blues"

Personally, I don't know of any person who has shot a man in Reno, or any other place for that matter, just to watch him die. Johnny Cash does, however, make me wonder why somebody would kill another person. This song was playing once when I flipped the TV on to watch an episode of *Dexter*, and it got the gears in my head turning. Why does Dexter kill the particular people he chooses to kill?

Dexter's victims belong to one of two groups: killers who manage to escape the justice delivered by the Miami legal system or people who threaten Dexter or those close to him. Save for one accident and one crime of passion following the death of his wife, Dexter has never killed a person who falls outside of one of these categories. This choice of victims is no coincidence. There must be some reason behind it.

There are those who would have you believe that Dexter is a vigilante fighting for justice. He kills other killers because he feels it is his civic duty to ensure that the killers get what they deserve. These people are arguing that Dexter is a deontologist. This means that he kills the people he kills because he genuinely feels he has a moral duty to do so. For deontologists, the consequences of actions are not the central factor in determining whether an action is right or wrong. Other factors such as intent and a sense of moral duty are more important.

I don't believe that Dexter is a deontologist, because it's not entirely accurate to classify him as one. Moral considerations are not what not primarily guide his blade. He doesn't frame his killings as moral duties. Rather, Dexter's select killings of other killers serve his emotional needs as well as those of his father. His deontology has an emotional foundation.

The Mind Thinking about Its Sense of Duty

What exactly does it mean to be a deontologist? Deontologists don't think that the consequences of an action are primarily what determine whether or not the action is moral. Immanuel Kant, who many consider to be the father of deontological ethics, pioneered the idea that the results of an action alone do not determine its moral rightness. He even went so far as to argue that certain actions, such as lying, are categorically wrong, even if they save somebody's life. To say Dexter is a deontologist is to say that Dexter is not guided mostly by considerations regarding the consequences of his actions, but that he feels he has a moral duty to rid the world of the people he kills.

In order to classify Dexter as a true deontologist, his moral code should be the product of moral reasoning. Psychologically speaking, Dexter must be primarily motivated by a sense of moral duty over anything else. There's no doubt that Dexter abides by a code, initially Harry's Code and eventually his own. The question is whether or not this Code is the product of moral considerations or whether there is something else that actually guides him, and his morality is placed on top of that underlying foundation.

Philosophy and psychology are related. Long before today's neurosciences, philosophers like Thomas Hobbes, Friedrich Nietzsche, and David Hume questioned how and why people make their moral judgments. They addressed questions about human cognition, motivation, and the course of human psychological development. More modern philosophers like Walter Davis, Ernest Becker, and William Campbell use psychological analysis to analyze why people believe in religion or how people view their own identities. Recently, this relationship has taken a turn. Psychological research suggests that moral judgments, like Dexter's choice of victim, may not in fact be the product of actual moral reasoning. We may make these judgments and act upon them for unconscious reasons, reasons we may not even have access to.[1] When it comes to deontological judgments specifically, there is evidence to suggest that they "tend to be driven by emotional responses and that deontological philosophy, rather than being grounded in moral reasoning is to a large extent an exercise in moral rationalization" (p. 360). A rationalization is a reason we come up with, to explain or justify something we were going to do anyway, for quite a different reason.

Donald Davidson explains that "a desire and a belief of the right sort may explain an action, but not necessarily. A man might have good reasons for killing his father, and he might do it, and yet the reasons not be his reasons for doing it."[2] In some cases, a sense of moral duty may not be the product of actual moral reasoning. Instead, people may make judgments about what to do based upon intuitions and institute moral codes after the fact to rationalize their behavior.[3] This is what Dexter does. The Code Dexter follows is instituted as a suitable justification for his killings. But these killings serve deeper emotional needs for Dexter, and his morals are instituted, largely by Harry, as post hoc rationalizations. He has a natural desire or intuition to kill, and Harry's Code is constructed to justify and guide Dexter.

Dexter Doing His Duty Dutifully?

I admit that there is some evidence to suggest that Dexter is a deontologist. The best evidence is his strict adherence, at least initially, to Harry's Code. Before he has a family, Dexter operates stringently under this Code. Every aspect of every kill, from victim selection to body disposal, is controlled by it. He chooses to kill other killers, particularly those who manage to escape the Miami legal system with minimal or no consequences. He follows a precise and exact procedure in each of his kills and makes sure to gather evidence to confirm his victims' guilt. He was taught all of this by Harry, and

---

[1] Joshua D. Greene, "The Secret Joke of Kant's Soul," in *Moral Psychology: Historical and Contemporary Readings*, edited by Thomas Nadelhoffer (Blackwell, 2010), p. 359.

[2] Donald Davidson, in *Readings in the Philosophy of Social Science*, edited by Michael Martin and Lee C. McIntyre (Massachusetts Institute of Technology, 1994), p. 81.

[3] J. Haidt, "The Emotional Dog and Its Rational Tail: A Social Intuitionist Approach to Moral Judgment," *Psychological Review* 108 (2001).

it would seem as if Harry's Code is the sense of duty that drives Dexter to choose his victims.

Dexter's relationship with Miguel Prado seems to be further evidence that Dexter kills other killers because he feels he has a moral duty to do so. Upon learning who Dexter truly is, Miguel wants Dexter to help kill his chief legal rival, Ellen Wolf. Dexter refuses to assist in Wolf's murder, arguing that she doesn't deserve to die—she's not a killer. Dexter doesn't provide other reasons for his refusal to assist Prado, just that killing Wolf wouldn't be the right thing to do. This indicates that Dexter does have a sense of moral duty.

Dexter's remorse for killing Miguel's brother, Oscar, also indicates that Dexter is operating according to deotological considerations. His remorse grows after he discovers that Oscar worked with disadvantaged youth and had never truly harmed anyone. Oscar is the first killing Dexter carries out outside of Harry's Code. The important thing is that Dexter frames his remorse in terms of violating the Code. He does not necessarily express regret for the consequences of his actions, but rather for going against the code he operates under.

Dexter's impressions of the Skinner, a chief antagonist in Season 3, also demonstrate that Dexter does have some understanding of right and wrong. He finds the Skinner to be a deplorable person, a sick individual. Dexter almost feels some degree of remorse for the Skinner's victims and feels that the Skinner is being unfair. These opinions demonstrate that Dexter has some understanding of a distinction between a right killing and a wrong killing, potentially believing that his killings are right because he is carrying out a moral duty.

The Mind Serves the Heart

Dexter definitely has a code that he follows. The code begins as Harry's invention, and eventually evolves into Dexter's own. The code he follows, however, has a primarily emotional foundation.

Dexter's instinct to kill exists prior to any moral principles he has. Harry's Code is instituted after Harry discovers that Dexter has a propensity toward killing. In his teenage years, Dexter kills animals and buries their bodies. He tells his father that he desires to do this often. Recognizing Dexter's natural desire to kill, Harry decides to train his son to channel that desire toward what Harry believes to be a greater good. If Dexter's moral compass is truly what guides his syringe, then this sense of morality had to have been present prior to Dexter's desire to kill, or the two had to have appeared and evolved simultaneously. Dexter did not decide the world was full of bad people and then decide he had a duty to kill these bad people, to ensure they got what they deserved. Rather, he already had a desire to kill, and his father directed him with a "may as well use this to kill bad people" type of instruction.

Dexter's brother, Rudy, is clear evidence that Dexter's deontological drive is instituted as a suitable justification for killings he would carry out anyway. Rudy shares Dexter's life experiences, the exception being that Rudy was not raised by Harry after their mother's murder. He witnesses the same horrific incident, sits in the same pool of blood, and develops the same dark desire to take human life. However, without Harry to guide him, Rudy develops a different justification to legitimate his killings. Rudy kills in an effort to find his brother, Dexter. This is the imperative that guides Rudy's killer instincts, the same instincts that are present within Dexter. The two brothers have the same desire to kill, but Dexter has learned to operate under a code through Harry's instruction. This demonstrates that there's an emotional foundation underlying Dexter's deontology.

Dexter finally sheds Harry's Code when he discovers the truth about who Harry was and who his own mother was. Dexter begins his own family and begins to feel emotions he has never felt before. At this point, Dexter's conflict with the voice of Harry reaches a pinnacle, and Dexter ends up rejecting Harry's ways and developing his own. He learns to accept his Dark Passenger and reconcile it with his new family. Although he finds it very difficult at first, Dexter does manage to placate both his Dark Passenger and the desire to have a family. The important thing, though, is that all these desires, after rejecting Harry's Code, are emotional desires that Dexter seeks to satisfy. His actions are not principally guided by a sense of moral duty, but by his own needs and desires that he wants to serve.

The people Dexter identifies with the most show that his emotions are what truly control him. Dexter's connection with Trinity, for example, shows that he is seeking some emotional satisfaction. Trinity clearly doesn't have a moral code guiding him. He seeks to recreate three traumatic deaths from his earlier life, and he travels the country fulfilling that emotional desire. Yet, Dexter associates with Trinity and admires him initially. He begins observing Trinity, seeking to learn how to improve his own craft. Dexter's interactions with Trinity are not motivated by considerations of a moral duty involved in his killings.

Dexter also relates to Miguel more on an emotional level than a moral one. After Miguel kills Ellen Wolf, Dexter scolds Miguel for the murder and the way in which it was carried out. Miguel initially responds by arguing that Dexter is too restrained, that society is in a terrible condition and it's up to them to fix it. Once Dexter begins to walk away, however, Miguel quickly switches to an emotional justification, telling Dexter that he feels the same darkness inside himself, and he cannot control it. At this point, Dexter becomes slightly more accepting of Miguel and decides not to terminate their tenuous friendship immediately. Dexter does not respond to Miguel's moral appeal, but rather the emotional one. With Miguel, Dexter sees an opportunity to develop an emotional connection with somebody else, helping Miguel learn and evolve. The development of this friendship occurs in concert with Dexter's rejection of Harry's Code. Dexter's principal motivation is emotional, and his interactions with Miguel demonstrate that.

Dexter's interactions with the Skinner at the end of season three are also evidence that Dexter's deontology has an emotional foundation. He demonstrates throughout the course of the show that he has a better understanding of people that are similar to himself. He does not understand Masuka's sexual dispositions, nor does he understand Rita's desires in the family. This is largely because, as he admits himself, he does not share any similar emotions, and he hasn't experienced such emotions in his life. Dexter understands the games that Rudy plays with him and also understands how Trinity operates. At the end of Season 3, Dexter is kidnapped by the Skinner. He escapes by stripping the Skinner of control by playing emotional games, telling the Skinner that Dexter has in fact already killed Freebo. Dexter identifies with the look in the Skinner's eyes, saying that it is the same look he gets right before a kill. All these individuals that Dexter understands, and more, do not have genuine moral compasses. Or at least, they are portrayed as characters who do not have a genuine sense of moral duty. Dexter is much the same. A sense of moral duty doesn't figure into Dexter's life equation to any great degree.

Dexter also shows his emotional self in dramatic ways when he deviates from the Code to help others. This is most evident when

Dexter interacts with children or adolescents. For example, he deviates from his usual killings in order to kill a pedophile who begins following Astor, Rita's son. Dexter shows a great degree of consideration for the way his actions will affect Rita's children. The first victim Dexter spares is a teenager named Jeremy Downs. Dexter spares him because he empathizes with the teenager and feels that letting him go may be the best course of action. He also protects Trinity's adolescent son from Trinity's abuse. Dexter places the adolescents' welfare above his own mission of observing Trinity and learning from him. Again, however, Dexter does not frame any of these actions as moral duties, but rather just as feelings. His arguments with Harry's ghost regarding these incidents consist of him justifying his emotional responses. At these times, Dexter is operating upon emotional considerations that lead him to stray from his deontological Code.

Dexter also goes through a great deal of trouble to protect his sister, Debra. Dexter takes the life of his own brother to protect her. He hides the truth about his father and mother in order to protect Debra from the emotional trauma she would experience. Dexter also lets Debra stay with him after her ordeal with Rudy until she gets back on her feet and feels safe enough to resume living on her own. Time and time again, Dexter strays from his standard *modus operandi*.

Harry's House

Harry uses his stepson's urges to carry out his own idea of justice. Harry is a police officer disillusioned with the legal system and with the society around him. He's constantly faced with the shortcomings of law enforcement, and has resigned himself to accepting that the system is flawed and does not truly work. Harry was also a cause of the death of Dexter's biological mother. Harry cannot help but continue to blame himself for her death even during Dexter's adolescence. He sees an opportunity to take a step toward rectifying this situation when Dexter reveals his desire to kill.

Harry uses his experience as an officer to train Dexter to kill, and more importantly, to avoid being captured. He teaches Dexter how to avoid leaving forensic evidence and to avoid being caught in the act. Dexter's first victim is a nurse that treats Harry very poorly in the hospital and has killed several patients during her time. Harry oversees and encourages the killing of the nurse. Harry firmly believes that he has created a positive force in the world, and for a short time, he finds himself satisfied with the prospect of his son being such a positive force in the world.

Eventually, though, when Harry comes face to face with his handiwork and sees Dexter carrying dismembered body parts, he cannot accept the reality of what his son has become, what he has turned his son into. This shock leads Harry to commit suicide.

Dexter Is a Needy Ned

Dexter's killings serve emotional needs that developed as a result of his childhood trauma. As a helpless infant, he watched his mother get killed by a chainsaw in front of him, and had to sit for days in the resulting pool of her blood. What are the emotional needs that Dexter's killing serve?

First, Dexter seeks to establish control over his environment. This deep-seated need for control is a direct result of the trauma Dexter experienced in his childhood. Dexter blames himself for his mother's death and seeks to establish control over this situation. The greatest evidence of this desire for control is the ritualistic way in which Dexter leads his life, and the corresponding breakdown of the rituals when Dexter is faced with things that challenge his worldview.

Every kill Dexter carries out, with few exceptions, follows a meticulous and precise methodology. In the first two seasons, the viewer never sees Dexter depart from this methodology. While there are times when he's uncertain and anxious, he's never careless. He likes to be in control, and rarely shows his hand. Dexter is always sure to lay out his plastic coverings and seclude his killing lair. He always cleans up after himself, and he is always sure to draw a blood sample from each of his victims. Dexter likes his apartment to be arranged in a particular fashion, and he becomes irritated when Debra disturbs it. He likes his office at work to be arranged to his preferences, down to the blood spatter pictures he has up on his wall.

It's no coincidence that Dexter exhibits these obsessive-compulsive tendencies and a high desire to control his environment. Studies demonstrate that childhood trauma does correlate with an increased development of obsessive-compulsive behaviors.[4]

---

[4] P. Toit, "Childhood Trauma in Obsessive-Compulsive Disorder, Trichotillomania, and Controls," *Depression and Anxiety* 15:2 (2002).

Dexter's trauma has likely led to his neurotic impulses to control the environment around him, and to control every aspect of his killings. Futhermore, Dexter does not conform to the customs and practices of those around him. Although he puts on a good face for society, he does not truly understand why others behave the way they do, as vividly illustrated when he pushes Rita's daughter Astor into the pool at a neighborhood get together. Those who experience a greater desire for control also tend to exhibit a diminished tendency to conform to the norm behaviors around them.[5] Dexter's trauma has led him to be an outcast in society, leaving him largely incapable of being normal, and leaving him without the desire to be like those around him, as well.

Dexter's desire for control, however, weakens when he faces new situations that challenge the way he lives. When Dexter starts his own family and begins feeling attachment that he has never experienced before, he rejects Harry's Code. His desire for control diminishes slightly, and he becomes vulnerable with some of the people in his life such as Lila, Rita, and Miguel. This is further evidence that Dexter's childhood trauma has developed an emotional desire for control inside him. Research demonstrates that those who have a high desire for control tend to diminish that desire when they are faced with something that challenges their worldview.[6] Dexter's worldview, Harry's Code, is challenged by the new emotions and desires Dexter experiences after becoming part of a family, and his desire for control diminishes accordingly.

Recall that the first time Dexter remembers the details of his mother's death is when he decides to see a therapist. The doctor makes Dexter examine his emotional core, the reason behind his actions, and Dexter envisions the shipping container and the pool of blood from his infancy, the situation in which he was stripped of all control and was completely helpless. Dexter seeks to recreate scenarios in which he can become the killer. He becomes the very thing which made him feel so helpless as infant. This is the core strategy by which Dexter struggles to gain control over his childhood trauma. No wonder he identifies so much with Trinity, a

---

[5] J. Burger, "Desire for Control and Conformity to a Perceived Norm," *Journal of Personality and Social Psychology* 53:2 (2002).

[6] J. Burger and S. Solomon, "The Control of Death and the Death of Control: The Effects of Mortality Salience, Neuroticism, and Worldview Threat on the Desire for Control," *Journal of Research in Personality* 37 (2003).

man who seeks to recreate deaths from his past. All this evidence clearly shows that Dexter has a deep-seated emotional core that guides his actions. His killings, and the way his lives his life, do not follow mainly from logical or moral justifications. They follow from emotions that Dexter himself does not understand.

The second emotional need Dexter serves through his killings is the desire to belong. While he initially chooses to distance himself emotionally from society, he eventually begins integrating himself into a family and neighborhood, sacrificing some of his prized control. Dexter begins to appreciate belonging and being accepted, especially in the lives of Rita's children. He seeks to become a meaningful part of the lives of others. The only way he knows to do this, however, is through killing. He kills to protect Rita's children. He uses killing to connect on a deeper level with Miguel Prado. He kills to protect Debra. Dexter even admits that he needs these people in his life, something that he initially denies. He feels more secure with others in his life.

Showing these emotions, Dexter finally shows a human part of himself. Ernest Becker, a famous cultural anthropologist, explained the unique way in which humans develop a security blanket through interactions with people around them. He argued that most creatures perform effective actions, meaning that they do things that have some purpose. They don't do things just for the sake of doing them. Humans, however, are different. They need to interact with other people to fully realize the purpose of their actions. This begins with an initial attachment to one's parents, and later develops into a desire to become a valuable and meaningful part of others' lives.[7] This is Dexter's path—initially being attached to Harry, and then letting go as he finds value with others in his life.

De-Deontologizing Dexter

Dexter's killings, and particularly his victim selections, are not primarily the result of logical moral reasoning. Dexter does not deeply consider any moral duty he may have toward other people, nor does he incorporate many considerations of justice into his plans. Instead, Dexter's killings serve deep emotional needs resulting from the trauma of witnessing his mother's death. He has developed a desire to control the feeling of helplessness in his infancy.

---

[7] Ernest Becker, *The Birth and Death of Meaning* (Free Press, 1971).

He therefore recreates scenarios where he becomes the meticulous calculating killer.

Dexter's traumatic childhood has affected him emotionally, and it is that emotional development which guides his blade as an adult. Dexter also shows a human desire to belong as he develops and grows. This desire, though, is still strictly emotional and does not follow from any logical thought process. In fact, logically speaking, it is fairly dangerous for Dexter to attempt to placate this desire. Nevertheless, emotional impulses—not genuine moral reasoning—continue to guide his actions.

BODY PART IV

Bad Blood and Bad Behavior

16
The Discipline of Dexter's Punishment

ERIC HOLMES

Is there anything more enjoyable than seeing jerks get what they have coming? The guy who passes you on the shoulder of the freeway and then gets pulled over down the road. The co-worker who steals your idea and pitches it to the boss, only to have the boss crush her and the idea. The bully who picked on you all through school getting whipped by the new kid in front of the entire class.

This is what makes *Dexter* so enjoyable. Sure, the cat and mouse between Dexter and each season's Big Bad is delightful, but the ultimate pleasure comes from seeing the wicked punished as only Dexter can do it. The films *Let The Right One In* and *Inglourious Basterds* feature applause-worthy retribution scenes in which the loathsome are punished, and *Dexter* gives its audience the same pleasure. Can you think of anything more satisfying than when Dexter pops out of the back seat of the Trinity Killer's Mustang and gives him a syringe full of gotcha? How about when the Ice Truck Killer breaks into Dexter's apartment to kill Deb, only to find a bed stuffed full of pillows and Dexter playing possum? What about when Lila discovers a postcard from Miami on her end table and realizes that Paris isn't outside of Dexter's reach?

We like poetic justice. In fact, we love it, and *Dexter*, while featuring tight scripting, great acting, and witty dialogue, is made by the payoff that comes from seeing the wicked punished. Sure, nearly all of Dexter's victims are wicked, but single-episode prey like Zoey Kruger or Roger Hicks lacks the punch that comes from finally seeing Miguel Prado get what he has coming. But it isn't just knowing that the bad guy gets it in the end; it's seeing the bad guy realize that he's getting what he deserves that truly floats our boat.

The joy that you and I feel from Dexter's art isn't that he kills, but that he punishes.

The Wimpiness of Modern Punishment

In the not too distant past, punishment for crimes such as murder was swift, vicious, public, and common. Philosophers as broad in ideas as Thomas Hobbes (whose opinion of humanity can only be described as less than zero) and John Locke (the primary inspiration for the American system of governance) both agreed that punishment, whether coming from the ruling power or from your peers, had to be unrelenting in order to truly be effective. Locke takes it as far as to claim that in the event that no government exists, any man has the right to kill a murderer both to deter others from committing murder and to prevent the murderer from doing so ever again.

When executions were held publicly, the citizenry was able to see the villains of its community taken to task for their crimes. But this has changed. In his landmark work *Discipline and Punish*, French historian and philosopher Michel Foucault writes about earlier methods of punishment and the transition to the modern style that focuses more on incarceration and less on physical punishment. Starting in the eighteenth century, according to Foucault, "the body as the major target of penal repression disappeared."[1] If so, Dexter's a throwback to that time when criminal justice was far simpler and brutal in its execution—and more satisfying for the public.

Of the consequences that come from this change from physical punishment (what Foucault calls torture) to the modern method of largely incarcerating criminals, the most important is that punishment moved from concrete to abstract in its delivery. Murderers, rapists, heretics, and other weirdoes of centuries past knew what was coming: the sweet release of death from being broken on the rack, hanging, beheading, disembowelment, quartering, or some combination thereof. How did they know what was coming? Because executions were held in public before massive crowds that delighted in the violence, and everyone had seen at least one execution. If you were caught being a bad boy or girl, the punishment was absolute and final.

---

[1] Michel Foucault, *Discipline and Punish* (Vintage, 1995), p. 8.

Now, however, murderers sit in relative comfort on death row for years or even decades due to the appeal process and, if infamous enough, get to enjoy the attention that comes from the books, television programs, and online devotionals that make up the serial murderer industry. And when they are finally executed for their crimes (that's if execution is even part of the punishment), they will likely be given a mixture of narcotics that painlessly puts them to sleep before a small audience. As a result, contemporary murderers see little if any reason to demonstrate restraint of their homicidal desires, so why not take a life to get what you want? The best-case scenario is that you are never caught, while the worst case is a state subsidized three hots and a cot. Never can they imagine that there's someone like Dexter who is waiting to go medieval on their asses.

The focus of punishment has moved away from the crime and toward how effectively the punishment prevents the criminal from acting out again. In the past, murderers were murderers, rapists were rapists, and no amount of soul searching or rehabilitation would change that. Dexter doesn't believe in the contemporary view that penalties like imprisonment reduce crime; he was born in blood, and it's a part of him more than anything else in his life is, be it Rita, Deb, Harry, Astor, Cody, or even little Harrison. As a killer, Dexter knows that he and others like him are beyond redemption and that only true punishment of the corporal kind is the cure. Someone who is willing to murder an innocent person is a problem, and Dexter knows just how to solve it. And just like any good project, punishment needs a good set of instructions.

Following Harry's Code

Dexter has a very specific guideline that he follows when it comes to his craft. We know this as Harry's Code. Its rules are, first, never get caught. Second, only kill those who deserve it. Third, always be sure that the victim is guilty.

Dexter's life would be much easier without Harry's Code, as there have been many people (and animals) that have caused him inconvenience. They range from the personal (Rita's obnoxious neighbor and her even more obnoxious dog) to the professional (James Doakes and Joey Quinn, both Miami police detectives who independently come to the conclusion that Dexter has something to hide). However, Dexter is incapable of breaking Harry's Code merely to make his life easier. When Doakes discovers that Dexter is the Bay Harbor Butcher, Dexter attacks him and locks him in a ramshackle cage in a swamp shack, unsure of what action to take next. By Harry's Code, Dexter can't kill Doakes despite the fact that that doing so would eliminate the one person who can tie him to the Bay Harbor Butcher murders. As we know, Dexter leaves Doakes trapped until Lila murders him in a massive explosion at the shack.

Dexter's belief in Harry's Code is so deeply imbedded in him that even the fact that Lila murdered Doakes in an attempt to protect Dexter's secret is irrelevant. Dexter tracks Lila across the globe in order to exact punishment upon her for the murder of Doakes, who is eventually blamed for the murders that Dexter has committed.

As a killer who follows Harry's Code, Dexter has no tolerance for the proclamation from his victims that they can't help themselves, that the crimes are part of some sort of addiction. In *Dexter*'s pilot episode, we see Dexter confront child murderer Mike Donovan about his crimes. Donovan replies that he can't help himself, to which Dexter notes that, "I can't help myself either." but that when it comes to killing children, "I have standards" ("Dexter," Season 1). This standard also extends to the innocent.

You Can't Always Kill Whom You Want

In Season 1, The Ice Truck Killer leaves limbs of a man named Tony Tucci all across Miami, along with a Polaroid photo of the crime scene where the limbs are found. Dexter quickly notices that each photograph has something to do with his own childhood with Harry. After a tryst with Rita on Halloween night, Dexter realizes that the Ice Truck Killer has been nosing through his photo albums, and that the key to finding whatever remains of Tony Tucci is in his apartment. Dexter finds a photograph of himself and Harry in front of the long since abandoned Angel of Mercy hospital, and notices that a smiley face has been drawn on the back of the photo.

Arriving at Angel of Mercy, Dexter finds Tucci blindfolded and strapped to a surgical table with a whole palette of surgical tools just off to the side. He is given every incentive that he needs to take Tucci's life: a helpless victim, a table full of surgical tools, and a seeming absence of witnesses. As Dexter puts it, Tucci was "gift wrapped, begging for death, tools at the ready. He was left here so I would kill him." Of course, Dexter passes on the opportunity, and gives Deb an anonymous tip about Tucci's location. "I can't kill this man," he says. "Harry wouldn't want it, and neither would I . . . I'm not the monster he [the Ice Truck Killer] wants me to be, so I am neither man nor beast. I am something new entirely with my own set of rules. I'm Dexter" ("Let's Give The Boy A Hand," Season 1).

Dexter's claim that he's neither man nor beast suggests again that his primary function isn't to kill, but to punish. After all, a genuine killer with no regard for life would've delighted in killing Tucci. But the victim didn't deserve the torture that Dexter provides, so the kill does not take place. Dexter, as a killer, is a force that is unemotional and impartial, a force of punishment, not cruelty. Dexter tortures his victims not because it pleasures him, but because they deserve it.

One Minute, You're on Top of the World, the Next, Dexter's Table

Foucault writes that the main function of torture is to produce pain and that, unlike the days of old, the modern system of punishment seeks not to inflict pain but to deprive the guilty of liberty through imprisonment. Dexter doesn't believe in such nonsense, as he purposefully waits until his victims are conscious before carrying out his duty. And while cutting the cheek of his victims is to draw blood for Dexter's collection of slides, it also gives the victim a coming attraction of the main event. Finally, the *coup de grâce* inflicts pain, be it a stab to the midsection, being beaten to death with a hammer, or having any number of power tools used upon your skull. However, the slicing of the face and the actual murder are far from the only methods that Dexter uses to cause his victims pain.

Dexter sets up each crime scene so that the victim must encounter his or her own crimes head on. This is done by exposing the perpetrator either to images (photos or videos) of his or her victims or in certain extreme cases, such as child murderer Mike Donovan, to the corpses of the victims. For those of Dexter's victims who feel shame for their crimes, this is an especially powerful reminder of their transgressions. And while many of Dexter's victims have shown no remorse for their crimes (and the crocodile tears shown by others are obviously disingenuous), Dexter's requirement that his victim see the faces of their own victims is a form of torture. The experience of seeing the faces of people that have been raped or murdered informs Dexter's victims that the party is over, and that the check is due.

Dexter's choice to remind his victims of their crimes prior to their execution is deliberate. He takes great efforts to compile the photos and videos that he presents to his victims. The use of these visuals does nothing to increase Dexter's efficiency as a killer, but it does a great deal to increase his efficiency as an agent of punishment. It tortures his victims as much as possible.

In fact, every aspect of Dexter's kill ritual is designed to cause the greatest amount of torture possible. Dexter's choice to strip his victims nude serves several functions: Aside from the logistical purposes of unclothing his victims for the inevitable dismemberment that is part of Dexter's ritual and the fact that it just makes good sense to avoid blood soaked clothing at all times, the nudity that his victims feel upon awakening in the kill room makes them feel as vulnerable as possible, making the torture all the more unbearable. Next, the harsh glow of the light overhead shines brightly in the faces of his victims, throwing them off balance and adding to their discomfort, but that isn't the only kind of disorientation that Dexter causes.

Dexter's favorite method of capture is a syringe full of tranquilizer to the throat. This gives him time to unclothe and incapacitate his victims. Logistically, this is the best method for him to use, as it all but eliminates his victims' ability to fight back or to scream for help. However, this is not the primary purpose of the old M99-to-the-jugular trick. The disorientation that comes from eating a cheeseburger and then suddenly waking up nude tied to a table is as awful of an imbalance as you can face—but, for Dexter's purposes, it's a way to start off the ritual on the right torture-based foot. Dexter is no stranger to letting the punishment fit the crime, whether that be murdering drunk driving killer Matt Chambers in an old liquor store or beating Trinity Killer Arthur Mitchell to death with the claw hammer that Mitchell himself used to commit a murder. As the agent of punishment, Dexter knows exactly what form of torture will inflict the most pain upon his victims, and nothing makes that more clear than the case of Miguel Prado.

In Season 3, Dexter takes District Attorney Miguel Prado under his wing and tutors him on the art of the kill. However, Prado soon finds himself with ideas of grandeur regarding his own invulnerability, and takes it upon himself to kill his nemesis, the prominent Miami defense attorney Ellen Wolf. Much to Dexter's dismay, he realizes that he has created a far greater menace in Prado than any other menace that Prado as a punisher would eliminate. Prado has stepped away from killing the guilty in favor of killing those who merely stand in his way. Naturally, Dexter has to kill him.

Dexter entraps Miguel in the usual way, but he murders him in another: the way of the Skinner, who strangles his victims with wire. This, however, isn't the true moment of torture in this kill. The true torture comes when Dexter reveals that he's the murderer of Miguel's brother Oscar. In fact, this was an entirely accidental killing that Dexter perpetrated in self-defense as Oscar interrupted his pursuit of the murderer Fred "Freebo" Bowman. But Dexter knows that this news will send Prado into a whirlwind of emotions ranging from rage to sorrow. Not only is Prado forced to relive his brother's murder, he realizes that the man that he has been searching for, the man whom he has wanted to kill more than anyone, is Dexter himself—his new friend and closest confidant. Dexter's choice to tell Prado that he killed Oscar is the most gruesome torture that he could've inflicted. And Dexter did it without blinking.

Everything that Dexter does in his ritual, from the reminders made of his victims' crimes and his victims' forced nudity to the harsh lighting and even the taking of his beloved slide of blood (not to mention the murder itself) is done with the intent to torture his victims. After all, Dexter lives his life around the efficiency of his craft, and if he were focused solely upon the kill, he wouldn't take the effort. He would simply drug his victims and kill them while they were unconscious. If Dexter's sole function were to merely quench his homicidal thirst, then none of his ritual would exist aside from the initial attack, the murder, and the eventual dismemberment. Dexter's not like that. He believes in the virtue of actual punishment, where the victim knows exactly why he or she is being punished, and that is what makes us love him as much as we do. He's the physical embodiment of our desire to see and believe that there really is justice in the world.

Dexter Is the Sovereign We've Been Waiting For

Both Hobbes and Foucault identify the force that punishes as the Sovereign. The Sovereign exists because it has to: people without rules become animals that war and kill and rape. The Sovereign isn't emotional, isn't vengeful, and isn't remorseful. It punishes wrongdoing, and Dexter lives his life along those very lines.

We know that everything in Dexter's life, from his graduating at the top of his class in medical school to his advanced training in martial arts to his complete lack of credit cards or rental of adult movies is all in place for a single purpose: to ensure that he's as efficient a punisher as possible. His medical training ensures that he knows human anatomy so that his murders are clean and error-free. His advanced martial arts training allows him to effectively attack and subdue his victims without their immediate knowledge as to what's happening. Finally, his lack of credit cards and rental of porno movies allows him to remain free of the electronic leash around each of our necks in this modern, plugged-in, data-mining society. After all, how long can Dexter kill without suspicion once Visa takes notice of all of the surgical tools and black plastic trash bags that he purchases?

Dexter is bound by Harry's Code that dictates that he never get caught. Dexter's method of dispatching his victims (a clean room draped in plastic, surgical implements, and the trademark stab wound to the midsection) are all in use as they are the most efficient and the safest in regards to Dexter's possibility of getting caught. They don't indicate that Dexter seeks to avoid inflicting gruesome, physical punishment. They just reflect his first objective: to never, ever get caught so that he may continue to dispense punishment for as long as possible.

In fact, several of Dexter's greatest foes, such as the Ice Truck Killer and Miguel Prado, were killed with methods inconsistent with Dexter's usual style. But this was only to frame the deaths as something other than what they were. Dexter made the murder of the Ice Truck Killer look like a suicide, while he designed the murder of Miguel Prado by strangulation to look like the work of the Skinner. In both cases, this sleight of hand serves a greater purpose: to throw all possible scents away from Dexter. After all, the disappearance of The Ice Truck Killer wouldn't have closed the case; in fact, it would have led to a nationwide (if not global) manhunt, which would only lead to greater scrutiny of the Ice Truck Killer case—scrutiny that might possibly reveal that he and Dexter are brothers. The only way to effectively end the case would be the appearance of a suicide. Any obvious murder of the Ice Truck Killer would only add to the attention that Dexter doesn't want.

As for Miguel Prado, Dexter had to eliminate him due to his newly discovered love of homicide. But the murder had to appear as something other than the standard disappearance that Dexter provides his victims. Prado's power in the Miami area wouldn't allow for him to simply vanish and be forgotten. Instead, he's strangled to death ala The Skinner, which provides a tidy, unquestionable ending to Miguel Prado's life without the scrutiny that his disappearance would cause.

But, you may ask, why does Dexter choose to keep his craft a secret? After all, wouldn't some potential killers hold off if they knew that they would be strung up (or sawed up, to be accurate) for committing their crimes? Wouldn't public knowledge of Dexter's talents (but not necessarily his identity) work in favor of deterring other murders?

It might. But Dexter lives in a modern society that, according to Foucault, no longer accepts public punishments or executions. Except for handful of victims or relatives who are permitted to witness modern executions, for example, punishment is now "a spectacle that must actually be forbidden" (p. 15). Dexter's happy to oblige. He punishes privately, away from the gaze of a judging society. This isn't due to any sort of shame about what he does. Dexter makes no effort to hide his identity from his victims. He allows his victims to see his face upon waking and engages them in conversation prior to the kill (in many cases, the victim is shocked to discover that Dexter is who he is and not one of the many characters that he has played in order to get closer to his prey). Dexter only takes such effort to cover his tracks because failing to do so would violate the first rule of Harry's Code, and would make him an ineffective agent of punishment. How much punishment could Dexter deliver behind bars? Not much.

The Final Thrust to the Abdomen

With his medical training, experience as a crime scene investigator, and relentless patience, Dexter has every opportunity to bring his victims to justice in the contemporary sense. They would be incarcerated and perhaps even executed by the state for their crimes, but that isn't good enough for Dexter. A life spent on death row can't inflict the type of pain that Dexter's victims have inflicted on others, and it's his duty to make sure that the wicked are punished appropriately. Harry taught him first-hand that the modern system of punishment doesn't give society's worst what they truly deserve, which is one reason why our adoration for Dexter and his Dark Passenger runs as deep as it does. We need to know that evil will be punished, and that's exactly what Dexter provides: a one-way ticket on the *Slice of Life.*

17
Dexter the Busy Bee

DAVID RAMSAY STEELE

Be brutal. Tell the truth. Would you rather live in Miami with Dexter than without him?

I think we'd all have to agree. Miami with Dexter would be a safer and healthier place than Miami without Dexter. To know that someone is unobtrusively and efficiently disposing of really, really bad guys—especially really, really bad guys whom the official law enforcers can't or won't touch—can only be reassuring. The fact that this highly conscientious executioner is somewhat more painstaking than the police in refraining from hurting us good guys is an additional comfort.

It's part of Dexter's M.O. that we wouldn't know this was going on. Dexter's discreet way of working loses the tremendous social advantage of deterrence: if everyone knew what Dexter was doing, that would cause some of the bad guys to become less bad, or at least to behave less badly. Murders would be prevented by discouraging the murderers, not just by eliminating them before they could murder again. Once you're on Dexter's table, you don't get to call your lawyer, so deterrence wouldn't be pissed away by the uncertainty of retribution. Unfortunately, that very salutary deterrence has to be given up, for the sake of Dexter's secrecy (the first rule of Dexter's Code: Don't Get Caught).

Killing Killers, Saving Lives

Despite the absence of deterrence, the elimination of the really, really bad guys can only be judged really, really good. Just think about it. If each of the bad guys dismembered by Dexter would have killed one more person, then Dexter's actions would save just as many lives as he deleted. And if each of the bad guys would have killed two more persons, then each of Dexter's disposal operations would save one net life.

Given the quality of Dexter's targets, that we've been able to see, that would be a conservative estimate. Let's suppose that the average Dexter target, but for Dexter's timely intervention, would have gone on to kill six more people, which seems about right. Say Dexter kills twenty of these bad guys a year, which also appears to be in line with what we've been shown. That means Dexter saves one hundred net lives a year! Can any Miami fireman or heart surgeon say as much?

And that's counting the lives Dexter terminates as equal with the lives saved. But we all know perfectly well that the lives of Dexter's targets are not worth the same as the lives of the people Dexter rescues from death. The targets deserve to die, whereas the targets' prospective victims deserve to live. Can you deny that Dexter's a public benefactor? If so, just what kind of a twisted monster are you?

Back in the 1930s when Ronald 'Dutch' Reagan was a teenager in Dixon, Illinois, and everyone still pronounced his name 'Reegan', he worked as a lifeguard on the Rock River and was credited with saving seventy-seven lives in seven years—eleven lives per year. That's a suspiciously high figure, and it's been suggested that local damsels contrived to put themselves in a position to be saved by this dishy hunk, which may have somewhat inflated Dutch's life-saving, umm, score. But making all due allowances, it was highly creditable. Obviously, that boy would go far. But it couldn't begin to approach the magnitude of the public benefit conferred by Dexter Morgan. Maybe this boy will go farther.

Without deceiving himself about his motives, Dexter clearly understands his contribution to human welfare. After Special Agent Lundy has commented that there's but one justification for killing, "to save an innocent life," Dexter observes (not to Lundy, of course, but to us):

> How many bodies would there have been if I had not got to those killers? I didn't want to save lives, but save lives I did. Motivation aside, I think Harry and Lundy would agree on this one. ("An Inconvenient Lie," Season 2)

Wait, wait. Is Dexter an unmitigated social benefit? He doesn't respect habeus corpus or the Miranda rule. We need habeus corpus, the Miranda rule, trial by jury, and a slew of other checks on the powers of the official enforcers because we need to be protected against the official enforcers becoming bad guys themselves. We need the official enforcers to stop bad guys attacking us, and we need the Bill of Rights to stop the official enforcers attacking us. (That's the theory. Some of us anarchists are not completely sold on the theory, but it does have its points. And, like it or not, it is the theory.)

But don't we need protection against Dexter? No, no, no! Dexter is driven by an irresistible force, a passion as remorseless and unreasoning as a tornado, to kill the guilty and save (or at least, avoid killing) the innocent. Oh sure, Dexter makes mistakes. Who doesn't? But he tries as hard as he can, and a lot harder than any government employee on a pension plan ever would, not to screw up. As Dexter tells Doakes:

> My Code requires a higher standard of proof than your city's laws, at zero cost to the taxpayer. If you ask me, I'm a bargain. ("There's Something about Harry," Season 2)

But wouldn't we need protection against a real-life Dexter? Yes, of course. But Dexter isn't real-life, silly. He's all made up. That's why he's so marvelous. A real-life Dexter might become a bad guy. A real-life Dexter might start slicing and dicing folks according to their race, their religion, their sexual preferences, their astrological signs, or their musical tastes. (Musical tastes? Hey, wait a minute . . .) A real-life Dexter might go after children or cats, or, like the Unabomber, after exceptionally talented and productive people.

Even more ominously and more probably, a real-life Dexter might become a Miguel Prado, classifying as guilty people like defense attorneys who sometimes help to get the guilty off. But we and Dexter understand what the late Miguel didn't: that occasionally getting the guilty off is the price we pay for not convicting the innocent. And we all know what happened to Miguel. Dexter got to him and administered the *coup de grâce*. "This isn't over," says Miguel. "It is for you," says Dexter, swiftly garroting him. Did I mention that our Dex is witty?

So, to those people who're puzzled or distressed by the fact that we want Dexter to keep getting away with it: There's no contradiction between passionately wanting a fictional character not to get caught and quite decidedly wanting his real-life counterparts to get caught.

If you don't want Edmond Dantes, the Count of Monte Cristo, to impose the most humiliating misery and death upon those douchebags who conspired to have him falsely imprisoned, then don't bother to check your pulse. I can tell you there's nothing there. At the same time, and without contradiction, we don't want a legal system that would permit rich men with fancy titles to get away with some of the really cool things the fictional Count does. A work of art is not a manual of ethics or self-help. If you find this too tricky to wrap your head around, maybe it'll be safer for all of us if you stay away from fiction. Oh, and stay away from the Bible and the Quran too.

The Thrill of the Kill

But one thing might still worry us about Dexter Morgan. And this is the element that makes Dexter such an astounding innovation in the history of fiction and drama. Dexter's fundamental motivation, so we're repeatedly told, is arbitrary, amoral, inhuman, inherently malign, fearsome, and revolting. It's an addictive imperative. Dexter has an urge to ritualistically kill warm-blooded creatures. As a child, he begins with non-human animals, but he soon graduates to those opposable-thumbed naked apes who flow so expendably through the streets of Miami.

This urge, this drive, this hunger owes nothing to a sense of justice or any other kind of disinterested intention. Dexter does not kill to fulfill a mission. He kills because of his addiction to the thrill of killing. Usually it has to be killing by sharp steel implements. Shooting, poisoning, strangling, rigged auto accidents, we feel, just don't (pardon me!) cut it. Miguel Prado is dispatched by garroting— but that's only because it has to look as if the Skinner (a serial killer without a Code) has done it.

But then there's something else: Harry's Code, which becomes Dexter's Code. The Code controls and restricts Dexter's howling appetite for blood. Dexter's Code doesn't modify the primal urge to butcher people for the sheer joyous gratification of butchering them. It doesn't change that motivation to one of justice or benevolence or concern for public safety. Fundamentally and intrinsically, Dexter doesn't give a rap about these notions, one way or the other, though as an intelligent observer keeping tabs on that wondrous beast, *Homo sapiens non-serial-killerensis*, they do mildly interest him as worthy of his urbane and amused comments.

What the Code does is to impose a rigid pattern, like a superstition or an obsessive compulsion, on top of the naked urge. The Code takes a terrifying, mindless, brutal force and channels it into a solid benefit for humankind.

The exact relation between Dexter's hunger to kill and the Code bequeathed by Harry has yet to be (if you'll excuse the expression) fully fleshed out. Maria Montessori was an educational theorist who believed that there's a point in time when a child is just ready to learn some particular type of thing. Maybe Harry Morgan, Dexter's step-father, caught Dexter at just the right Montessori moment where the Code would 'take' with Dexter. Maybe Dexter would go to pieces without the Code. As Dexter says, "I know I'm a monster."

His wistful, secret, impossible dream is to be normal, fully cured, with normal headaches and normal heartaches, just like all those millions of non-serial-killers out there. Although this doesn't bother him enough to put him off his knife stroke, it does seem possible that complying with the Code makes it easier for Dexter to live with himself. And so the two parts of Dexter's make-up, the basic instinct to chop up humans and the Code, may support and sustain each other. But maybe not; we don't really know.

In the novels, Dexter is a sadist who has fun torturing his subjects before he recycles them. In the TV show, Dexter only tortures them mentally, for a minute or two, by reminding them of their horrendous crimes. The physical process is not protracted. Though both Dexters have their engaging side, the TV Dexter is more thoroughly likeable, more charming, and more of a wag than the Dexter of the books. We feel that any *gratuitous* inflicting of pain would be entirely foreign to the TV Dexter.

Not that he's a softy. He's capable of acting with impressive ruthlessness, as when he frames Rita's husband for breach of parole to get him sent back to jail. Come to think of it though, this may be more a matter of opportunity than motivation: as a highly trained ambusher, abductor, and eraser of forensic clues, at the top of his game, Dexter can easily get away with exploits that just wouldn't be practicable for those of us who maintain our upper-body strength mainly by pushing the buttons on the remote.

But Dexter lacks even normal spitefulness, just as, we're repeatedly informed, he lacks much of normal sentimentality and human warmth (though he sincerely if half-heartedly regrets his lack of these). This can lead him to send the wrong signals, as when he responds to Quinn's overtures with profound indifference, after Quinn knows that Dexter has seen him steal money from a crime scene. Quinn just doesn't get it: Dexter simply doesn't care the teeniest bit about Quinn, except that Quinn should leave him alone. (Oh dear, Quinn, me boyo, do I see Hefty bags and duct tape in your future? Just try not to murder anyone, there's a good police officer, or you'll become a legitimate target under the provisions of Dexter's Code.) The vengeful payback motive, among many conventional emotional responses, seems pointless and barely intelligible to Dexter.

The uniqueness of Dexter as a character in drama is that he totally does the right thing for totally the wrong reason. (Shut up, all you ADHD cases. We've established it's the right thing, okay? Just get used to it.) He's a good guy, a hero, whose primal driving force is dangerous, ugly, monstrous, terrifying—everything that we've learned to call *evil*. So maybe (as Milton Friedman said of Henry Ford) he's a bad man who does a lot of good. But if he does a lot of good, can he really be so bad?

Bad Motives, Good Actions

Dexter's unique. He's a sympathetic character whose fundamental motivation is totally creepy, while the consequences of his actions are predominantly benign and protective.

For thousands of years, the ruling assumption has been that if you want to encourage good actions, you'd better encourage good motives. At first blush, this makes sense. If people feel it's wrong to kill other people, for instance, they're less likely to kill other people. But there's always the possibility of motivation and behavior working in opposite directions. People may do the right thing for wrong reasons, or they may do something appalling for decent and good-hearted reasons.

Christianity gave a new importance to motives as opposed to actions. Jesus angrily denounces the Pharisees, the inventors of what we now call orthodox Judaism, those Jews who were especially concerned to follow every detail of the Jewish law, but no more than that. Jesus came out with such remarks as:

You've heard that it was said, 'Don't commit adultery'. But I tell you that anyone who looks at a woman with lust has already committed adultery with her in his heart. (Matthew 5:27–28)

(What the actual? God's going to bill you for the goodies before you've even opened the wrapper? Might as well go the whole hog, then.)

So Christianity makes you responsible for your thoughts, even if unacted upon. The real test of a person's morality is not their actions nor the results of their actions but what goes on, unseen by their fellow-humans, inside their skulls. By this standard, hypocrisy (outwardly being good while inwardly having bad thoughts) becomes one of the worst of sins.

A moral dilemma is no longer simply 'What ought I to do?' but more importantly, 'Am I thinking and feeling the right way? Are my intentions pure?' This opens up a vast new scope for self-examination, guilt, self-flagellation, and self-doubt, especially as thinking is, by its very nature, frolicsome and uncontrollable.

Enter the Man-Devil

In early eighteenth-century England, Dr. Bernard Mandeville was denounced as the most evil person alive. His enemies—almost everyone—branded him "the Man-Devil" (Get it?). Nearly all the most eminent thinkers of his day wrote ferocious denunciations of the Man-Devil. Just as anyone who wants to be recognized today as a stand-up guy has to denounce racism, Islamicism, or sexual abuse of children, so anyone who looked for minimum cred in the eighteenth century had to express their horror and detestation for the Man-Devil.

His bad reputation was only to be matched by Jack the Ripper, nearly two centuries later. Dr. Mandeville was Public Enemy Number One. No, he wasn't a ritual serial murderer. He was something far more dangerous than that!

The Man-Devil's great crime was to say something that had never been said before. He proclaimed that wicked behavior by individuals is good for society as a whole, or as he put it, private vices are public virtues. And he made it sound very convincing.

Far less is now known about the life of the mysterious Man-Devil than about anyone else of comparable importance at the time. But we do know that he made his living as a doctor specializing in nervous diseases. He was married and had children. He was at home in four languages and had read a lot in each of them. He died of the flu in 1733. As far as we know, aside from what he wrote, he led a blameless life.

This was an age of new media and information explosion. The thousands of London coffee houses were like today's Facebook. The thousands of London bookstores, with a printing press in the back, and with a coffee house attached, were like today's blogosphere. Printers were the IT nerds. The presses turned out a flood of new leaflets, pamphlets, and magazines, soaked up by the denizens of the coffee houses, who debated them endlessly. Mass literacy had arrived, and with a sure instinct the masses turned to the vile and disgusting. The world had seen nothing like it before. Could the human mind possibly withstand the weighty burden of information overload?

Many of the new printed works were irreverent, mildly but persistently erotic, and satirical. Their goal was entertainment, but their authors understood, with the Dexter scriptwriters, that to truly entertain people you have to make them think.

The coffee houses charged one penny admission. "Runners" went round the coffee houses, from table to table, reciting the latest news reports. There was a turmoil of new ideas. No one could predict where it was all going. One coffee house, Jonathan's, started posting stock prices on the walls, and this coffee house eventually became the London Stock Exchange. People of different walks of life and social standing mingled and debated in the coffee houses (which, however, did maintain minimal standards: women were excluded, except for professional ladies who looked after customers in some of those little rooms in the back). A powdered wig and a penny a day—and you were online!

The new media were effectively unregulated and we all know what that means: something terrible's bound to happen. As the anarchist Dave Barry says, without government people will start having sex with dogs. Well, that didn't happen in eighteenth-century London, but something almost as appalling did occur: the coming of the Man-Devil.

A Poem that Will Live in Infamy

Dr. Mandeville came over from Holland at the age of twenty-nine, and fell in love with London. Within a few years, no one who met him would believe he wasn't a native Englishman. He wrote a number of satirical publications before he penned *The Grumbling Hive* in 1705. This is not a poem of polished elegance like those of Alexander Pope (who like nearly everyone else stole some of Dr. Mandeville's ideas while personally attacking the Man-Devil) but conversational and street-wise, in line with coffee-house chatter.

The Grumbling Hive tells of a fabulous beehive in which all the bees do, in miniature, exactly what eighteenth-century English people do. The bees are immoral though hypocritical: they practice all kinds of vice, while paying lip service to virtue. The hive flourishes, and becomes a beacon of prosperity, much like England.

Every part was filled with Vice
But the whole Mass a Paradise.

Then, overnight, the bees all become virtuous; they begin to practice what they preach. The economy of the hive collapses, and the hive is depopulated. A tiny remnant of the original population of bees leaves the hive and flies off into a dead tree-trunk. Since the bees remain completely virtuous, there is no indication that they regret the catastrophic consequences of their reformed behavior.

The Grumbling Hive did not immediately make Dr. Mandeville notorious. In 1714, he republished the poem with an extensive commentary, under the title *The Fable of the Bees, or Private Vices, Public Benefits*. Still no scandal. In 1723 he brought out a new edition, with even more added material, including "A Search into the Nature of Society." A few months later, the Grand Jury of Middlesex referred this book, as a public nuisance, to the Court of King's Bench, recommending prosecution of the publisher.

No prosecution went ahead, but the hour of the Man-Devil had struck. *The Fable of the Bees* was reprinted five times in the next few years. Suddenly, everyone in Europe (and its outposts like the North American colonies) had heard of the Man-Devil, and every respectable person felt obliged to make outraged comments about him. All across Europe, people became aware of the horror perpetrated by the Man-Devil, as printed translations of his work appeared in every civilized language. When a French translation of *The Fable of the Bees* came out in 1740, a copy was ritually burned by the public executioner.

The leading philosopher of the moment, George Berkeley, living in Rhode Island at the time, wrote a vigorous denunciation of the Man-Devil (this was before Berkeley had been made a bishop and long before the town of Berkeley, California, had been named after him, immortalizing his name in a mispronounced form). Berkeley's attack unfairly misrepresents Mandeville's argument, but then, exactly what Mandeville's argument was is still being debated.

A few things are clear. Dr. Mandeville did not think that morality was a crock, and did not want to encourage people to practice vice. He thought that morality was useful, and that it made its impact by appealing to people's desire to gain the approval of others. He thought that people would always naturally practice vice (love themselves more than their neighbors and try to satisfy their own appetites before caring about anyone else). People need no special encouragement to practice vice: they are naturally vicious. Mandeville could have said that what was generally thought to be vice was not really vice, but was partly morally neutral, in itself neither good nor bad, and partly good. But that would have ruined the joke.

Only a few of the Man-Devil's literary contemporaries did not denounce him. One was Sam Johnson, compiler of the first dictionary. Reading Mandeville opened his eyes and changed his life. He reported that every young man believed *The Fable of the Bees* was a terribly wicked book, and therefore had to have a copy on his shelves. Another was Ben Franklin, on a visit to London, who had a few drinks with Mandeville, and called him "a most facetious, entertaining companion." So in the flesh he seemed just as he does on the printed page.

The Man-Devil wrote many satirical pieces. It's not always clear just where he's coming from, for two opposite reasons. First, he's careful to avoid saying anything that would get him executed or imprisoned, so we can't always be sure when he's pulling his punches. Second, he's trying to be entertaining by being shocking, so we can't be sure when he's exaggerating his own audacity to keep up the reader's interest.

There's also the fact that what he wrote was mostly either in verse or in the form of dialogues, and in dialogues we can't be sure whether he completely agrees with what any one of his characters is saying.

Mandeville wrote a fun piece called *The Virgin Unmask'd*, a long conversation, with a touch of mild pornography, between an elderly woman and an adolescent female, in which the older woman tries to convince the younger to have nothing whatsoever to do with men, ever. Mandeville published this piece without finishing it, and we don't really know where he's going with it, except that it would be amusing to get there.

Among his other productions was a hilarious piece arguing for the provision of public stews. (A stew, at this time, was the popular name for a house of prostitution. Brothel—stew, get it? Those witty Londoners.) In this pamphlet "by a Lay-Man," pun intended, Mandeville pointed out that the suppression of prostitution would naturally lead to an increased incidence of rape. So harlots, by doing it for money, are incidentally helping to protect and defend virtuous women. As *The Grumbling Hive* put it,

> The worst of all the multitude
> Did something for the common good.

Or as Mandeville explained with mock-earnestness:

> I am far from encouraging Vice, and think it would be an unspeakable Felicity to the State, if the Sin of Uncleanness could be utterly Banish'd from it; but I am afraid it is impossible. The Passions of some People are too violent to be curb'd by any Law or Precept; . . . If Courtezans and Strumpets were to be prosecuted with as much Rigour as some silly People would have it, what Locks or Bars would be sufficient to preserve the Honour of our Wives and Daughters? . . . some Men would grow outrageous, and Ravishing would become a common Crime.

At this time the penalty for rape was death, and neither Mandeville nor anyone else expected that was going to change.

Did Dr. Mandeville really want government-run bordellos? We can't be sure. His more serious arguments for this policy are phrased as comical parodies of the then-fashionable arguments for economic policies that promote national greatness. But the Man-Devil was nimble enough to make fun of arguments he actually believed in.

Later in the eighteenth century, most of those who could read (eighty percent of males and twenty percent of females) had read Dr. Mandeville, and even as they fumed with righteous anger, many of them pirated his ideas. The Man-Devil invented economics, sociology, social anthropology, sociobiology, utilitarianism, liberalism, evolution, postmodernism, psychiatry, sex education, the social philosophy of Rousseau, the ethical theory of Nietzsche, and the class theory of Marx. In the spirit of the Man-Devil, I'm exaggerating only very, very slightly. He also, sad to say, invented Keynesian economics and the theory of the stimulus package, the dumb notion, refuted many times since in a recurring nightmare, that government spending can get you out of a slump. But here, I like to think, the Man-Devil was just kidding around.

Many of Mandeville's ideas are developed fifty years later by Adam Smith in *The Wealth of Nations*, especially the idea that acting out of self-love and self-interest can lead to the public benefit. Smith wrote that:

> It is not from the benevolence of the butcher, the brewer, or the baker, that we expect our dinner, but from their regard to their own self-interest. We address ourselves, not to their humanity but to their self-love, and never talk to them of our own necessities but of their advantages.

Smith finally comes out with what Mandeville had only slyly hinted at: that so-called private vices are not really vices at all. It's ethically okay to love yourself, to be predominantly self-interested. Smith replayed a riff that had done the rounds of the coffee-house chatter: "A man is never more innocently employed than when making money." And Smith described how an individual could be

> led by an invisible hand to promote an end which was no part of his intention. Nor is it always the worse for the society that it was not part of it. By pursuing his own interest he frequently promotes that of the society more effectually than when he really intends to promote it.

In his first book, *The Theory of the Moral Sentiments*, Smith had included an entire chapter devoted to a rebuttal of Mandeville. Smith, unlike Dr. Mandeville, had to make sure he could keep his university teaching post. While sharply criticizing Mandeville, taking the Man-Devil's provocative over-statements with deadpan seriousness, Smith commented that *The Fable of the Bees* couldn't have impressed so many people "had it not in some respects bordered upon the truth."

Mandeville's and Smith's theory that everyone will benefit if each person acts in his own self-interest can easily be misunderstood. A more complete statement of what Mandeville and Smith believed is that since most people are going to act predominantly in their self-interest anyway, laws ought to be designed so that, as far as possible, everyone will benefit if each person acts in his own self-interest. This is, they believed, the test of good law.

So the point Mandeville and Smith are really making is one about which laws are best. It's easy to overlook this because both Mandeville and Smith believed that the laws of England and Scotland in the eighteenth century had come quite close to being the best laws, and could easily be brought closer. Whereas Mandeville believes (or pretends to believe—you never quite know with the Man-Devil) that good laws are devised by clever politicians, Smith has a theory that law, especially judge-made common law, evolves and tends to improve as it evolves.

A country's laws fulfill a function like Dexter's Code: they direct individual human appetites that are very far from benevolent into actions which benefit other people, without trying to change the appetites themselves. The Man-Devil's insight now dominates most of the world and is rapidly mopping up the few remaining holdouts. If you want living standards to keep rising, then you have to give up the idea of making people morally better, in their inmost souls, by law. Instead, you design the law so that it takes people as they are, and gives them an incentive to be productive—to serve the good of other people.

We live in a world the Man-Devil has made. In some ways, the Man-Devil is like Jesus: he draws attention to the difference, and the possible antagonism, between inner thoughts and outward behavior. In other ways, the Man-Devil is just the opposite, a true Anti-Christ: he teaches us something we can never forget: that what really matters for humankind is not the purity of people's intentions but the actual results of their actions, results which may be, and most often are, no part of their intention.

A Second Look at Dexter's Motives

So far I've been assuming that Dexter is a psychopath reined in by a Code. His motives are foul, though his deeds are salubrious. This is the way Dexter thinks of himself. Dexter continually tells himself this, and as he does so, continually tells us. But could Dexter be misled himself and then misleading us?

The show's appeal hinges on the fact that we both accept this story and simultaneously feel it to be false. We know that Dex is no soulless psychopath. How do we know it?

Here's one example. Dexter kills both Jorge Castillo and his wife Valerie. The chopped up Jorge goes into the regulation six Hefty bags, but Dex doesn't chop up the wife because she's a bit of an afterthought and he can't afford the precious minutes. This dreadfully impolite and inconsiderate couple certainly deserve to be disassembled (though my inner economist can't help wondering whether it could possibly be profit-maximizing for them to murder *so many* of their clients), and there's the hilarious bit where Dexter asks them for the secret of their successful relationship, and then murmurs, "Thank you, that's very helpful," just before slaughtering them both.

Then what does Dexter do? He walks up to the door of the shed where the Cuban immigrants are imprisoned without food, water, or sanitation, and unlocks it. A brief pause. As we watch, we automatically think, 'Thank God those poor people will now be able to get out, but maybe they won't notice the door's unlocked and will still spend hours of torment in there.' Dexter obviously has just the same thought, and opens the door wider, before driving off to dump the Castillo corpses in the ocean. We see one immigrant come to the door and peer out, fearfully and wonderingly.

Dexter has nothing to gain by this spontaneous action. He's very pressed for time, and the quicker the disappearance of the Castillos is reported, the more danger he'll be in. As it turns out, there were actually two eye witnesses to Dexter's capturing the Castillos and loading their bodies into his car. Admittedly, Dexter couldn't be expected to know that one of them would dive down to the ocean bed, recover Valerie's corpse, and replace it just where Dexter had killed her, but still, he has informed us that his motto is 'Be Prepared'. Someone with no empathy, a psychopath, or even someone who over-rides his empathy in pursuit of pure self-interest, would have left the door locked and let the Cubans perish miserably, without giving it a thought.

Dexter keeps telling us he has no feelings, but we keep seeing that he does have feelings. It's true that his feelings are not entirely typical, and he's not fully in touch with them. Dexter, in fact, belongs to that procession of characters which includes Pechorin (in Lermontov's *A Hero of Our Time*), the narrator of Dostoevsky's *Notes from Underground*, and Meursault (in Camus's *The Stranger*). These characters are all very different, but in their different ways they have problems with their feelings. Meursault gets his head chopped off because he doesn't make a conventional display of the feelings he's expected to show in conventional settings, while Dexter, more intelligent and more controlling than Meursault, chops off other people's heads while working hard to simulate the appropriate feelings, to blend in and appear normal.

Dexter's interpersonal mis-steps are at worst only a slight exaggeration of hackneyed stereotypical situations: the male who doesn't understand what women are feeling, the non-macho male who doesn't quite know how to make macho talk, the person at the funeral whose mind is on matters other than grief. Often he is socially awkward because he doesn't know what feelings it is conventionally appropriate to display in certain situations.

One of the first things Dexter tells us in the first episode of Season 1 is: "It has to happen." He has to kill, he has no self-control, his Dark Passenger must seize the reins. And in that first episode we see Dexter and Harry's conversation, in which Harry explains why Dexter must follow the Code. One of the remarkable things about this conversation is that Harry doesn't merely deliver the Code: he assures Dexter that his urge to kill cannot be cured, that he's fated to be a killer. Dexter is puzzled and wonders if possibly he might be able to change, but Harry nixes that one. And it's little Dexter, not Harry, who comes up with some semblance of an ethical rationale for Harry's Code: "They deserve it."

Why is Harry so certain that Dexter can't recover? Remember that at this point Dexter has not yet physically harmed any human person. He kills a dog because it is keeping his seriously ill stepmother awake at night. Harry's an intelligent cop but he doesn't look like the type who would spend his spare time keeping up with the latest research into childhood development, and if he did, he would have come to a different conclusion anyway. As an infant, Dexter saw his mother cut to pieces in front of his eyes, and we're expected to suppose that this is what turned him into a serial killer governed by an involuntary compulsion. The plain fact, of course, is that most serial killers did not have extreme childhood traumas and most people who do suffer such traumas don't go on to become serial killers. At the age of three, seeing your mother horribly slain and then sitting for a couple of days in the pool of her blood is going to be upsetting, and your school grades will probably suffer, but it simply will not make you a serial killer.

And when Dexter does begin killing humans, it's on the direct orders of Harry. Dexter has done nothing to commence a career killing humans, and is horrified when Harry instructs him to kill

Nurse Mary, who makes a practice of killing her patients with drugs and is now trying to kill Harry. Dexter is appalled and resistant, but Harry firmly insists ("Popping Cherry," Season 1). Harry makes it seem that killing Nurse Mary is necessary to save his life, but instead the police could have been informed of what she was up to, and she would have been suspended pending an investigation. Or Harry could simply have moved to another hospital (surely Miami police health benefits would run to that). However Harry has determined that Dexter must take the step of killing his first human. Harry quite deliberately sets Dexter on his path as a serial killer, while without Harry's pro-active intervention, there's no guarantee that Dexter would ever have slain or physically hurt a human.

So while we keep being fed the line that Dexter is a predetermined killer and that Harry gives him the Code which guides and constrains his killing, the facts of the narrative tell us that Harry both gives Dexter the Code and deliberately turns him into a killer. What's Harry's motive? We know that Harry the cop was breaking departmental rules by having sex with Dexter's mother, the CI (confidential informant) up to the time when she was brutally slain. Further dot-connecting is scarcely necessary. There's somthing poisonous about Harry.

Like many people, Dexter has bought the theory that he's subject to an irresistible compulsion. Since he firmly believes that, he doesn't seriously try to fight it. When he lays off killing for a few weeks, he gets irritable and concludes that he can't do without it. But of course he can. He just has to persist for a few more weeks or months—if he really wants to kick the habit. Then the urge will die down and become easier to control. Addiction is always a choice.

But maybe he doesn't want to kick the habit just yet. Maybe he's having too much fun. We certainly are.

18

You Hurt Her, You Hurt Me

EVERITT FOSTER

Season 1 of *Dexter* is about the struggle between Dexter's love for his adoptive family, Harry and Debra Morgan, and his biological brother Brian Moser. The story broaches many topics people deal with on a day-to-day basis, though in far more dramatic and extreme ways.

We can understand Dexter's psychological and sexual evolution over the course of the first season with the help of the French philosopher Michel Foucault, especially his *History of Sexuality*. Foucault can help reveal how we reach a sort of completeness in our lives, and an understanding of not just how, but why, our families function in the twenty-first century.

For Foucault sex, power, and knowledge are three inextricably linked aspects of the human experience. Power as expressed through sex, is a means to knowledge, and knowledge is the key to understanding who we are. This connection makes is possible to use Foucault's philosophy to understand the root of Dexter's "Dark Passenger" and how his search for a family and normalcy (as contemporary Americans understand the term) is rooted in sex.

Why Does Dexter Need a Family if Blood Is His Life?

If sexuality is the very essence of our being, indicative of our soul, then Dexter's initial apathy towards sex (he describes it as being "so . . . undignified") is easy to understand. And if sexuality is a key to understanding someone's psychology then Dexter is in danger of being exposed as a killer if others realize his personal life is a little unorthodox.

When we're first introduced to Rita, Dexter describes her as being "perfect" because she is "in her own way, as damaged as me" ("Dexter," Season 1). Because she's been horribly traumatized after her soon-to-be ex-husband Paul beat and raped her in front of her children, she developed an aversion to sex, which suits Dexter just fine. As he explains, every time he gets close to a woman and makes himself vulnerable she sees through his mask forcing him to move on. Because of her past, Dexter is free to maintain the façade of what he believes to be a typical relationship without risking the exposure that comes through intimacy.

Dexter's Awkward Sexual Advances

In *The History of Sexuality*, Foucault uses the concept of "deployment" to substantiate his repressive hypothesis. He divides society into spheres, calling one the "deployment of alliance" and the other the "deployment of sexuality." The deployment of alliance ties individuals together via kinship bonds, blood relations, ancestry and family, ultimately arrives at a sort of consensual social law. The deployment of sexuality helps individuals understand the changing social standards (including standards of sexual pleasure) around them. In a way, this is Foucault's reply to Freud's claim that sex is a function of biology.

For Foucault, the family helps nurture sexuality. It's nurture, not nature that dictates our understanding of pleasure and power. The deployment of alliance and the deployment of sexuality really only meet in the context of family, culminating in an intuitive understanding of love. In the Morgan family, for example, Harry's so preoccupied with Dexter's training that he fails to realize his adoptive son is more than just a killer, and leaves his biological daughter Debra feeling neglected and unimportant in her father's eyes, resulting in her own relationship problems.

As Season 1 progresses, Rita begins to feel comfortable enough with Dexter to want sex. At first this is because she's afraid of losing "the one truly decent man in Miami" but later it is because she is a sexual being who wants to express her love for him. Dexter, being the ethical yet socially stunted serial killer that he is, begins to worry about how to deal with Rita's advances. When most people encounter relationship problems, they can rely on their "deployment of alliances" for support. Dexter has Debra and some of the guys of Miami Metro, specifically family oriented Angel Batista and resident pervert Vince Masuka.

In the presence of Debra, Dexter appears to be a protective brother by doing everything from checking out her boyfriends to lending assistance in getting out of Vice and into Homicide; in short being the one guy who has never let her down. To Vince, Dexter is a fellow geek and someone he can brag about sex with after Dexter announces Rita gave him oral sex while dressed as Lara Croft. To Angel he is a shoulder to lean on when we learn Angel's wife left him. And it's Angel who, though obviously no better at romance than Dexter, he has no qualms about advising Dex to learn to "reciprocate" when Rita wants, you know, something . . . *more*. Dexter tries, but proves himself to be arguably the most sexually inept man in America when he tries to give Rita something . . . *more* . . . as she is crying and watching a DVD of *Terms of Endearment*. When Dex attempts to "reciprocate," he is affirming his sexuality and illustrating Foucault's point about how these spheres intersect (if comically, in this case).

Focusing on the relationship between Dexter and the Bennetts helps us understand what Foucault meant by the interplay between the deployment of alliance and sexuality. In entering a platonic, though potentially romantic, relationship with Rita, even as a mask, Dex inherited a pre-made family and settled into the "human bonds" that came with it. By showing the kids a kind of fatherly love, the Bennetts begin to nurture Dexter in return." Thus the family, even if it is not biological, forms the basis of his sexual identity and ultimately defines Dexter's soul. As the season progresses we understand how this surrogate family has really come to mean everything to him and in fact actually gives his life meaning and direction that his adoptive family did not. It also forms the foundation for the inevitable choice Dexter will have to make: is he Dexter Morgan or is he Dexter Moser? In other words, Dexter no longer needed to fake a life when a real one had evolved from the cover. The really interesting question then is, how did he decide which life was more important?

Sex, Power, and Knowing Thyself

Another important concept from Foucault's *History of Sexuality* that plays out in *Dexter* is "the spirals of power and pleasure." Foucault uses this idea to reveal how sex and power are connected. It's all about the relationship between observer and observed. When the two objects (in this case people, Dexter, Rita, Rudy/Brian, and others) engage each other by openly discussing their sex lives, they become connected in a search for knowledge. The unspoken goal is to gain power over oneself by knowing others. To be more precise, Dexter as observer increases his power by examining a subject, "drawing out its sexual pleasure" and, in turn, increasing his own power. By highlighting the observed object's pleasure, the observer actually increases those pleasures.

Foucault's knowledge-power paradigm is based upon several basic notions. First, power and knowledge are "always connected." Second, power changes over time. And third, discourse connects knowledge and power. Dexter seems aware of at least part of this, too. As the investigation progresses, he realizes the relationship between he and Rita has changed him. "My days are numbered," he says after nearly being caught at a crime scene, "so I better make the most of what I have left."

On some level, Dexter realizes that the discourse between himself and the objects he observes is really a power struggle. The more he knows, the more power he has. But conversely the more he observes, the more power he grants to those who observe him.

Two moments connect Dexter's new knowledge to Foucault's "spiral of power and pleasure." The first comes when Dexter is about to kill a couple who have been extorting and murdering Cuban refugees ("Love American Style," Season 1). As Jorge and Valerie Castillo are about to die, their last thoughts and words to each other are, "I love you baby!" and "I love you so much!" Dexter pauses and asks, "How do you make it work?" Their answer, "We want the same things," provides him with some insight into both his life and his relationship with Rita (but he doesn't desist from slaying the couple. Hey, he's still a killer).

The second happens when Dexter reveals to the young killer Jeremy Downs ("Popping Cherry," Season 1) how he finally managed to feel "less bottomless." For fans to believe the transformation is genuine and to make the psychological choice between Moser and Morgan seem truthful and logical, it is necessary to reveal a crucial piece of Dexter's newly developed self-awareness. "Pretend," he says. "You pretend the feelings are there for the world, and for the people around you. Who knows, maybe one day they will be."

While the audience has already seen Dexter's capacity for humanity, he still seems to doubt that it is present within himself. Dexter is still not sure of who he is. If the hero lacks self-knowledge, then the modern solution is therapy, which, as Foucault suggests, is just another aspect of the transformation of sex into discourse. People talk about sex instead of doing it. It is the increasingly accepted method by which we subjects exercise control over ourselves.

In his session with Dexter, Dr. Emmett Meridian ("Shrink Wrap," Season 1) attempts to broach Dexter's sex life, a topic Dexter simply turns around on his psychiatrist in "an attempt to take control of the situation" because he has trouble letting others get close. When Rita gains more inner strength and self-assurance stemming from taking control of the situation with Paul, she becomes more sexually assertive. Dexter rebuffs her advances fearing that he will lose her. Really though, Dexter is afraid of losing power in their relationship. If knowledge is power and she has carnal knowledge of him, it follows that Rita will have control over Dexter, and he will have to relinquish some of the control he needs to exercise to keep his mask in place.

Meridian knows that Dexter has been living a dishonest life (though he is clearly unaware of the killer's intentions) and attempts to bring him back to a point where he first felt powerless. Dexter's life has been about being a Morgan. But this identity was superimposed on a boy found in a shipping container sitting in a pool of blood. Harry Morgan was not only Dexter's father, he was his maker.

To know who he is, Dexter must relinquish some of the power he has. This happens precisely when Dex and Rita finally consummate their relationship, just moments after the traumatic revelation of the boy in the blood and the origin of the dark passenger is revealed.

It seems unlikely that this juxtaposition of blood and sex is simply a coincidence. For Foucault, there is a long, historical relationship between blood, power, and sex. What he called the "right of death" had been historically exercised over a population by ruling classes and kings. The specific method of killing is usually some combination of war and justice, but in both instances blood and power are linked via death. It's no surprise that after seeing the boy in the blood, and after having sex with Rita, Dexter is able to confess who he is for the first time. In giving up some power, Dexter was able to gain control over other parts of his life and confess (albeit to the doomed psychiatrist) who he is.

Morgan or Moser?

Throughout Dexter's story, identity and power are exercised through sex. Just as Dexter seems to be comfortable with acknowledging who he is, those around him start to wonder who he really is. A man named Joe Driscoll from Dade City, claiming to be his biological father, deeds him a house. As Dexter delves into Driscoll's life, old memories re-emerge and the long held deployment of alliance centered on the Morgan family is thrown into question, especially when Debra introduces her boyfriend "Rudy" (really Brian Moser, the Ice Truck Killer) to her brother.

In Foucault's philosophy of sexuality the relationship between observer and observed leads to knowledge and ultimately to power and control. So as Dexter explores his life before Harry, Deb begins to question where she fits in his alliance. She wants to exert power to keep what is left of her family intact; while Rudy exerts power (based on his knowledge of Dexter's past) in an attempt to reassemble the family he was denied.

When Debra learns that Dexter sent Vince material for a DNA test, she confronts him, angry and hurt. They learn that Harry lied to them about Dexter's father being dead. Dexter tries to reassure his sister that he isn't questioning Harry's motives, but he just had to know the circumstances of Driscoll's death. Debra is hurt by her brother's search for knowledge because to her it implies that if he can question their dad, perhaps he can start questioning what she means to him as well. Knowledge is power, a power that might threaten the sanctity and bonds of Dexter's deployment of alliance.

While looking at the "thank-you-for-the-good-blood card" that Dexter made for his anonymous blood donor as a kid, it occurs to him that, "I had a father, someone other than Harry who called me son. The thought never even occurred to me. . . . Harry always had the answers. . . . I built my life on Harry's Code, lived by it. But Harry lied. What else don't I know? My concrete foundation was shifting, turning to sand." The only way for Dexter to find out what is missing is to plunge back into the blood bath.

When a hotel room covered in blood proves too much for Dexter, Deb tries to connect with him. Yet he shuts her out. Though he has attained a certain comfort with his mask, and finds fulfillment in his relationship with Rita, Dexter is still unable to connect with his sister. The solution to the problem can be found in more discourse. In this case it is Deb who reaches out to Dexter to speak with Rudy/Brian on her behalf. This dialogue reveals Dexter's level of commitment to his sister: "You hurt her, you hurt me."

In the end, Dexter chooses to save Debra ("Born Free," Season 1) to cement his traditional deployment of alliance and identity as a Morgan. She hugs him and thanks him, not for saving her, but for finally being emotionally available when she needs him. With his choice made, he couldn't just leave Brian alive, and so "for the safety of his sister" murdered his brother, severing the only remaining blood tie to the Moser family and affirming the Morgan alliance.

"She's not your real sister. She's a stranger to you and she always will be. I tried to help you by killing her," Brian tells Dexter, who responds, "I know that!" before slitting Brian's throat and whispering "I'm sorry. I can't hear anymore. But you're right."

Dexter Moser, brother of Brian, was born to Laura. He died one day in a cargo container on the Miami docks. But at that same moment, Dexter Morgan was born and his family, his "alliance" came into being. Like most families they have their problems and like many adopted children Dexter did go looking for his birth family, but returned to those who loved him enough to hide the truth. The murder clearly happens for dramatic reasons, but in Foucault's world this act is an example of the "right of death" and is a symbol, and affirmation, of Dexter's power over his life.

For Foucault, the modern world places such an emphasis on sexual expression (and the power that goes with self-discovery) as the key to healthy mental development in a society that seems to have forgotten its own history and that consequently remains subject to the power of our sexual history. Just as Dexter's power to choose who he is could only be acquired by plunging deep into his past, knowing himself as both a Morgan and Moser, Foucault teaches that we each must embrace the search for knowledge in order to know who we are, behind our own masks.

19

Dexter's Whiteness

EWAN KIRKLAND

Dexter is a very white television character.

By this I mean that so much of what defines him is bound up in qualities, historical activities, and philosophical perspectives traditionally associated with white masculinity. As an emotionally empty, anally retentive, Harvard graduate, forensic scientist and serial killer, there seems to be a clear fit, intentional or not, between Dexter's characterization and his ethnicity. Emotional repression, in contrast to the passion, excitement, and exuberance attributed to other races, is a particularly white thing. A fussy attention to detail also seems a personality trait of predominantly white film and television characters. Notwithstanding recent efforts within academic institutions to broaden their intake, higher education remains associated with white privilege. Science, forensic or otherwise, is historically a white man's field. And serial killing, as represented in fiction, is practiced primarily by white men.

Think of Hannibal Lecter, listening to classical music in his cell, extolling the virtues of fine wine and fine eating. Think of the yuppie monster in Bret Easton Ellis's *American Psycho*. Think of the white-faced masks of Jason, Leatherface, or the killers in the Scream series. Now try to think of a fictional black serial killer. If any exist, they are absent from the canon.

This is not to say that the role of Dexter could not be played by a black man, a Hispanic, or a Native American. But if this happened, he would be cast against type. Dexter, ethnically speaking, plays to type—so much so that exploring Dexter from this perspective provides an insight into the nature of whiteness itself.

Of course, the characteristics that define Dexter's ethnicity are stereotypes, not a reflection of what white people actually are. Race is understood to be a social, historical, political, and representational construction, and references to race throughout this chapter should be read as something defined by culture and not by genetic heritage. In addition, whiteness connects with other kinds of categorisation, such as class, gender and nationality. Nor is whiteness a single cluster of traits: there are different kinds of whiteness. The particular whiteness exemplified by Dexter is different to that of, say Michael Douglas's character in *Falling Down*, Mr. Burns in *The Simpsons*, or Edward the romantic vampire of the *Twilight* series. Dexter expresses a specific form of whiteness, overlapping with other popular images, but distinct unto itself.

To say that Dexter engages with white identity is not intended as a criticism. The series contains an admirably multiracial cast. While occasionally touching on the subject of illegal immigration, or racial tensions within Miami, it does so with sensitivity and respect. In *Dexter* we see no celebration of white identity. Dexter himself is no racist. As he clearly states, his murderous impulses do not discriminate ("Its Alive," Season 2). Dexter's whiteness is not extreme. He's no white supremacist, racist redneck, or collector of Nazi memorabilia. Instead his is a whiteness in part rooted in banality, ordinariness, transparency. For this reason, it is a whiteness that is extremely hard to see.

The ways in which *Dexter*, both serial and serial killer, throws this ordinary everyday whiteness into relief—contrasting it with other ethnicities, sardonically reflecting on its invisibility and emptiness, revealing its visual constructedness, playing with the association between whiteness, death, and sexual dysfunction—is part of what makes the show such an intelligent and fascinating example of popular television.

The Problem of Whiteness

Whiteness in culture is a tricky business. Critics of film and television so often explore images of marginalized groups—black people, lesbians and gay men, women—while those at the center—Caucasians, heterosexuals, men—often go unconsidered. It's easy to identify the racial stereotypes that circulate 'minorities' and the ideas behind those representations. These characters stand out. They're different. Historically, on the screen they are defined by their race in ways that reflect limiting assumptions about the nature of such groups.

In contrast, identifying the stereotypes that surround white people in popular culture is much harder. Richard Dyer, one of the first critics to start interrogating whiteness, argues that "white power secures its dominance by seeming not to be anything in particular"[1] and not anything in particular is particularly hard to define. White people are just that—people, unencumbered by the burden of representation. Whiteness, as an ethnicity, defines so much of what it is to be normal in Western culture, and normality is bland, characterless, without form. Seeing whiteness, identifying what whiteness is, and how it is represented in film and television, requires looking very hard indeed.

One way Dyer suggests whiteness becomes visible is in moments when white people are depicted alongside non-white characters.[2] *Dexter* certainly presents plenty of instances where its protagonist's white masculinity is thrown into relief by characters who seem more defined by their gender, race, or sexuality. Debra Morgan, Dexter's sister, is introduced working on the vice squad, and initially struggles to gain respect and acceptance in a man's world. Maria LaGuerta is a Hispanic woman whose success is constantly jeopardized by the machinations of her white male superior. She even states on a number of occasions that her struggle is gendered and raced. Angel Batista, with his distinct, slightly lisping accent, and occasional exchanges of unsubtitled Spanish, is colored by his ethnicity with every word he utters. James Doakes's abrasive manner is consistent with notions of black men as aggressive and confrontational, even if he turns out to be more insightful than any of his colleagues. And Vince Masuka's Asian ethnicity is partnered with a perverse non-normative sexuality, albeit one that is played for laughs.

Of course, Dexter's colleagues are more than stereotypes. But there's no value in a racially diverse cast who are not allowed to reflect that diversity in their performance, and it is to the writers' and performers' credit that these characters never seem tokenistic. The point is that against this background of multiculturalism, Dexter, the white heterosexual male, seems at first to be devoid of

---

[1] Richard Dyer, *The Matter of Images: Essays on Representation* (Routledge, 2002), p. 126.

[2] Richard Dyer, *White* (Routledge, 1997), p. 13.

character. He has no political ax to grind. He has no distinct accent. He is polite, unobtrusive, and quietly professional. He has no sexual peccadilloes, as far as anyone knows. And at the same time, just as white paint is only noticeable when placed on a non-white surface, this 'colourful' environment allows Dexter's ethnicity to become visible.

A broad-strokes comparison of Dexter with his Season 3 partner in crime Miguel Prado illustrates how such racial juxtapositions make Dexter's whiteness apparent. Dexter is cool and calm, but his Hispanic colleague is emotional and hot blooded. While the practiced killer remains detached and aloof, unclouded by emotion, the DA pursues a personal vendetta against Ellen Wolf whom he messily murders then dumps into an open grave. Dexter sleeps soundly in his bed untroubled by the atrocities he has committed, but Miguel has restless nights. While Dexter has a granite set of ethics, Miguel has no dead white man's Code to live by and, as a consequence, spirals out of control. Again, Miguel is more than his ethnicity, but exploring the character in such terms throws light on the contrasting nature of Dexter, the white serial killer. Dexter is defined by cold, calculating, dispassionate logic, exemplified in his meticulously sterile method of murder. In this respect, Dexter confirms Richard Dyer's speculation that whiteness is about "tightness . . . self-control, self-consciousness, mind over body" (p. 6). Miguel lacks this control, which Dexter has practiced all his life.

The Invisible Killer

There is an invisibility to whiteness. This is not the invisibility suffered by minority groups within the media, who are routinely ignored or marginalized. Rather it's an invisibility that comes from saturation, normalization, non-particularity. Dyer says that this invisibility derives from "the sense that whiteness is nothing in particular, that white culture and identity have, as it were, no content" (p. 9). White people appear to own no distinct heritage or history to characterize who they are. Consequently, and because they are so pervasively present within popular representations, white people do not stand out.

There is a similar invisibility to Dexter. Even in multiracial Miami, the white man whose ethnicity has been largely overlooked within discussion of racial identity, cannot be seen. When stalking his victims, Dexter has the uncanny ability to move unnoticed by his quarry. He can break into cars, homes, offices, apartment buildings, stalk tattoo parlours and used car lots seemingly undetected by surveillance systems, human or electronic. When Dexter is spying on his mother's killer in "Morning Comes" (Season 2), the retired thug emerges looking decidedly agitated, glancing furtively up and down the street. Yet he entirely fails to spot the man he attacked only two nights earlier, sitting in broad daylight, in his huge car, ominously putting on a pair of brown leather gloves. As a white man, someone who has been historically regarded as above suspicion, Dexter projects a prima facie blamelessness. More than being simply beyond scrutiny, Dexter seems at times to be literally invisible.

Leaving no trace is his area of expertise. There is something ghostly to Dexter's activities, something that invokes a non-corporeal quality of white identity. This is an extension of the requirement that white people master, control and in a way transcend their bodies. Dyer sees the idea of corporeal transcendence in the Christian symbol of Mary and Christ ("a thumbnail sketch of the white ideal"), in the Kantian notion of the "subject without properties" who remains always the subject, rather than the object, of scientific racial investigation, and in the myth that white people are distinguished by some intangible invisible 'spirit' which sets them apart from other, more bodily races (p. 23). This spirit, Dyer argues, often translates into a form of imperialistic 'enterprise' or 'will' that entails "the control of self and the control of others" (p. 31).

Dexter is without doubt an extremely enterprising individual, mobilizing all the resources that his privileged position lays at his disposal in his search for victims. His killings represent the channelling of his own murderous desires for the greater good, the end result being a control not only of his own body but also the bodies of rapists, murderers, and pedophiles whom he transforms into clean little packages, wrapped neatly in garbage bags, and deposited where they will never be found.

Clearly, Dexter gets away with his crimes not simply because he's a white man. He is also very clever. He is very clean. He is meticulous in his methods. But these characteristics—cleverness, cleanliness, care and attention to detail—are themselves connected to white people and white identity, evident in the stereotyping of many non-white races as stupid, dirty, and sloppy.

Dexter also illustrates one of many paradoxes of white identity. Whiteness is ordinary, banal, unremarkable—the very qualities from which Dexter's invisibility derives. At the same time whiteness is supposed to be special, superior, admirable. This contradiction can be understood as resolved in the superhero archetype, where the Clark Kent/Superman dyad allows both incompatible meanings to reside in the same white body, and Dexter flirts with the image of himself as a caped crusader figure.

Dexter might be ordinary on the outside, but he is extraordinary on the inside. He is extremely intelligent, a graduate of Harvard Medical School, admired amongst his colleagues for his professionalism, prized as a brother and as a boyfriend. Dexter is also remarkable because he kills people, he kills only those who deserve it, and he is able to do this so well that for four seasons he has avoided detection by the authorities. The extraordinariness of whiteness also incorporates extraordinary atrocities, the spirit and enterprise of white people allowing them the potential to achieve remarkable things, both wonderful and terrifying.

In Dexter we see a common theme in tales about white people: secrets lying beneath the surface. Bodies buried in basements, abuse hidden behind respectable front doors, psychotic impulses disguised by tight white smiles and implacable white faces, like Dexter's fellow white suburbanite who smashes up his own neighbourhood under cover of darkness. These stories suggest something sinister about what white people keep hidden, as if the invisible something that makes white people so special might not be very nice at all.

The theme of the mask recurs throughout *Dexter*, in every soliloquy about the mantle of normality, ordinariness, conformity that Dexter wears to conceal his true nature. As the only main character on the show who might be considered 'black', Doakes seems to be the one most able to penetrate the layers of Dexter's whiteness, suspecting that there's something sinister at the center of his supposedly vice-free alter ego. Observing one of the many ways in which their difference is ethnically coded, Doakes tells Dexter, "Unlike you I do everything out in the open" ("That Night a Forest Grew," Season 2).

There is another, arguably 'black', character in Dexter, one suggested by Toni Morrison's analysis of how darkness is often used in American literature to represent the chaotic, uncivilized, savage aspects which white culture finds within itself, but cannot deal with (Dyer, p. 80). Behind the mask of his white ordinariness lurks Dexter's "shadow self," his "Dark Passenger," the Dark Defender. But despite such black metaphors, Dexter's other self is white at heart.

Murder and the Mise-en-Scène of Whiteness

If whiteness and the qualities which distinguish white people from other races are invisible, there's also the problem that, as Dyer points out, white people are not actually white. Caucasian skin is rather a yellow-pink tone. It makes no more sense for white people to be labelled 'white' than for other races to be termed 'black'. For this reason, the drawing, painting, photographing, lighting, and application of cosmetics and digital manipulation to white skin and white bodies historically works to reinforce the tenuous connection between pale skinned people and whiteness.

White pervades Dexter. Across the range of DVD box covers, promotional stills and publicity material defining the show, actor Michael C. Hall is consistently presented dressed in white against a white background, smiling conspiratorially from a toneless canvas which is as much—maybe more—a component of his ethnicity as his own blood flecked skin.

There are undoubtedly aesthetic reasons for this visual design. Red against white provides dramatic contrast of colour, and a recognizable visual motif that runs throughout the series. Dexter is repeatedly associated with white spaces. The "intoxicating ritual" which accompanies every execution involves surrounding himself and his victims in an unreal cocoon of transparent plastic that has the effect of bleaching colour from any environment. The plastic-bag interior of Dexter's kill room ironically echoes the white space where he practices blood spatter patterns. Amid white-skinned manikins, walls hung with white paper, stands Dexter dressed entirely in white. Season 3 opens in a dentist's surgery. A succession of images includes a blinding white electric light, a row of silver instruments on a reflective surface so clean they are barely visible, and white hands made unnaturally so by talcum powdered latex gloves. The location is entirely devoid of colour: white walls, white floor, white panel ceiling, white chair, on which lies white Dexter.

One of the problems with interpreting this imagery in racial terms—a practice commonplace in analysis of dark visual imagery and non-white characters—is that there is slippage between whiteness as hue, whiteness as skin, and whiteness as symbol (pp.

45–46). In other words, there are different spheres of whiteness at play, some only tangentially related to race. For example, there is an exaggerated, expressionistic quality to many of Dexter's visually white scenes that draws upon the symbolic dimensions of whiteness to characterize the protagonist's mental state. The icy bleached blank design of these settings underlines Dexter's cold, emotionless, hollow, deadly nature. But these qualities, the symbols of whiteness, are not divorced from the construction of whiteness as a race which is aloof, emotionally controlled, culturally empty, and which enjoys a symbolic relationship with death. Dyer speculates that this slippage underlines all images of white people in Western culture, and is the potential source of white power and authority.

By depicting the killer in such overtly white spaces, *Dexter* makes visible the invisibility of white identity at the same time that it parodies it. *Dexter* exaggerates, almost to an unreal breaking point, visual strategies for depicting white people that are common in traditional painting, early photography, political cartoons, and classic Hollywood cinema, and that continue to appear in detergent commercials, suburban serials, romantic comedies, and horror movies. Surrounding Dexter with such hyperbolic, ironic white imagery serves to demystify the myth of whiteness and its protagonist's association with the various meanings of the tone.

Death, Sex, and Dexter

Death is a recurring theme in the imagery and iconography of whiteness, both historically and culturally. Death is present in the crucified Christ as figure of white male aspiration, in the sight of the white-clad Ku Klux Klan riding to the rescue in *Birth of a Nation*, in sub-Saharan Africans mistaking the first Europeans for the living dead, in the Holocaust's conception as a clean, scientific, purification through the extermination of 'dirty' people (pp. 209–210)—a disposition Dexter shares towards the disposal of undesirables.

This alignment between whiteness and death recurs throughout *Dexter*. It's present in the cut to white which signifies the death of a character. It's present in the scenes where Dexter chats to his dead adoptive father, where every surface seems to radiate uncomfortable over-exposed phosphorescence. It's evident in the bright, translucent plastic glow of Dexter's kill room, the last thing his victims see.

Sometimes the white color of death appears with other Caucasian killers, such as the Ice Truck Killer whose very name points to the frosty whiteness of frozen water, the emotional coldness of ice, and the immaculate preservation of dead things. Dexter admires the "clean, dry, neat looking dead flesh" that his brother leaves behind, and the blood-draining process which renders the skin bleached of colour, irrespective of its victim's ethnicity. And Trinity, like Dexter, hides in plain sight, moves like a ghost, and seems able to penetrate spaces—an office block, his old family home, Dexter's place of work—largely unseen and unchallenged. Blending into the background with his facade of middle class heterosexual Christian normality, dressed in beige jacket and pale slacks, with grey hair and blue eyes, Trinity does an even better job than Dexter at conforming to the generic tradition of the white ordinary-looking serial killer.

Sex presents another paradox at the heart of whiteness. As Dyer puts it, "To ensure the survival of the race, they have to have sex—but having sex, and sexual desire, are not very white" (*White*, p. 26). There's something awkward about white sexuality. White people have historically seen themselves as less sexual than other races, as if sexuality, along with bodies and bodily instincts, were something that white people are supposed to transcend.

So, Dexter has a problem with sex. When we first meet him, we learn that he has taught himself, using the same cold and emotionless precision with which he dismembers a corpse, how to perform heterosexual desire. Dexter admits he has no problem with bodily fluids, only the emotions they entail. In a nod to the dispassion of whiteness, the functional approach to copulation his ethnicity has inherited, and the perverse associations between sex and death, Dexter approaches his first time with Rita as a necessary ordeal—something that may even kill their relationship.

Dexter's white sexuality is also reflected in the women he has sex with. The virginity or frigidity that characterised Rita in her early interactions with Dexter eventually gives way to symbols of glowing white femininity. In Dexter's preliminary wedding vows, she is aligned with the qualities of sunlight, prayer, and Anglo-Saxon mythology. Rita is a Martha Stewart beacon of civilization, the redemptive white blonde woman who might tame the darker, hidden impulses of the white male. Her yellow hair is frequently given a halo effect, and her fair skin covered typically with light grey pants, beige cardigans, and pale suits. And despite this being her third marriage, Rita's wedding to Dexter is white.

The ghastly alternative to Rita's redemptive white femininity is femme fatale Lila. Defined from the start by her coloring, Lila is described by Debra—to whom, in the frosty light of Dexter's refrigerator, she has already shown too much skin—as a gross, pale, titty vampire. White as a corpse, Lila is Dexter's perfect woman. And it is perhaps no surprise that Rita and Lila end up dead.

In his various relationships with these women—one an angel-unicorn, the other an "emotionally colour blind" sociopath—Dexter dramatizes anxieties about white sexuality that are only one aspect of the general ambivalance of whiteness. As Dyer observes, whiteness is riddled with paradoxes, inconsistencies, and anxieties. So it is fitting that in Dexter we see so many expressions of white identity's problematic relationship with the its own corporeality, the self-serving but ennui-inducing sense of whiteness as devoid of character or substance, and white people's discomforting relationship with death and their own far-from-white history.

20
Happiness, Dexter Style

MIKE PIERO

Dexter Morgan, everyone's favorite serial killer, seems to have it all: the great job, friends, and a killer beachside apartment. But his secret—his Dark Passenger—complicates who Dexter is *as a person* and adds to his isolation from others. Can we even think of Dexter as a genuine human being, given his out-of-work activities? Let's face it, if Dexter's chums at the Miami Metro Homicide Department knew about his need to kill, they would, at the very least, think twice about taking one of Dexter's daily morning doughnuts. Somewhere between evil serial killer and avenging force for good, Showtime's *Dexter* sets us up to question not only the legitimacy of his humanity, but also how we define good and evil.

In the first five minutes of *Dexter* ("Dexter," Season 1) we learn that he loves Cuban food, pork sandwiches, and killing people. But, he doesn't kill just anyone—not prostitutes like the Ice Truck Killer or young women like Trinity—he has "standards." Right away, the Code that Harry Morgan taught his adopted son is given center stage. Yes, he kills because he can't help himself, but he does so with a specific set of rules that keep him safe from being caught and given the electric chair. That's the overarching rule: Don't get caught. What about Dexter's other needs as a person, a human being? How much fulfillment can Harry's Code bring to Dexter? In Season 1, Dexter is portrayed as a lone wolf who has no feelings and keeps everyone at a safe distance. As Dex says in "Popping Cherry," he must "maintain appearances to survive." No doubt, there is more to this serial killer than meets the eye.

One Code to Kill Them All

To learn more about Dexter, we have to take a close look at his reverence for the Code of Harry as well as how his needs evolve throughout the series. Dex is a changing man; he's growing up. It's how he changes from Season 1 to the later seasons that shows how "normal" he actually is. To begin, let's lay out exactly what we know about the Code that Dexter follows when choosing and killing his victim. Harry's Code boils down to the following four rules:

1. **Don't get caught—the ultimate rule**

2. **Be absolutely sure he's guilty; never take an innocent life**

3. **Make sure he will kill again; killing that serves no purpose is murder**

4. **Blend in, maintain appearances, and pretend to be like others**

These rules govern not only Dexter's kills, but his entire life. In Season 2, upon learning of Harry's infidelity and shortcomings, Dexter begins to question whether or not the Code is right. Harry could have been wrong, or worse yet, lying. He lied about Dex's biological parents. In the season finale, "The British Invasion," however, Dexter makes peace with the Code and takes ownership of it: "The Code is mine now, and mine alone."

Another interesting change begins in the last few minutes of Season 2; Dexter continues his commentary on his Code by admitting more changes: "So, too, are the relationships that I cultivate. They're not just disguises anymore. I need them, even if they make me vulnerable." Dexter is realizing that he is his own person and is capable of having a regular life, even with the Dark Passenger inside. He progresses through what psychologist Abraham Maslow called the five basic needs that innately motivate a person in life; these are oftentimes referred to as "Maslow's Hierarchy of Needs." You may have seen this concept expressed visually as a bright, rainbow-colored triangle.

These universal needs are arranged in a hierarchy, or what Maslow calls "hierarchies of prepotency," which means that in order to move on to fulfilling the second need, you must first meet the first one.[1] Maslow believed that "man is a perpetually wanting animal," and was interested in what motivates such wants and behaviors. He came up with five basic needs, in order: Physiological, Safety, Love, Esteem, and Self-Actualization. The "normal" human being moves from the first need through the others to self-actualization. From *Dexter* season one to season five, we see Dex progress through these needs as he learns more about what he wants out of life for himself.

The reason the Code exists is to keep Dexter physically safe—to stop him from getting caught. (A secondary purpose, of course, is to protect the world from Dexter, to channel his urges for good instead of evil.) In "Resistance is Futile" (Season 2), Dexter recalls when Harry once took him as a teenager to an execution to instill in him that the Code is, first and foremost, a code of survival. Maslow's hierarchy lists *physiological needs* as the most basic, the most essential, to survival. Physiological needs include food, water, shelter, and clothing, the basic needs for survival. When we meet Dexter, all of these needs are met already. He has his apartment, shares with us his favorite foods and drinks, and is obviously clothed. He is, however, always on the verge of losing all of those things; with each kill, he risks being caught and having his very life taken away from him. The Code protects him from being caught and, therefore, enables him to preserve his physiological needs.

The first season of *Dexter* is largely a matter of survival: of controlling the chaos with the blood, of hiding in order to keep safe. In "Love American Style," Dex says, "I like to pretend I'm alone . . . no one left to act normal for." He is emotionless and without concern, aside from maintaining his lies and not getting caught. It's not until Season 2 that he begins to realize that he actually does want more out of life. Perhaps Harry left out the possibility that Dexter could have a chance at a relatively "normal" life. As we get more comfortable with Dexter, he seems to be getting less comfortable with himself and the life he's quite literally *carved* out for himself according to his Code.

Dexter: The Family Man?

We all live by codes, whether or not we choose to articulate them. In fact, many tenets of our personal codes (of ethics, morality,

---

[1] All Maslow quotations are from "A Theory of Human Motivation." *Psychological Review* 50 (1943).

belief and the like) operate in the background of our everyday life, or in other words, unconsciously. Maslow's five needs are also at work all the time without us being aware of them. We might infer that these needs had been secretly working in Dexter when we first meet him and learn about his childhood. The cargo container where he spent days sitting in a pool of his mother's blood as a toddler had a profound impact on him.

That traumatic event would upset what Maslow calls *safety needs*, the second set of basic needs. With our physiological needs satisfied, we'll seek safety and security from violence and harm, largely through family. This is why children have, as Maslow puts it, "a preference for some kind of undisrupted routine or rhythm . . . a predictable and orderly world." When infants hear loud, unknown noises, they interpret them as a threat to their safety and respond by crying. Maslow even says that "death within the family may be particularly terrifying," let alone watching your mom sawed up into little pieces with a chainsaw. Despite Harry's best attempts to raise Dexter properly, he could never recover from the horror he witnessed that day. While many adults in our society have these safety needs largely met already—through a safe upbringing—Dexter is at a great disadvantage in this area from the start.

With everything considered though, Dexter is remarkably well adjusted in this department. He needs his privacy because of his secret, but he's not neurotic about safety needs except when he's in danger of being caught, which would be a normal reaction. He is secure in his job and his finances. His health is top notch as far as we know. Security remains a great mobilizer for us, but usually only in emergencies that severely threaten our way of life. At the beginning of the series, Dexter admits that killing people helps control the chaos of his world. This is similar to the way someone with obsessive-compulsive disorder works, in Maslow's words, to "try frantically to order and stabilize the world so that no other unmanageable, unexpected, or unfamiliar dangers will ever appear." The Code helps him fulfill his safety needs.

For Dexter, Rita and the kids also become that kind of protection for him. He tells us in "Circle of Friends" (Season 1) that he needs them because he feels the need to connect with someone. By pretending in order to make the emptiness within feel less bottomless, he actually begins to feel genuine care for those close to him, including his friends and family. This embodies his *love needs*, the third of Maslow's basic needs. This is where the Code begins to fail him. Dexter's safety needs are largely met, albeit with deficiencies, but he is secure in his job, his "work" for the time being, his health, and his relationships. Evidence of love needs can be seen, according to Maslow, when "the person will feel keenly, as never before, the absence of friends, or a sweetheart, or a wife, or children." Dexter is moving towards having more friends—even dangerous friends like Miguel Prado and Trinity—and of course his family. He learns, episode by episode, what it means to have one's love needs met.

Dexter shows more sincerity and wears fewer masks as the series advances. Even in Season 1, he realizes that his days are numbered and remarks, "so I better make the most of them," and is seen in the last few shots playing with Cody—swinging him around with a big smile on his face. He saves Deb because of some human bond between them, even when it means killing his biological brother. When Dex lies to Rita about being a heroin addict, quits the program, and then Rita refuses to see him anymore, what does he do? He goes back to the Narcotics Anonymous meetings to be part of her family, or as he says in Season 2, "An Inconvenient Lie," "the mask is slipping . . . People who never mattered before are suddenly starting to matter." There are many instances of Dexter starting to realize his love needs; needs which he always denied he had or thought were impossible to satisfy in his situation.

Is Dexter Morgan going soft on us? I think we can safely answer with an emphatic "No way!" Harry's Code could not take him past his security needs, and Dexter resents that (and Harry) for a while. Then he realizes that he is in charge of his own life and can make choices about how he wants to live. Lila (or perhaps we should call her Lie-la because she was one lying, manipulative person!), his sponsor-turned-sex buddy, shows Dexter how to pay attention to what he wants out of life. When he was content with being a loner, he sneered at love. But now, a brave new world he thought previously unknowable has been opened to him.

Beyond the Code, Beyond the Lies

One thing that I love about *Dexter* is that Dex is not the only damaged person on the show. Every main character struggles with tragic, life-altering issues. Deb has some cold-blooded boyfriends. Sergeant Doakes has the demons of his past that haunt him. Angel is recently divorced and picks up an undercover officer he thinks is a prostitute. Rita is a single parent with two failed marriages behind her. And the list goes on. We all have secrets, Dark Passengers as it were, and we all work toward obtaining some sense of normalcy.

Maslow's fourth set of needs is the *esteem needs*, which includes the need we feel to have a stable and high evaluation of ourselves "for self-respect, or self-esteem, and for the esteem of others." This need emerges when we feel a strong urge to be liked, appreciated, and viewed as proficient in what we do; in short, to be respected by others. It's like when you spend hour after hour rolling before the first game of the bowling tournament. The point in all the practice is to improve your skill so you'll play stronger for your team, earn the esteem of your teammates, and feel a sense of worth about your performance. While some may seek out this validation by being part of a group, like Batista's and Masuka's bowling team, Dexter gets his esteem needs met in two other ways.

One could argue that Dexter's esteem needs are met mostly by the excellent blood spatter work that he does for a living. He is highly respected for his work by Special Agent Frank Lundy, Lieutenant LaGuerta, Deb, and nearly everyone else in his department. Now, is this all an act? Maybe. It does serve the purpose of helping him blend in; he's a regular guy who's good at his job. That doesn't change the fact that, whether Dex realizes it or not, he receives the esteem of his co-workers and it builds up both his self-esteem and the knowledge that he is appreciated in his work.

This need is also met in Season 3 by his nefarious friendship with Miguel Prado, Miami's Assistant District Attorney. Despite Miguel's truth telling being on a par with Lila's, Miguel gives Dexter the chance to take on a disciple. The mentor-protégé relationship involves esteem needs on both sides. In Season 3, "The Damage a Man Can Do," Dexter begins to teach Miguel the Code and how to stalk and kill his prey. He quickly realizes, however, that Miguel Prado is not the person he pretends to be, much like himself actually. Miguel spins out of control and decides, as was his plan all along, to learn the skills he needs to be able to kill anyone he sees fit, without what he sees as Dexter's "bullshit" Code. This decision ultimately costs him his life, at his old friend's hand. Despite the way that things turned out with Miguel, Dex learned a lot from that friendship. It also demonstrates his ability to absorb confidence and esteem from others, a basic human need according to Maslow.

There is one final need that appears at the very top of Maslow's hierarchy: Self-actualization. People have interpreted this need as many different things, such as morality, creativity, spontaneity, or acceptance of facts.[2] In the end, these experiences are merely cultural interpretations of what Maslow, quoting Kurt Goldstein, describes as the rule that "What a man *can* be, he *must* be." This refers to the need for self-fulfillment, that is, to fulfill one's potential. A self-actualizing moment could be, for example, when you've gotten Cs on most of your papers in high school, and then one day you get an A; and a light clicks on, "Oh, wow, I can get As on my future papers if I put enough time and work into them." Before you got that A, you may have thought your best was a C, but that A showed you your potential, which caused you to desire to do your very best next time as well. Perhaps this is why Dexter helps Cody do his best on his class presentation on Saudi Arabia.

Dexter's beginning to realize that he has more inherent potential than he saw before; indeed, more than Harry saw as well. At the end of Season 3, in "Do You Take Dexter Morgan?," when the Skinner, George King, has Dexter on his table, Dex actually cries inside (we see it as Harry in the vision crying), and forgives his father and wants with all of his heart to stay alive to see his son come into the world: "I've never wanted anything before so much in my life." It's not just a sense of belonging to a family (although that is part of it), but the realization that he can have a normal life, with genuine roles like that of a husband and father. This is something that he wants *for himself*—not as a smokescreen or a mask, but to be the best person he can be, despite his dark urges.

Can a Serial Killer Be Happy?

Achieving perfection is not what Maslow's theory is about though; instead, it reveals what makes us tick, what motivates us, and how we can live more fulfilling lives. It also proves that Dexter, despite the dozens of people that he's killed, is a person capable of human emotions after all. Damaged? Hell, yeah. But he has normal human

---

[2] Many Maslow pyramids available in textbooks and on the web include inferred descriptions of the five needs, often with some cultural bias. Maslow makes it clear that while he is treating these five needs as universal, that is, beyond cultural differences, "No claim is made that it is ultimate or universal for all cultures . . . Basic needs are *more* common-human than superficial desires or behaviors."

motivations that are being revealed to us, season by season, as we watch. Dexter is, as we all are hopefully, achieving what Maslow called "degrees of relative satisfaction."

To this point, we've dealt with these five needs as all-or-nothing categories in which you complete one fully and then move on the next, which is not entirely accurate. Maslow explains that one need can be satisfied, for example, only partially and that is sufficient for an individual to place importance on the next set of needs. To say that Dex is involved in some self-actualizing acts is not to say that he has totally, one hundred percent, met all of the four lower needs. He has met each of them to some extent, but only partially. And they fluctuate from time to time.

Season 4 presents new issues for Dexter; namely, how to juggle his many roles as husband, father, brother, friend, co-worker, and protégé (for a while to Trinity). He has doubts as to whether or not he can do it, unconscious doubts that manifest themselves in his visions of Harry. He remains steadfast that he can manage all these moving parts of his life. Maintaining his Code, even when he makes mistakes, is paramount. But let's face it, he's in dangerous territory now. In *Dexter*, the killers don't seem to treat their families that well. Brian (Rudy) ties his fiancé up to a table and tries to kill her. Miguel treats his wife coldly and then cheats on her. Trinity emotionally and physically abuses his wife and kids, despite his image as the perfect family man. Comparatively, Dexter looks pretty good, but the prospect of having a family is still fraught with many hazards.

Dexter's thoughts of suicide at the beginning of Season 5 indicate his mourning, guilt, and depression over Rita's death at the hands of Trinity. After that, Dex resumes feeding the Dark Passenger and realizes that he must stay strong for his kids' sake, and they also give him a reason to live. While I don't think we can say that Dexter is happy in any absolute way, he has his moments of happiness, such as when he holds Harrison and plays with him. The joy of parenthood, of being a father, still infuses happiness into Dexter's life despite all of the chaos that surrounds him. To tell whether or not Dexter is happy is a difficult task because he expresses his emotions differently from most of us. From what we have seen in Seasons 1 through 5, it seems that Dexter has a relatively happy, albeit complicated, life. As we've seen, Dex has moved up Maslow's hierarchy of needs and while with the death of Rita he risks retreating into his former ways of complete isolation, his children, Harrison first and foremost, will be his salvation.

Self-actualization is not about perfection and leading a totally happy life; it's about realizing one's potential in this brief time we have alive and achieving, experience by experience, moments of satisfaction, worth, and contentment.

Perhaps his biggest new challenge will be how to raise Astor and Cody, should they return from living with their grandparents, along with Harrison on his own. How will he deal with his son who may very well have the same urges that Dexter has, each having been baptized so young in his mother's blood? He will, no doubt, rely on his Code to see him through, but there must be more than that. The situation will require him to reach out to those he's close to—his friends and family—for help and support. Hopefully, he will move deeper into self-actualization in order to realize his full potential as a father and as a human being.

BODY PART V

Dexter's Bloodline

21
Dexter Unmasked

DEBORAH MELLAMPHY

> My name is Dexter. Dexter Morgan. I don't know what it was that made me the way I am, but whatever it was left a hollow place inside. People often fake a lot of human interactions, but I feel like I fake them all.
>
> —Dexter ("Dexter," Season 1)
>
> There are no secrets in life, just hidden truths that lie beneath the surface.
>
> —Dexter ("Crocodile," Season 1)

Dexter Morgan is a serial killer. You don't even have to watch the television show to know that.

Showtime's entire marketing campaign relies on advertising the show as one that centers on a serial killer. Posters and images invariably depict Dexter sprayed with blood, brandishing knives, coming into contact with dead bodies and limbs or "shushing" the audience, letting us know that we're in on the secret of his true identity. Taglines for the show—"America's Favorite Serial Killer," "Takes life. Seriously," and "A serial killer with a heart. . . . . Just pray it's not yours"—all flaunt the image of Dexter as serial killer.

People who haven't seen the show would expect that such a character would not be able to keep his secret safe for long because, as everyone knows, serial killers are "different"; they're outsiders, unlike the rest of us. Yet, those who know Dexter know how "normal" he appears to the other characters. He looks, acts, and sounds like an extremely hard-working, incredibly charming and likeable character. He has several friends amongst his co-workers at Miami Metro, including Angel and Masuka, who even throw him a bachelor party in Season 3. He also has a good relationship with his adopted sister Deb and is in a relationship with Rita and is close to her two children, Cody and Astor in the first four seasons. At work he is the "doughnut guy" who also joins a bowling team with his colleagues. In "All in the Family" (Season 3), he says that "pizza night" is the highlight of his week. He also gives a talk at "Dad's Day" in Cody's school in Season 2. Even Dexter's morning routine, shown in the show's opening sequence, is ordinary. He flosses, shaves, eats breakfast, and dresses just like everyone else.

But of course all this normality is simply a facade, constructed in an attempt to fit in with everyday society. Dexter has carefully designed and adopted the mask of normalcy to fool others, including the authorities and those closest to him, Deb and Rita. Following the revelation in Season 1 that Brian Moser/Rudy Cooper is his brother and Dexter's subsequent killing of Brian in compliance with Harry's Code, Dexter says:

> I drove away a brother who accepts me, sees me, for an adopted sister who'd reject me if she knew. . . . Sometimes I wonder what it would be like for everything inside me that's denied and unknown to be revealed. But I'll never know. I live my life in hiding. ("Born Free," Season 1)

This masquerade leads him to regularly ponder his sense of self and identity through voice-over and in his conversations, remembered or imagined, with Harry. Dexter persistently asks who he is. What is his true identity? Is it his hidden self, his everyday appearance or a combination of the two? Is it neither?

This links Dexter to philosophical questions that the brilliant minds have been trying to answer for millennia—what is a person's true identity, how is it formed, and how can we identify it? Since *Dexter* is a show about identity, truth, and masks, investigating the identities of the show's characters can help us to understand our own. Do we know who we really are?

Everyday Masks

> Human bonds always lead to messy complications . . . if I let someone get close, they'd see who I really am, and I can't let that happen. So, time to put on my mask.

> —DEXTER, ("Let's Give the Boy a Hand," Season 1)

We all have various "masks" that we wear in different social situations in the course of our day-to-day lives. For example, we act differently with our closest friends than with new acquaintances. Different situations and groups of people call for different "masks" or parts of our personality. We don't have split personalities, that's just how society works. Most of the time we're not even aware that we're doing it. That's also how killers are able to elude the police for years; they look and act like everyone else to the world at large.

Dexter embodies these conflicts but he is highly conscious of them and his are more pronounced. Dexter reveals to us that he believes the killer within him to be his "real" self and the everyday social personality to be the facade. We discover early in Season 1 that he crafted his everyday "persona" in childhood with the aid of his adopted father Harry Morgan. After rescuing Dexter as a child, Harry felt it necessary for Dexter to consciously construct the facade of an everyday person, with a normal life in order to fit in and to escape persecution. Instead of sending Dexter to therapy and attempting to control his behavior at an early age (as anybody else would naturally do), Harry guided the young Dexter to use his murderous instinct for good.

In a flashback, we see a teenage Dexter taking a girl to the prom, a rite of passage for young men in American society. In "Love American Style" (Season 1), Harry has a conversation with him about girls and dating, yet this is not the typical "father-son" talk, it's more of an instruction of how to appear normal.

"Shrink Wrap" (Season 1) reveals that perhaps Dexter might have benefitted from therapy. The burden of keeping his identity a secret is clear when he reveals himself to Dr. Meridian, a therapist whom Dexter is investigating due to the mysterious deaths of Meridian's patients. To Dexter's surprise, these sessions provide him with an opportunity to reflect on his life. In his last session he finally admits to Dr. Meridian, "I'm a serial killer. That feels so amazing to say out loud". When Meridian laughs the claim off as a joke Dexter continues, "I'm not joking. I kill people". Later in the kill room he tells Meridian "You helped me to accept what I really am. I'm grateful for that, but I was raised with a certain set of principles." This illustrates the separation between his two identities. He acknowledges that the personality that he projects isn't who he really is. This is also clear when he addresses himself in the third person, when he asks himself, "Where is the orderly, controlled, effective Dexter? How did I lose him? How do I find him again?" ("Waiting to Exhale," Season 2).

Dexter considers himself both a monster and a superhero. In the closing scene of Season 1, he fantasizes that his secret has been revealed and that he is considered a hero for his actions. In perhaps the most humorous scene of any season so far, he imagines himself walking through a ticker-tape parade, where admirers shout "You sliced him up good" and "Way to take out the trash, thanks buddy."

Dexter is highly duplicitous, as indicated by the secrecy surrounding many objects including his box of slides, his chest of weapons, and his apartment. He feels as if he can "take off" his mask in his apartment and (late in Season 4) in his garden shed. His panic when Doakes discovers his blood slides (his secret trophies) in Season 2 is clear. The discovery of the bodies of his victims and the subsequent investigation into the identity of the "Bay Harbor Butcher" brings Dexter closer than ever to being unmasked by the authorities. His panic throughout Season 2 is palpable as he frantically attempts to follow the latest findings in the case from Deb, who is part of the investigation.

Nietzsche's Masks

The German philosopher Friedrich Nietzsche can help us to better understand Dexter's dilemma. His theories can help us to comprehend Dexter's identity more fully and to relate it to ourselves in our own lives. Like Harry, Nietzsche was a firm believer in masks and considered them a necessary, justifiable, and unavoidable part of social life. For Nietzsche, "Mediocrity is the most successful mask the superior spirit can wear because to the great majority, that is to say the mediocre, it will not seem a mask."[1] Nietzsche's masks are the various aspects of our personality that we present to the world. He believes that all individuals express their "will to power" or reason for living, which will involve deception and the wearing of masks to avoid danger. The will to power constitutes life; "Where I found the living, there I found will to power; and even in the will of one who serves I found the will to be master"[2]

---

[1] Friedrich Nietzsche, *Human, All Too Human: A Book for Free Spirits* (Cambridge University Press, 1996), p. 352.

[2] Friedrich Nietzsche, *Thus Spoke Zarathustra: A Book for Everyone and Nobody* (Oxford University Press, 2005), p. 99.

In *Beyond Good and Evil*, Nietzsche describes masks as useful for the lower classes who need to represent themselves according to the conditions set in place by the ruling classes, in order to "blend in" with the middle classes and to stay alive. Dexter needs to do the same thing (on ethical and moral grounds) for he too would be sentenced to death if his secret was found out by the "ruling" class or authorities. Dexter's mask is both necessary and inevitable and must be carefully crafted and performed.

Nietzsche discusses masks not only in relation to the lower classes but to society in general; the everyday world is full of appearances. He proclaims that, "Every profound spirit needs a mask: what's more, a mask is constantly growing around every profound spirit, thanks to the consistently false (which is to say shallow) interpretation of every word, every step, every sign of life he displays."[3] Nietzsche praises the mask as a form of defense and self-preservation; everyone hides behind the mask of convention (everyone, that is, who wants to blend in with the rest of society). He praises such masks for their ability "to deceive other spirits and to dissimulate in front of them . . . the spirit enjoys the multiplicity and craftiness of its masks, it also enjoys the feeling of its security behind them" (p. 220). Nietzsche maintains that humans model themselves on others. They feel validated by believing what others believe. This allows them to belong and makes them feel less insecure.

Nietzsche also believes that man, as a social being, relies on social dress and deceptive masks to disguise immorality; individuals masquerade as moral and thus "normal" persons. He believes that these masks have become ingrained in society; "every surface is a cloak" (p. 122). Other philosophers have recognized this as well; individuals "simply cannot dispense with that masquerade which one calls clothes"[4] Dexter seems to have thought closely about how clothing is used as a metaphor for masquerade with the naked body representing truth. His victims are naked in each of their kill rooms, representing the "shedding" of their masks and the revelation that somebody knows their secrets.

Dexter's decoration of the kill rooms with photographs of each killer's victims points to each victim's knowledge of who they really are. These photographs serve as "audience" to the killing. The use

---

[3] Friedrich Nietzsche, *Beyond Good and Evil: Prelude to a Philosophy of the Future* (Cambridge University Press, 2002), p. 39.

[4] Sarah Kofman, *Nietzsche and Metaphor* (Athlone Press, 1993).

of clear plastic and cellophane is also significant—they are transparent, allowing each victim to see clearly their true identity as a killer. Dexter's killing of these individuals represents his own search for identity and his own desire to shed his mask and to appear "unclothed."

Dark Passengers

Nietzsche believed that the individual who loves masks "alone has the strength to look behind a mask to discover a man, the courage to mask himself in his individuality, and the playful innocence to choose a mask which not only hides, but represents him to the world."[5] This individual sees the masks that others wear and is able to look beyond these disguises. This seems true of the characters, throughout all four seasons, who see beyond Dexter's facade. These include Brian/Rudy and Doakes in Season 1, Doakes and Lila in Season 2, Miguel in Season 3, and Arthur in Season 4.

Each of these is also extremely conscious of how they themselves appear to others and are aware that they possess many different guises and personas. The most important of these is Doakes who suspects Dexter (as opposed to Brian) from the start. As an ex-Special Forces operative, Doakes is a trained killer who may be as bloodthirsty as Dexter and has inevitably murdered in the past. Doakes is also hiding the fact that he's having an affair with Kara Simmons, the soon-to-be ex-wife of a fellow officer. Since Doakes seems to be the only member of the police force who recognizes that Dexter consciously embodies various personas and he is extremely suspicious of him, even going so far as to spy on him in Season 2, he illustrates Nietzsche's point: those who are aware of their own masks are better able to recognize those of others. This is also true of Lila, in whom Dexter recognizes the lack of emotion he knows so well. "You're emotionally color-blind," he tells her.

> You use the right words, you pantomime the right behavior. But the feelings never come to pass. You know the dictionary definition of emotions. Longing, joy, sorrow. But you have no idea what any of those things actually feel like. ("The British Invasion," Season 2)

---

[5] Harold Alderman, *Nietzsche's Gift* (Ohio University Press, 1977).

Of all the other "villains" in *Dexter* who wear masks to disguise their alter egos, John Lithgow's character, Arthur Mitchell, is perhaps the most interesting as he appears to be an extremely "normal", church-going, family man. But he is revealed to be the "Trinity Killer," one of America's most prolific serial killers who has evaded the FBI for almost thirty years and who terrorizes and abuses his family within the confines of their home.

The fact that Arthur's identity has been kept secret for so long, even from his own family, illustrates how successfully a person can masquerade within contemporary society. Even the show's supporting characters know this, as they adopt various guises throughout the series. Angel disguises the breakup of his marriage. Deb puts on a brave face following the revelation that Brian is the Ice Truck Killer. In fact Deb's foul mouth can be read as a kind of mask that disguises her vulnerability. Rita appears to be strong in front of Cody and Astor in Season 1, following her husband Paul's release from prison. Even Harry, a police officer, is secretly harboring and managing a serial killer.

Dexter shows that we all wear masks and disguises and that doing so is not always a bad thing (as in the case of Rita, who pretends that everything is fine for the sake of her children). According to Sarah Kofman, Nietzsche realizes "how the removal of masks does not take one to the deepest level" of our true selves. For some, "she is but this veil itself" (p. 175).

So we need to ask, is Dexter just his veil? If masks are necessary and inevitable, is everybody "just this veil"? It may be that we all wear masks, but is there anything underneath them? Is there such a thing as "truth" about our identities?

True Blood

The very concept of masks implies that there is an opposition between reality and appearance and that there is an underlying truth that is hidden by the mask. Dexter, for example, believes that he has modeled his persona on normalcy. But Nietzsche would have doubts that there is an underlying truth that is more than a construction or fantasy. Dexter himself sometimes wonders whether there is anything beneath his mask; he asks himself, "If you play a role long enough, really commit, does it ever become real?" ("All in the Family," Season 3). Nietzsche was suspicious of empirical truth throughout his writing and begins *Beyond Good and Evil* by asking, "What in us really wants 'truth'?" He questions the value of truth through what can be called "perspectivism," the view that that our world, our opinions, and our beliefs are determined by our particular situation or outlook. For Nietzsche,

> there is only a perspective seeing, only a perspective 'knowing'; and the more affects we allow to speak about a thing, the more eyes, various eyes we are able to use for the same thing, the more complete will be our 'concept' of the thing, our 'objectivity'. (*On the Genealogy of Morality*, Cambridge University Press, 1994, p. 92)

In "Truth and Lie in the Extra Moral Sense,"[6] Nietzsche asks, "What then is truth? A mobile army of metaphors, metonyms, and anthropomorphisms . . . metaphors which are worn out and without sensuous power." Thus, everyone is inevitably bound to particular social, cultural, moral, and religious ideologies and so are their beliefs and identities. An individual's knowledge and truth, whether about the world or about themselves is never objective, as it is bound to their particular perspective. As a result, "truth" may be different for each of us; two people can have opposing views of the same thing because they have different perspectives and outlooks on life in general, on the situation, and on self.

The evolution of Dexter's character from bachelor, living on his own in Season 1 to married father, living with Rita and their three children in Season 4, to widower and again living on his own in Season 5 illustrates this changing nature of identity and truth. Dexter's shifting opinions of his relationship with Harry, Rita, and Deb also illustrate Nietzsche's perspectivism as new knowledge and information, as it comes to light, affects the core of Dexter and his relationships. As audience members, we too understand Dexter's identity in different ways as our perspective of his situation shifts.

Since there is no truth about the self, Nietzsche also rejects the idea that we can interpret the self. No individual can ever know completely or understand either ourselves or others and thus, every truth is only partial. Nietzsche rejects that "final" interpretations or truth itself exists, arguing that "truths are illusions we have forgot-

---

[6] Nietzsche, Friedrich, "Truth and Lie in the Extra Moral Sense," in *The Portable Nietzsche* (Penguin, 1982), pp. 46–47.

ten are illusions" (p. 47). According to this theory, it's impossible to ever understand any facet of our world or being.

Deeply Dissecting Dexter

Just like Dexter, we all also want to know "who we are." Self-help books, which are a multi-million dollar worldwide industry, attempt to teach us about who we are and how we can better ourselves. It is this conflict between what Dexter considers to be his "mask" and his "true self" that constantly leads him to question the "truth" of his own identity. He explains that he's not sure "where Harry's vision of me ends and the real me starts" ("Let's Give the Boy a Hand," Season 1). For Dexter, this is important because he wants to understand his unique place in the world.

His revelation in Season 1 that he "was born of blood" in the shipping container in which his mother was murdered when he was three years old gives him a way to understand, even justify, his behavior. In "Truth Be Told" (Season 1) Dexter says, "My mother was murdered before my eyes. It makes sense I choose a life where I find meaning in blood-when the sole memory I have of her is being covered in it." But we have to ask if this mask really excuses Dexter for the kind of life he chose.

Dexter's self-identity constantly changes according to his experiences. The many roles he plays and masks he wears—murderer, blood spatter analyst, husband, father, brother, friend, super-hero, victim—illustrate the complexity behind his search for understanding of himself. He comes close to understanding when he asks, "Am I evil? Am I good? I'm done asking those questions. I don't have the answers. Does anyone?" ("The British Invasion," Season 2). As Nietzsche challenged his readers, Dexter challenges his fans to question whether and how our identities can be more than various masks. Yet Dexter may have taken this question a step farther than Nietzsche by realizing that there is still a fundamental truth about each of us—one made up of many layers and many costume changes that are in fact the "truth" of everyday life.

22

Neither Man nor Beast

PHILLIP DEEN

> But he who is unable to live in society, or has no need because he is sufficient for himself, must be either a beast or a god.
>
> —ARISTOTLE, *Politics*, lines 1253a27–30
>
> I'm neither man nor beast; I'm something new entirely with my own set of rules. I'm Dexter.
>
> —DEXTER ("Let's Give the Boy a Hand," Season 1)

Every week, millions of people who are presumably not sociopaths tune in to watch the adventures of a serial killer. Inevitably, we're led to wonder if there's something really wrong with us. As a loyal viewer and someone who, it will soon become clear, has spent too much time thinking about this, I would like to believe that there isn't. I'll assume you feel the same way.

These opening remarks from Aristotle and Dexter express the tension that allows us to follow Dexter's exploits without immediately retreating to therapy. Dexter is a conflicted monster, one caught between the ethical life fit for humans who should live with one another and beastly desires that exclude him from the full company of humanity. He's murderous, yet like us. He's trying hard to be a good person, yet unlike us.

Dexter is a monster (a self-described "wooden boy") who aspires to be a real boy. This aspiration makes him interesting. He wants to do good, maybe, but he's unable to stop killing and channels his dark desires into socially beneficial acts of murder. In an earlier barbaric time, Aristotle asked why we do things that we know we shouldn't. He explained that there's a difference between being wicked and being morally weak. When confronted with an extreme example like Dexter, it's natural to wonder if he is really bad or, despite all the murdering, a morally strong person.

Being Bad Feels So Good

Aristotle developed the concept of moral weakness as a response to his predecessors Plato and Socrates. In Plato's dialogues, Socrates argues that virtue is ultimately a matter of knowledge or wisdom. People do virtuous things because they know them to be good, and they do vicious things when they are ignorant. We always act with some good in mind, but we may be wrong about what we're pursuing. When we eat chocolate cake for breakfast rather than a healthy, well-balanced meal, it's because we have made an error of knowledge. Like the person who thinks their hand is larger because it blocks out a distant sun, we mis-measure the goods of nearby delicious cake and distant health. If we truly knew which was the larger good, then we would pursue it. Vice is always a matter of ignorance.

But to Aristotle, and probably to many of us, that seems too simple. Often, we do bad things even when we know them to be bad. I may know that I shouldn't eat chocolate cake for breakfast and that health is a greater end to be pursued, but I eat it anyway. I act against my better judgment. To explain scenarios like that, Aristotle introduced the idea of moral weakness in Book VII of his *Nicomachean Ethics*—calling it *akrasia*, a lack of self-rule. He offers various explanations for why we act this way, but however we explain it, it certainly seems true that to know the good is not necessarily to do the good.

A person may be reasonable and know what ethics demands of them, but still succumb to temptation. Aristotle understood virtue to be a matter of our relationship to pleasure. The noble find pleasure in the proper things and to the proper extent; the base enjoy the wrong things and to the wrong degree. The difference between them is that the noble are governed by reason while the base have excessive desires that overstep their proper place in a good life. Moral strength—*enkratia*, the opposite of *akrasia*—is the ability to give our various pleasures their correct measure, to do what we know to be virtuous even when we're tempted.

The Self-Controlled Person

But there are degrees of moral weakness and strength. Aristotle lays out four (and a half) levels of moral weakness in descending moral worth. Our question is how far down Dexter falls on this continuum.

The best type of persons are those whose pleasures are properly ordered. The Greek term has been translated as 'moderate' or 'temperate'. They're not tempted by base pleasures because they know them to be base. They know what human excellence means and they act in accordance with that ideal without being burdened by their baser nature. These are the people who do not cheat, steal, or murder because they would find doing such things to be shameful and a violation of their integrity. Think of Dexter's and Debra's image of their father. He is their moral ideal, a committed police officer and family man. (Of course, Dexter discovers that Harry was not as perfect as he thought, forcing him to re-evaluate the Code.) Rita is also a self-controlled person; at least once she comes to take the proper amount of pleasure in sex and in being courageous (among other things).

The Morally Strong Person

Most people would probably place themselves in the second category—the morally strong person. Such people have excessive desires and must work to maintain their integrity. This distinguishes them from the self-controlled person:

> While a morally strong man has base appetites, a self-controlled man does not and is, moreover, a person who finds no pleasure in anything that violates the dictates of reason. A morally strong man, on the other hand, does find pleasure in such things, but he is not driven by them. (*Nichomachean Ethics*, lines 1152a1–3)

Morally strong persons know what it means to be virtuous and really want to be so, but are tempted by laziness, gluttony, rage and other vices of excessive desire. Under the right circumstances, they might get drunk or "let their anger get the better of them," but these lapses do not define them. In Dexter's world, Detective Sergeant Angel Batista is the morally strong man. He cheated on his wife, but it was an isolated act he deeply regrets. He sought the services of a prostitute, but out of weakness and loneliness. He gets into a bar fight with another cop, but only because his wife was insulted ("Hello, Bandit," Season 5). Otherwise, he is the fundamentally decent man that his name "Angel" ham-handedly indicates. Dexter even tells Angel, "If I had to choose a person, a real person to be like, out of anyone it would be you" ("Left Turn Ahead," Season 2).

The Morally Weak Person

Third is the morally weak person.

> Here a man who pursues the excesses of things pleasant and avoids excesses of things painful (of hunger, thirst, heat, cold and of anything else we feel by touch or taste), and does so not by choice but against his choice and thinking is called 'morally weak' without the addition of 'in regard to such-and-such,' for example 'in regard to feelings of anger,' but simply morally weak without qualification. (lines 1148a7–11)

In the famous words of Oscar Wilde, morally weak people "can resist anything but temptation." Their desires are in disarray and they lack the integrity of the virtuous person. While it is not a tight fit, this could describe Deb. Though she's an excellent police officer and able, at times, to maintain healthy personal relationships, Deb takes excessive pleasure in booze, paternal fidelity, sex, smoking and, of course, swearing. In this, she is a foil for Dexter's lack of emotion.

The Self-Indulgent Person

Fourth, Aristotle discusses a more extreme form of moral weakness we might call self-indulgence. A morally weak person rationally chooses what is virtuous or excellent, but habitually succumbs to excessive desire. But self-indulgent persons don't know what is virtuous, or at least don't care. They openly choose excess.

> A man is self-indulgent when he pursues necessary pleasures to excess, by choice, for their own sakes, and not for an ulterior result. (lines 1150a18–21)

Self-indulgent persons don't choose human excellence; they choose the pleasures of the body alone. At least morally weak persons regret their actions. "A self-indulgent man . . . feels no regret, since he abides by the choice he has made. A morally weak person, on the other hand, always feels regret" (lines 1150b29–31). The self-indulgent person does not feel regret, and is therefore incorrigible, for "a vicious man is not aware of his vice" (line 1150b35). Unlike the morally weak, who aspire to virtue, the self-indulgent are simply wicked. With a consuming love of power and advancement that leads her to ruin Esmé Pasquale's career, Lieutenant Maria LaGuerta is a possible candidate. But Vincent Masuka is a better fit. His love of all things perverse suggests that he is interested in pleasure above all else. (This decadence also makes him a personal favorite.)

The Beast and the Saint

To round out our survey, there's the brute, who may lie outside the very idea of what it means to be a human. Brutes do not desire what is proper for humans, those things that are pleasurable by nature. Rather, they come to desire what is vicious "through physical disability, through habit, or through an innate depravity of nature" (lines 1148b17–18).

Aristotle recounts brutish acts that we have a hard time imagining even Dexter committing: "the female who is said to rip open pregnant women and devour their infant; or what is related about some of the savage tribes near the Black Sea, that they delight in eating raw meat or human flesh, and that some of them lend each other their children for a feast; or the story told about Phalaris [the tyrant who roasted people alive inside a hollow brazen bull]" (lines 1148b20–23).

Those who are brutish by nature rather than habit or accident are called beasts. The beast does not fall within the scope of "morally strong" or "morally weak." Where nature bears the responsibility, there is no moral weakness. They are not oriented toward human excellence and those things it is natural and good for humans to desire. We don't blame rabid dogs. We just put them down. Or, in the case of the beastly, criminally insane people, we do not hold them morally accountable. We just lock them up forever.

In this chapter, I'll lump brutes and beasts together as 'beasts'. We can set aside the question of whether Dexter is naturally homicidal or was "nurtured" that way.

Now that we've identified the beasts, a word on saints. Aristotle also criticizes those at the opposite extreme who are miserly with regard to the necessary pleasures. "There is also a type who feels less joy than he should at the things of the body and, therefore, does not abide by the dictates of reason" (lines 1151b23–24). Aristotle did not find pleasure itself to be wicked. It's all a matter of our relationship to pleasure that makes us virtuous or vicious. Both excess and deficiency are vices. The virtuous person represents a mean between two extremes. The world-denying, ascetic saint would be wicked as well. But then, there have always been far more people who overindulge in bodily pleasures than those who underindulge, so we can forgive Aristotle for focusing on the former.

Locating Dexter on the Scale

And so the range of character types extends down from virtuous individuals who embody integrity and measure in their relationship to properly human pleasures, through the persons who are sufficiently strong to exhibit virtue (despite lapses), the weak persons who try but cannot resist excessive pleasure, the self-indulgent persons who openly choose excess, and the beasts whose desires are so in-human that weakness or strength does not apply. Where does Dexter fit? Because he's a serial killer, it's tempting to toss Dexter in with the beasts and be done with it. But, of course, if he were the type to sit down for a meal of roasted Cody and Astor, I suspect that ratings would plummet. It's not that simple.

Before getting to the hard cases, let's eliminate some of the relatively easy ones. Dexter is clearly not a saint, nor is he temperate as Aristotle understands it. From an early age, Dexter has had a Dark Passenger who makes him need to kill. He also clearly takes pleasure in killing, as shown by the ecstatic look of relief that comes across him as he kills. (For the sake of argument, let's assume that serial murder is not part of the excellent, virtuous life.)

We should also eliminate the possibility that Dexter is a self-indulgent person. This may seem odd, given that he is a serial killer, but "self-indulgent," as we have defined it, means that Dexter lacks both discipline and an interest in virtue and pursues unfettered pleasure. He does not take pleasure in many human pursuits, such as sociability and intimacy (though that is changing). In fact, with the one notable exception, Dexter is an ascetic. And even in the exceptional case of murder, he abides by a rigorous Code. For that reason, we may also say that he is not a morally weak person. His Code seems to have a sense of the ideal, but he does not give in to temptation as a matter of habit. He may kill, but he does not give in to base desires generally.

So that leaves only two possibilities. He's either a morally strong person who is tempted to do wrong but disciplines himself in the name of a rationally revealed moral ideal, or he is an exceedingly unusual beast. And there are good arguments on either side. Like Aristotle's savage cannibals, Dexter craves death and butchers bodies. Like the moderate person, he disciplines his dark desires.

Fine, I'm a Sociopath, but Do I Have to Feel Bad About it?

Both gods and beasts lack a conscience, but for different reasons. To have a conscience, we must feel conflicted. We want something base, but our "higher nature" tells us is would be wrong to indulge it. The philosopher Immanuel Kant imagines conscience as a judge determining guilt. We propose rules for behavior and the tribunal of Reason either approves or condemns. But if we are god-like, then we do not have base desires. If we are beasts, we do not judge them.

For the moment, let's assume that neither of us is a god or a beast. That means we are people who want to live excellently and succeed or fail in varying degrees. We are capable of regret, even if we're morally weak people who never live up to the ideals we hold. Let's also assume that we are intrigued by Dexter not simply out of perverse fascination or a vicarious desire to do horrible things to horrible people. We follow him because, in some way, we relate to his struggles. We know what it is like to have dark desires, to fake social interactions, to worry about what we would be like were we to become parents, and so on. (Perhaps I am projecting, but I'm going to go out on a limb and say that since you're reading a book with the words "Dexter" and "Philosophy" in the title, you probably think too much and had a hard time in high school.) And we worry about such things because we have a conscience. A perfect person would see Dexter as pathetic and disgusting and wouldn't watch. A beast would be off killing, raping, and otherwise sating its inhuman desires by watching *The Hills* and *Dancing with the Stars*.

But is Dexter really like us? Does he have a conscience? Ultimately, this is linked to whether or not Dexter is a sociopath, as he claims. In popular understanding, the defining quality of the sociopath is the absence of conscience. And it is conscience and discipline that separate the morally strong person from the self-indulgent and the beastly. Therefore, if we are to understand whether Dexter is morally strong or beastly, then we must address whether he has a conscience, that is, whether he feels the tension between the moral ideal and his desires.

At first blush, this seems easy to answer. If we know anything about Dexter, it is that he has a Code. Handed down by Harry, the Code tells Dexter what to do if he is to be good. But there is a deep tension running down the middle of it. The Code has two vital parts: 1. Kill only those who deserve it, and 2. Don't get caught. On the one hand, the Code tells him how to be moral. On the other, it tells him how to be prudent.

Philosophers make a lot out of the distinction between morality and prudence. The first tells is what we must do no matter what. The second tells us what to do if we are to get what we want. If someone doesn't murder the innocent because they know it do be wrong and they find fulfillment in doing what is right, we admire them. If we learn, however, that they really want to murder the innocent but they are afraid that the risk to their life, liberty, and loved ones is too great, then we usually don't. So whether Dexter is morally strong, and therefore whether we should admire him, comes down to whether he recognizes that we shouldn't kill the innocent is a good rule in and of itself, and not simply because it allows him to attain other things he wants.[1] When he does good, is it because he recognizes its goodness, or is it that doing good allows him to survive? Is he moral or merely prudent? This is the central ethical ambiguity in the series.

Let's sift through some of the evidence that Dexter is merely prudent. Even as a child, he resisted the impulse to kill because he "thought [Harry] and Mom wouldn't like it" ("Dexter," Season 1). Why shouldn't he be a bully? Because it's wrong, but also because people, like cops, notice bullies ("Let's Give the Boy a Hand,"

---

[1] Those who have taken Intro to Ethicss will note that I have completely dismissed utilitarians and other consequentialists who argue that the goodness of an action has to do with consequences only, and nothing to do with the governing duty or character of the agent. Yep, I have.

Season 1). Hearing of the Code, his sociopathic brother Brian asks, "Like an absurd avenger?" and Dexter replies "That's not why I kill" but it is left unsaid why he does ("Born Free," Season 1). Reflecting on his victims, he asks "How many bodies would there be had I not stopped those killers? I didn't do it to save lives, but save lives I did" ("An Inconvenient Lie," Season 2). When he confronts the Cutter at the end of Season 3, Dexter disabuses the Cutter of the notion that they kill for some higher purpose ("I Had a Dream"). These and countless other examples undercut our hope that we are rooting for a morally clean protagonist. Just as we start to see him as just like us, the writers remind us that he may not be the person we want him to be.

But there is evidence on the other side as well. For example, Dexter believes that there is a moral difference between himself and other serial killers. Dexter's self-perceived superiority is not because he desires the highest human good. He clearly enjoys killing. But he also prides himself that he is better than those who kill kids, telling his first televised victim "I have standards" and that the world will be "neater" and "better" place without him ("Dexter," Season 1). He tells himself "Without the Code of Harry I'm sure I would have committed a senseless murder in my youth just to watch the blood flow" and refers to his killing as "taking out the garbage" ("Popping Cherry," Season 1). His killing "brings order to the chaos, builds civic pride" ("It's Alive," Season 2). And he sees himself as picking up the slack when society fails to enforce the social contract ("Our Father," Season 3). Lastly, he considers himself better than Rita's ex-husband because Dexter does not harm the innocent and says "I am not like you" as he is strangling a pedophile ("The Lion Sleeps Tonight," Season 3).

Dexter believes that some good other than the pleasure of killing is being served, such as protecting children. When he accidentally kills an innocent man in Season 4, it "eats at him" and makes him "uncomfortable." When he judges the act, he catches himself and says "I don't do 'should haves,' that's not me." But Dexter does judge himself. Remorse, the Trinity Killer explains, is what "separates us from the animals. Your conscience is eating away at you." Dexter is left to ask himself, "If erring is human then remorse must be too. Wait, does that make me human?" ("Road Kill," Season 4).

That ambiguity between prudence and morality was brought to center stage when Dexter had to consider killing Sergeant James

Mother-F##king Doakes, an innocent man who had come to learn Dexter's true nature and would surely punish him for it. Dexter comes close to turning himself in, making arrangements with Deb and taking Rita and the kids out for one last day together. But, when Doakes is killed by the Lila ex Machina and Dexter is spared being punished for his crimes, he is deliriously happy and relieved, bouncing along handing out donuts to a department full of inexplicably sad officers.

But Will You Still Love Me Tomorrow?

Perhaps the greatest bit of evidence that Dexter is more than merely prudent is that he seems to value some people in themselves, instead as merely a means to keeping him safe. Over the course of the entire show, Dexter extends his sympathies further and further. A sociopath incapable of empathy, and therefore of conscience, couldn't pull that off. Let's catalogue the evidence again.

Dexter certainly claims to have no feelings, saying he is "a very neat monster" and like a donut box, "empty inside" ("Dexter." Season 1). He reiterates this supposed emptiness again and again: "I see their pain. On some level I even understand their pain. I just can't feel their pain" ("Crocodile," Season 1); "If I had a heart it might be breaking right now" ("Popping Cherry," Season 1); "That must be what love looks like. The inability to feel has its advantages. Sometimes" ("Love American Style," Season 1); Deb is "bighearted, kind, nothing like me" ("Return to Sender," Season 1); and, when told that something is human nature, he replies, "I'm not human" ("Waiting to Exhale," Season 2). (Phantom Brian replies, "No, just f##ked up.")

Because of this supposed lack of empathy, Dexter claims to be incapable of genuine relationships and must fake all human interactions. The obvious case is Rita. He begins dating her because having a girlfriend is "normal" and, therefore, good cover. She had the added advantage of being emotionally scarred and incapable of intimacy. He claims that he can't have intimate relationships because he is eventually unable to hack it and the other person leaves. "Every time I sleep with a woman she sees me for what I really am—empty—and then she's gone" ("Shrink Wrap," Season 1). Dexter's lack of understanding is often funny, as when he doesn't get Doakes's joke and says "I didn't know you were Jewish" or when he doesn't know how to comfort Rita when she is feeling insecure and, when she is crying from watching *Terms of Endearment*, tries to offer her oral sex. (Season 1, "Crocodile").

But Dexter can't be trusted when he claims to have no feelings. Like Doakes when he heard the claim, we can ask "Who's lying now?" ("There's Something About Harry," Season 2). Dexter seems to care about some people. He clearly wants to please Harry. When he concludes that his practice of killing was the cause of Harry's death, Dexter is devastated. He cares for his sister: "I don't have feelings about anything, but if I could have feelings at all, I'd have them for Deb" ("Dexter," Season 1). When given the chance to embrace sociopathy by killing Deb and joining his brother, he replies, "I can't. Not Deb. I'm very . . . fond of her" ("Born Free," Season 1). He grows to care for Rita and the children and modifies the Code to include killing those who threaten his family. Referring to friends and family, he says: "They're not just disguises anymore. I need them, even if they make me vulnerable" (Season 2, "The British Invasion," Season 2).

Dexter has a Code, but at times he wants to be free of it. After realizing Harry committed suicide over him: "I'm flying without a Code here. I can unleash the beast anytime I want. . . . It would feel f##king great" ("Left Turn Ahead," Season 2). In every season, we find Dexter wanting to establish genuine human relationships, whether with a brother (Brian), a girlfriend (Lila or Rita), a friend (Miguel Prado), or a son (the fittingly named Harrison). Brian, Lila, and Miguel each offered him the chance to be purely self-interested and to pursue his base desires. Each would allow him to be a pure and accepted monster. His brother Brian, lacking the presence of a father to instill a Code, is unconflicted and true to himself. In an ironic twist on Heidegger's idea of authenticity as Being-towards-death, Brian tells Dexter that he never has to apologize for what he does or who he is, that he could be his "real, genuine self" if he kills Deb. "You could be yourself around me" ("Born Free," Season 1).

But, each time, he chooses to be conflicted, caught between his desires and the Good. What does this tell us? Dexter likes being conflicted. He feels the Code's weight, but carries it anyway. Granted, he realizes that he must modify Harry's Code as he internalizes it—something familiar to all people as they separate themselves from their parents—but that is further evidence of what Dexter aspires to be. He doesn't want merely to be accepted for what he is, but for what he wants to be.

Becoming a Real Boy

When Aristotle said that beasts and gods are no part of a state, he meant more than they are excluded from voting, holding political office, and other signs of citizenship. For the ancient Greeks, there was no line between politics and morality. It was the very purpose of the government to care for the moral character of its citizens. Likewise, it was not possible to imagine a moral person outside the city-state. Beasts and gods live outside the walls of the city not only because it is dangerous out there, but because they are not part of our moral community. They are either strangely perfect or profoundly corrupt. Humans have to live among other humans.

Friedrich Nietzsche, philosophy's resident smart-ass, pointed out a third possibility in his *Twilight of the Idols*: "To live alone one must be a beast or a god, says Aristotle. Leaving out the third case: one must be both—a philosopher." But the question of whether Dexter is a philosopher is put off for another day.

Dexter is quite aware that he is not part of humanity, but he is desperately clawing at the walls of the city. Acknowledging his need to fake grief at a funeral, he reflects: "The willful taking of life represents the ultimate disconnect from humanity. It leaves you an outsider forever looking in, searching for company to keep" ("Popping Cherry," Season 1). Dexter also learns the burdens of community once he gets married, has a son, and moves to the suburbs.

The over-arching issue is whether Dexter is a morally strong person or a immoral beast—that is, whether he's the sort of person who rationally knows the Good and, for the most part, disciplines his base desires and does the Good or whether he is a monster who has no conception of the Good and, on the occasion that he does it, it is only out of self-preservation. The creators of the show clearly want to keep this question open, since it keeps bringing us back on Sunday nights. We could leave it at that, but what fun would that be? Rather, let's take the hard case and assume that Dexter really is what he claims to be: a sociopath who wants to be human.

The fact that Dexter is capable of caring for the happiness of others may prevent him from being a strict sociopath, but it does not necessarily mean that he is capable of knowing the moral ideal or aspiring to human excellence. He's still a murderer fueled by a horrible desire. At the same time, he is not simply a beast who has no inkling of the human good. It would appear that Dexter has outdone Aristotle in his understanding of moral weakness and the types of moral character. It may be that there is a type of person that falls into both categories, both man and beast. He is a morally strong beast.

How does he pull that off? By faking it. Recall the conversation Dexter had with the budding sociopath in the first season. He tells the teenager that he shares a young killer's lack of feeling, feeling nothing except when killing. How does he deal with it? "I'm empty, but I found a way to make it feel less bottomless. . . . Pretend. You pretend the feelings are there-for the world, for the people around you. Who knows? One day they will be" ("Circle of Friends," Season 1). Or recall his conversation with the Trinity Killer. Trinity asks Dexter whether thinks he is morally superior. Dexter replies, "No, but I want to be" ("The Getaway," Season 4). By acting like a good person, Dexter hopes to become one.

Morally strong persons know and appreciates the nature of human excellence and because of it, they discipline themselves. Their Code has been internalized. The beast simply acts without Code or judgment. As a sociopath, Dexter really does not appreciate the inherent value of innocent lives. But he really wishes he did. And, by pretending he does, he hopes that his actions will become habitual, part of his true nature.

For Aristotle, humans fall between god and beast. Dexter locates himself between beast and human. Is there room for a moral being in that gap? Is an internal sense of the Good necessary for goodness, or is it enough to act in accordance with the Good on the hope that some day it will be your own? Dexter abides with that hope. He believes that there's a chance, if he only tries hard enough, he will turn into a real boy.

Maybe so, but I wouldn't let my sister date him.

23

Dexter SPQR

JAMES F. PONTUSO

Dexter is a contemptible television show. It's debatable whether moral people should watch it, never mind write books about it. The lead character, Dexter Morgan, is an amoral sociopath who gets away with murder. Indeed, Dexter gleefully slays his immobilized victims. After taking them to a secure location, he stabs them – their blood oozing into their clear plastic restraints—and then carves up the bodies (thankfully off camera) for disposal. *Dexter* is all the more disturbing because it is so entertaining.

It's not immediately obvious why *Dexter* is enjoyable. At first blush, it could be that the Dexter-character is engaging because he is an outlaw-hero, one who goes beyond the law to pursue justice. But the anti-hero who bends the rules for worthy causes has become a hackneyed formula, one followed by almost every contemporary "superhero." In fact, the anti-hero as model is an old and well-worn idea tracing its lineage to Lord Byron's *Childe Harold's Pilgrimage* (1812) and *Don Juan* (1819) and through such iconic films as Clint Eastwood's *Dirty Harry* (1971) or Charles Bronson's *Death Wish* (1974). By itself, the bad-guy-doing-good-narrative would make Dexter more of a cliché than an interesting show. As Rudy explains to his brother Dexter, "You can't be a killer and a hero. It doesn't work that way!" ("Born Free," Season 1).

Another suggestion for the show's appeal is Dexter's lack of authentic emotion or empathy towards other people. As Pinocchio, the puppet who wants to become a little boy; *Star Trek*'s Mr. Spock, the half alien; and Data, the robot, indicate, the timeless quest to discover our inner humanity is oftentimes revealed best through those who do not have it.

Here again, we have followed the wrong path. Because of a trauma as a two-year-old in which he watched his mother dismembered by a chain saw and then was trapped amidst the blood and gore for two days, Dexter neither can nor desires to find an inner self. "No wonder I've been so disconnected my entire life. If I could feel, I'd have to feel . . . this," Dexter says to his brother ("Truth Be Told," Season 1). Rather than trying to become human, Dexter embraces his inhuman Dark Passenger, as he calls his compulsion to kill. Because Dexter does not have inner feelings of pity and remorse he is not psychologically unbalanced by homicidal activities. He's not like Pinocchio or Data wishing to become human. Even after the most heinous butchery, his emotionless "mechanical" heart allows Dexter "to sleep like a baby" ("Waiting to Exhale," Season 2).

Dexter occasionally wonders what it would be like to be like the people around him and he even pretends to be normal, but he finds it impossible to be like other normal folks.

> I find people around me are all making some kind of connection. Like friendship, or romance. But human bonds always lead to messy complications. Commitment, sharing, driving people to the airport. Besides, if I let someone get that close they'll see who I really am—and I can't let that happen. So time to put on my mask. ("Let's Give the Boy a Hand," Season 1)

Despite his emptiness, Dexter is not unbalanced. Rather, he is extraordinarily intelligent, as we learn from the suspicious Sergeant Doakes, who finds out that Dexter finished at the top of his class in pre-med but decided against life as a physician in order to become a forensic blood-spatter expert. We learn from Dexter's monologues that his chosen profession enables him to discreetly uncover the criminals he longs to slaughter. Dexter says that he "can kill a man, dismember his body, and be home in time for *Letterman*. But knowing what to say when my girlfriend is feeling insecure—I'm totally lost" ("Crocodile," Season 1).

Dexter's soliloquies confirm that he is rational in everything he does. He has no inner feelings, but he does have an inner voice, one that carefully weighs and assesses his actions. If Dexter has been damaged by his past, his infirmity is not derangement, untidiness, or carelessness, but rather cold, meticulous ferocity.

Dexter's most absorbing characteristic is the absence of an inner life. He does not truly experience love, pity, guilt, or remorse—although he sometimes identifies with and admires those with skills on a par with his own. Dexter is amoral, but what sets him apart from ordinary sadistic killers is that he follows strict ethical rules set down by Harry Morgan, the policeman father who adopted him. Dexter kills only when he has unquestionable proof that the victim is guilty of reprehensible crimes—ones that are unlikely to be punished by the legal authorities. Dexter gratifies his blood lust in a grotesque, yet socially responsible way—he follows the "Code of Harry." As Dexter explains that "there were so many lessons in the Code of Harry. Twisted commandments handed down from the only God I ever worshipped" ("Our Father," Season 3).

Nietzsche's Bay Harbor Beast

Harry Morgan recognizes the killer in Dexter when he is just a boy. The policeman knows that people with Dexter's urges can never be changed or cured. Instead of trying to make Dexter normal, Harry teaches the boy skills necessary for survival: stealth, concealment, and disguise. Dexter learns to carefully pick his victims. Not only must they be culpable of odious misdeeds, ones they are likely to repeat, they must also be the kind of people who won't be missed by friends or relatives. Harry shows Dexter how to kill and dispose of the remains without leaving behind incriminating evidence. Harry's Number One rule is: "Don't get caught," a lesson he hammers home by taking the eager teenage Dexter to witness an execution in the electric chair.

Harry can't make Dexter normal, so instead he teaches the boy to fit in. Harry insists that Dexter behave as if he were the product of an average suburban upbringing. He smiles during family photos, plays sports without resorting to confrontation or violence, appropriately teases his younger sister without really hurting her, and pretends to be having a good time at school outings, all the while silently imagining how best to slaughter those he is with. Dexter even passes a psychological exam by thinking about the answer that first enters his head and responding in exactly the opposite way. "People fake a lot of human interaction, but I feel like I fake them all" ("Dexter," Season 1). Harry's so successful at making Dexter average that he would outscore Supermen's Clark Kent on the Geek meter.

Harry seems to have understood Nietzsche's argument that "the real meaning of culture resides in its power to domesticate man's savage instincts."[1] But why would Harry permit and even promote such amoral behavior? Perhaps if we comprehended the origin of morals, we would get a better understanding.

Conscience and Guilt

Unlike most people, Dexter does not seem to have a moral sense. He does not feel the pangs of conscience when he commits acts of cruelty. Nietzsche would argue that Dexter is not abnormal. The sense of guilt and regret that most contemporary people experience after having done something wrong is certainly not a sentiment imprinted on our souls. Rather, the human experience of guilt developed historically as a consequence of successfully taming our animal instincts.

Nietzsche begins by asking how it is possible for animals to keep promises. Of course animals cannot keep promises, because they never make any. Human beings need to make promises because their actions are not motivated by pure instinct. They do not have to eat when they are hungry or drink when they are thirsty. They can say one thing and do another. Humans need not behave in a straightforward manner, making it possible for them to mislead. Because humans can deceive, they need to make promises to each other not to deceive. They must swear to keep their word. But in order to keep their promises they must bind their future actions with their present words. To adhere to their words, humans must propel themselves into the future and control their actions in a time that does not yet exist. How then did the peculiarly trait of forethought arise in humans?

In the beginning, Nietzsche claims, there was no guilt. People just did as they pleased and felt no remorse for stealing, killing, lying, or cheating. They made promises and reneged on them with no second thoughts or regrets. Nietzsche explains the primitive compulsion that is similar to that which overcomes Dexter on those nights when he pursues his victims:

> **For these same men who, amongst themselves, are so strictly constrained by custom, . . . tenderness, . . . and friendship, when once**

---

[1] Friedrich Nietzsche, *The Birth of Tragedy and the Genealogy of Morals* (Doubleday, 1956), p. 176.

they step outside their circle become little better than uncaged beasts of prey. Once abroad in the wilderness, they revel in freedom from social constraint. . . . They revert to the innocence wild animals; we can see them returning from an orgy of murder. . . . and torture, jubilant and at peace with themselves as though they had committed a fraternity prank. (*Genealogy of Morals*, p. 174)

How then did bad conscience come to be? Unlike the Biblical account, Nietzsche argues, guilt did not arise because the first humans consumed fruit forbidden by the deity. Rather, when people started living together they needed some kind of rules. The regulations were simple and fierce. We can imagine that if thieves were caught they lost a limb, murderers lost their lives, and adulterers suffered equally harsh treatment.

These conventions were not meant to reform the guilty or even to prevent crime; they simply were ways in which primitive societies compensated the party who had been wronged. What did the aggrieved person receive? According to Nietzsche's account, the great good of seeing another person suffer was a compensation for the injured party. "My crops are ruined but I will feel better about it after hearing the bandit squeal in pain," Nietzsche's archaic people might have thought.

Those punished felt little guilt for their misdeeds; they accepted their penalty as "if some terrible unforeseen disaster had occurred, if a rock had fallen and crushed" them (p. 215). Dexter is very much like these pre-morality primitives. He does not feel guilt and is surprised that he feels some shame for making a mistake. "A changed man at peace with himself. Maybe only monsters feel no regret." Dexter wonders to himself, "If erring is human, then remorse must be too. Wait—does that make me human? Huh!" ("Road Kill," Season 4).

At some point, Nietzsche argues, people began to engage in cost-benefit analysis. They tried to avoid the pain associated with violating the rules. But what happened to the natural animal instincts? What happened to the desire to take what one pleases— to rape, plunder, and murder? No longer able to inflict these urges outwardly on external foes, civilized humans turned their passions against themselves. Nietzsche explains:

Hostility, cruelty, the delight in persecution . . . all turned against their begetter. Lacking external enemies and resistances, and confined

within an oppressive . . . regularity, man began . . . persecuting, terrifying himself, like a wild beast hurling itself against the bars of its
cage. This languisher . . . who had to turn himself into an adventure,
a torture chamber . . . became the inventor of "bad conscience." Also
the generator of the greatest and most disastrous of maladies, of
which humanity has not to this day been cured: his sickness of himself, brought on by the violent severance from his animal past. (p. 215)

Morality is the unique human capacity to decide what ought to
be done. Moral codes guide us in making choices in the present and
dictate how we should behave in the future. Morality often inhibits
our longings and desires; it tells not to be gluttonous, lascivious,
egotistical, or cruel. Since the baser inclinations are powerful, we
need a supernatural ally to help tame them. Nietzsche explains:

The phenomenon of an animal soul . . . taking up arms against itself,
was so novel . . . that the whole complexion of the universe was
changed thereby. This spectacle . . . required a divine audience to do
it justice. It was a spectacle too sublime and paradoxical to pass
unnoticed on some trivial planet. (p. 215)

Nietzsche's analysis reverses the traditional order of the moral
universe. For him, it was not God who provided moral commandments to control the baser aspects of human nature, but the inner
compulsion of humans to justify the cooping up of instincts that
created both God and the metaphysic of morality. Moreover, there
is a clear path from the *Genealogy* to Sigmund Freud's concept of
the sublimation of the Id for the sake of the Ego and Superego.
Dexter, of course, never really learned as a child to sublimate his
deepest drives, he only pretended to. Reflecting on his childhood
Dexter says, "Role playing—such an important part of growing up.
When we were kids, whatever role Deb assigned me: evil monster,
treacherous Nazi, horrible alien, I played them to perfection" ("All
in the Family," Season 3).

If Nietzsche's social anthropology of archaic societies is accurate, it is evident why ancestor worship has been so widespread in
almost all societies. Those who established the first conventions
actually created human consciousness. Without such rules humans
would simply do whatever came into their heads. Perhaps it is this
realization that makes Dexter so loyal to the Code of Harry. "Harry
taught me to lie and keep my darkest secrets from those around

me" ("The British Invasion," Season 2), he says. "He taught me to hide, and that's what kept me safe" ("Let's give the Boy a Hand," Season 1). Without Harry's Code, Dexter's Dark Passenger would have gotten him killed.

But how do we pay back our forbearers for the ability to think in temporal ways? How do we repay the debt of being human? Nietzsche claims that rituals venerating founders become more elaborate, complex, and awe inspiring until ancestors become gods. Yet the capacity of people to stage ever-more sophisticated ceremonies only shows how far civilization has advanced, making the debt to past generations who established civilization's beginnings even greater. People feel guilt because they can never pay back what is owed to the godlike founders. Civilization's advances establish an unfunded mandate of guilt.

Here Christianity developed its most important and powerful principle. Christ the redeemer absolved humans of their sins.

> We come face to face with that paradoxical . . . expedient which brought temporary relief to tortured humanity, that most brilliant stroke of Christianity: God's sacrifice of himself for man. God makes himself the ransom for what could not otherwise be ransomed; God alone has power to absolve us of a debt we can no longer discharge; the creditor offers himself as a sacrifice for his debtor out of sheer love (can you believe it?), out of love for his debtor. (*Genealogy*, p. 225)

Who can repay such a selfless deed as this, who but the almighty? Human beings are driven ever further into guilt and despair. They can never live up to the example of a crucified Christ. They can never rid themselves of the debt and must perpetually submit to humbly obeying divine commands that require the taming of their strongest passions.

Christianity changed the way people thought about their lives. It turned them inward, making them aware of their inner thoughts, not merely their outer actions. In the New Testament St. Paul denigrates the outer physical self and celebrates the inner spirit which is closer to God.

> For we know that the law is spiritual: but I am carnal, sold under sin.
>
> For that which I do I allow not: for what I would, that do I not; but what I hate, that do I.

> If then I do that which I would not, I consent unto the law that it is good.
>
> Now then it is no more I that do it, but sin that dwelleth in me.
>
> For I know that in me (that is, in my flesh,) dwelleth no good thing: for to will is present with me; but how to perform that which is good I find not.
>
> For the good that I would I do not: but the evil which I would not, that I do. (Romans 7:14–25)

Dexter is certainly aware that there are standards of good and evil. But since he does not believe in God—in fact doesn't "believe in anything"—and cannot rid himself of his compunction, he utterly rejects New Testament morality ("The British Invasion," Season 2). "I'm Dexter. I'm not sure what I am. I just know there's something dark in me. I hide it. Certainly don't talk about it, but its there. Always. This Dark Passenger" ("An Inconvenient Lie," Season 2).

Nietzsche explains that the psychological and metaphysical effects of Biblical religion both deepen and weaken the human soul. The Biblical God is universal and perfect. Such a doctrine undermines civil religion, as it did the pagan religions of the ancient world. The laws and traditions of a nation no longer define what is right or wrong. Instead, individuals are personally responsible for observing the moral codes commanded by the deity. Biblical religion intensifies anxiety, for people are continually led to wonder whether their actions and even thoughts live up to the example embodied in a perfect being—what was once consciousness become self-consciousness. Humans owe a duty, not just to their family, friends, and country, but—following Christ's example—to all people.

As for these Christian virtues of empathy and compassion, Dexter is a man out of season: "Most people have a hard time dealing with death—but I'm not most people. It's the grief that makes me uncomfortable. Not because I'm a killer. Really I just don't understand all that emotion, which makes it hard to fake. In those cases, shades come in handy" ("Popping Cherry," Season 1). Nor will Dexter have anything to do with the humane principles originated by Christianity and preached by the human rights doctrine of the contemporary era. Peace and pity aren't high on his to-do list. As he puts it, "I've never been great at conflict resolution—not without a blade and several rolls of plastic wrap" ("Easy as Pie," Season 3).

What Have the Romans Ever Done for Us?

Edward Gibbon became controversial for maintaining that Christianity undermined the martial spirit of Rome, leading ultimately to the collapse of the empire. So formidable were the Roman legions that until the time of the Napoleonic Wars, military historians debated whether they could defeat armies equipped with firearms. Much has been written about the tactics and discipline of perhaps the greatest fighting force in history, but few people have considered the psyche of the legionnaires. Roman soldiers were highly disciplined and well-trained warriors, proud of their ability to dispatch an opponent with a thrust of the Gladius—the short sword that conquered the world.

Although fierce in combat, Roman soldiers had a strong sense of civic duty and loyalty to the ancient laws of Rome. There was little guilt or remorse for the carnage they visited on their enemies. Roman soldiers did not fall prey to anxiety and doubt about their brutality toward others. If they wondered at all about the rightness of their actions, they were comforted by a religion that justified their conduct. Since Roman deities were gods of the city, the fate of the legionnaires' souls was measured by the success of Rome.

Poor Dexter was born in the wrong age. Had he been a Roman, he would not have been a social outcast; a monster, as he calls himself. No one would have noticed that he lacked an inner life or conscience, since hardly anyone else had one. Those few who understood the shortcomings of dedication to a civil religion pretended to be average citizens and "with a smile of pity and indulgence," says Gibbon, "they diligently practiced the ceremonies of their fathers."[2]

Dexter too practices an ironic devotion to the lessons of his father. He too disguises his true intentions. As he puts it, "Harry taught me that. Secrecy. Self-reliance. And a well stocked cupboard of Hefty bags" ("Seeing Red," Season 1).

Instead of prowling around at night to fulfill his yearning, he would have joined the legions where the opportunity for slaying was ever-present. Dexter would not have to live by a secret Code. In the legions Dexter would have enjoyed the camaraderie of other born killers who, like Miguel Prado, would have seen him for what

---

[2] Edward Gibbon, *The Decline and Fall of the Roman Empire*, Volume 1, Chapter 1, <http://ancienthistory.about.com/library/bl/bl_text_gibbon_1_1_3.htm>.

he "truly was" and instead of being "repulsed" would have been "proud" of his friendship ("Turning Biminese," Season 3). Rome would have channeled Dexter's passions and celebrated his dedication to the "fathers" of Rome—its ancient ethical code. Rather than the imaginary parade that Dexter fathoms up in "Born Free," the final episode of Season 1, he would have been honored by thankful citizens for his skillful blood-letting—perhaps even with a real parade through the center of Rome. After all, he would have been completely justified in slaughtering the enemies of the Senate and People of Rome (SPQR—Senatus Populus Que Romanus).

The Ethics of Dexter's Appeal

One of the greatest texts on moral philosophy written in the ancient world, Aristotle's *Nicomachean Ethics*, really wasn't about morals at all. The *Ethics* certainly teaches a code of conduct, but the rules laid out have to do with conduct not conscience; the principles have more to say about what people do than what they think; more about outward behavior than inner motivations. Perhaps Dexter is so entertaining because he is an ethical, if not a moral man. He follows rules, which, although far from humane, do aim at Aristotle's highest ethical principle—justice.

Or maybe there's something darker in Dexter that appeals to us. We live in an age when the public philosophy promotes peace, humanity, co-operation, kindness and respect for all things, even objects without consciousness such as trees and glaciers. Contemporary morality demands that we treat everyone alike without consideration of outer qualities. But by concentrating on what is most common among us, we actually might promote what is lowest and least attractive in us. Nietzsche worries that "the leveling and diminution of . . . man is our greatest danger; because the sight of him makes us despondent." It could be that in such an age we secretly crave what Nietzsche craved, that "if there are any such in the realm beyond good and evil grant me now . . . the sight of something perfect, wholly achieved, happy, magnificently triumphant, something still capable of inspiring fear!" (*Genealogy of Morals*, p. 177).

Personally, I hate to think that Dexter merely represents destruction for its own sake. Perhaps instead, Dexter is so appealing because, even though he's a serial killer, there is something decent, even noble about him. As Deb says, "You are the only one I can count on, jack ass!" ("There's Something about Harry," Season 2). Since I'm such a fan of the show, I like to think of Dexter in a place where he could thrive. He really would be better off in the legions: Dexter SPQR.

24

Dexter's Look

REBECCA STEINER GOLDNER

The series premiere of Dexter opens with the title character cruising the city of Miami, looking . . . watching. Within two minutes, Dexter is demanding of his victim that he "look!"; "open your eyes and look at what you did!"; "look or I'll cut your eyelids right off your face!" ("Dexter," Season 1).

Scenes like this are repeated throughout the series; Dexter looking, observing, and demanding that someone both recognize and become accountable for what he's done. Dexter's relationship to other humans is often defined by this looking, followed by his call for shame, recognition and responsibility. He reduces the other to an object before his eyes, to a body on a table, to a thing to satisfy Dexter's own needs and purposes.

In his foundational work *Being and Nothingness*, Jean-Paul Sartre describes the relationship between human subjects as antagonistic, hostile, and limiting, and his exploration of this relationship begins in the moment when one subject sees another. The other, for Sartre, is always a limit to my freedom, to my possibilities; the look of the other crystallizes me into something fixed, nameable, and un-free. Though on some level I crave and seek out this identification, insofar as the other limits me to it, I resent and am ashamed of it. When Dexter reduces his victims to rapists, murderers, pedophiles and abusers, he likewise restricts their freedom, and he does so not only with duct tape and plastic wrap, but by robbing them of their possibilities, by stealing from them the openness of their existence, of their choices.

267

Bad Faith

The basic premise of existentialism, Sartre says in the essay "Existentialism Is a Humanism," is that "existence precedes essence."[1] But what does this confounding claim actually mean? It means that we are, that we exist, before we are any given thing. It means that we do not have "a nature" or any "essential identity" or "destiny." It means that from the moment we exist, we are radically, painfully, free, and that, as such, we are responsible for each and every choice we make and activity in which we engage. It means that I can't excuse my behavior by saying, as Dexter might, that I was "born that way" or that my childhood or past "made me that way." However, Sartre tells us, this freedom is not liberating, it is frightening and overwhelming. "We are condemned," Sartre writes, "to be free." Human existence is a constant tension of the desire to simply be something, as a table is simply a table, and our ability to go beyond that, to escape what we are, and to choose our world and ourselves. Bad faith is the primary way in which we try to be some one thing.

Sartre uses a number of examples to illustrate his concept of bad faith. The common theme to all of these examples is the central claim of bad faith, that "we have to deal with human reality as a being which is what it is not and which is not what it is."[2] Understanding this claim, which looks self-contradictory but is actually quite meaningful, is essential to understanding bad faith and Sartrean freedom. It is also a perfect description of Dexter himself.

Sartre describes a waiter in a café like this:

> His movement is quick and forward, a little too precise, a little too rapid. He comes toward the patrons with a step a little too quick . . . all his behavior seems to us a game . . . he is playing at being a waiter in a café. There is nothing there to surprise us. The game is a kind of marking out and investigation . . . the waiter in the café plays with his condition in order to realize it. (Being and Nothingness, pp. 101–02)

The waiter in the café, in one sense, is a waiter in a café. It is his job, he does his job sufficiently well, and he is recognized by those

---

[1] Jean-Paul Sartre, "Existentialism," in *Basic Writings of Existentialism* (Modern Library, 2004), p. 344.

[2] Jean-Paul Sartre, *Being and Nothingness* (Washington Square Press, 1992), p. 100.

around him as being a waiter. However, the waiter in the café is, in another sense, not a waiter in a café. There is some part of the waiter that is able to step back, outside, or beyond his role as waiter and be aware of himself as a waiter. And, insofar as a part of the waiter is engaged in thinking about himself as waiter, that very part escapes being a waiter. Unlike a table, or a water bottle, which can be nothing beyond a table or a water bottle, simply because the waiter is able to reflect, question, affirm, doubt or deny that he is a waiter, he is not (merely, or only) a waiter. In this way, the waiter is not what he is (a waiter).

For the most part, however, the waiter ardently desires to be a waiter; he yearns for an identity. The identification "waiter" provides for his life a meaning, a paycheck, a structure, and a situation that determines most or many of his choices. Should he get up at 6:00 A.M. when his alarm goes off? Yes, because he is a waiter, and being a waiter means arriving at work in time to set the tables. For Sartre, without the structure provided by an essential identity (waiter, teacher, even serial killer), our lives threaten to overwhelm us with the openness of the possibilities, with the anguish of our own radical freedom. If the waiter is not a waiter, he is free to sleep through his alarm, to deny that the alarm has any meaning for him at all, to leave Paris altogether, to abandon all responsibility.

Is Dexter in bad faith? Like the waiter in the café, Dexter is playing a role: caring, kind, polite brother/boyfriend/police analyst. Dexter, however, as we learn through the voice over narratives, is well aware of his role-playing. "People fake a lot of human interactions," he tells us, "But I feel like I fake them all. And I fake them very well. And that's my burden, I guess" ("Dexter," Season 1). These moments of self-awareness, of reflection on his own activities, are what Sartre refers to as pre-reflective consciousness. In our everyday interactions with the world "consciousness is consciousness of something" (p. 23). Our basic, usual, conscious activity is located in the way in which we are directed towards objects, it is always a relational activity directed at some thing in the world. When I think, I think about some object. If I doubt, I doubt the existence of some object or idea. Pre-reflective consciousness, on the other hand, takes up the activity of being conscious in the place of the object; it takes the thinking, doubting self as object. When Dexter reflects, through the voice-over narratives, on his inclinations, his past, or his activities, he takes himself as object.

Unlike most people, however, Dexter is fully aware of his role-playing, and that the identities into which he forces himself—Deb's supportive brother; Rita's caring boyfriend; Miami Metro's diligent blood spatter analyst—are choices that he must work to sustain at every moment. Dexter is constantly aware of the possibility that he could (and often does) behave completely differently—even in contradictory ways—from that other Dexter. Does his awareness that he is merely "playing at" being Dexter allow us to claim that Dex is not in bad faith? We'll get there.

Dexter as Master

Faced with endless, open possibilities and choices, we flee into essential identities that define and limit us. This wish, however, that a series or pattern of activities could crystallize us into a "thing", something which simply is, can ultimately backfire on us when we encounter the other. While my freedom might be apprehended in anguish, Sartre says, "by the mere appearance of the Other, I am put in the position of passing judgment on myself as on an object, for it is as an object that I appear to the Other." (p. 302). Dexter's victims see themselves in many ways; some are hardened criminals, others are upstanding citizens who believe they possess a fatal flaw that drives them to molest, rape, or kill. Rarely, however, do they confront themselves with the kind of reckoning they undergo on Dexter's table. Each of these criminals has, until Dexter enters their lives, enjoyed a kind of freedom—the freedom to get away with bad acts, to behave one way but often be seen as something else by society. When Dexter turns his gaze upon them, however, they are robbed of this freedom, the freedom to change, reform, start anew—all of this is taken from them from the moment we see Dexter begin to watch. As Harry tells the young Dexter "When you take a man's life you're not just killing him, you're snuffing out all the things he'll ever become" ("Popping Cherry," Season 1).

Dexter is rarely mistaken in his choice of victims. Most famously, perhaps, the events of Season 3 are inaugurated by a mistaken, hasty kill, but, in general, as his audience, we can be fairly certain that when Dexter begins investigating a victim, we will see it end in blood. Whatever else these people might be—teachers, nurses, car salesmen, valets, district attorneys—when Dexter begins to watch them, to him and to us they take on one essential identity: criminal. All other possibilities narrow to the point of invisibility, so that in spite of their promises to change, to reform, or claims that they can't help themselves, that they're sick, Dexter forces them to reckon with what they are. He has documented their acts, and the acts can't be denied or taken back. Thus, instead of a human being with open, endless possibilities, the acts that confirm their guilt become their definition.

A paradigmatic example, Matt Chambers, the drunk driver from the episode "Crocodile," has changed names and cities after every incident where he killed someone. There's a Sartrean freedom in this; he re-creates himself anew in every place he goes and does not allow the obligations and exigencies of a life to trap him into some chosen identity. When Dexter begins to observe him, however, Matt's freedom is taken from him—he will never go to a new city, assume a new name, kill another person. He is a drunk driver. That's all. He's trapped in the identity he did not and would not have chosen. Thus, it is Dexter who becomes the source of his identification. Typically, in bad faith, I choose the identity into which I flee and I require that the other confirm or validate me in this identity. Dexter, however, as often happens in the encounter with others, limits his victims to precisely the very identity they deny as being essential to them. To the other, I am just a thing—a particular kind of thing, yes, but a thing in the sense of an object, one among many. The look of the other robs me not only of my possibilities to be something else, but it also takes from me the belief that I am the foundation of my own world, that I am the one in control.

This loss of control starts with being watched. Being looked at presents me with the suggestion that the world is not entirely my own or of my own making. Dexter, from the moment he chooses a victim, controls the world of that person. When the victim realizes he has been under observation—should this moment occur on the kill table or even before it—he realizes, as Sartre says, that "I am no longer master of the situation" (p. 355). To be looked at, then, is far more than merely to be seen, it is to be reduced, objectified, and threatened. Even if the one watching you is not a serial killer, the fact that the other robs you of your possibilities and steals the world from you is sufficient to signify that the encounter with the other is a danger to you. As Sartre writes and Dexter well knows, the look can be given not just by someone turning their eyes on me, but by "a rustling of branches, or the sound of a footstep followed by silence, or the slight opening of a shutter, or a light movement of a curtain" (p. 346), and the result is the sudden awareness that I am being looked at. What occurs to me, upon this awareness, is "that I am vulnerable, that I have a body which can be hurt" (p. 347). Indeed when that noise behind you, that rustling in the bushes, or that man staring at you from the family minivan is Dexter, you will surely end up hurting.

Caught in the Act

Dexter's goal, however, is not merely to hurt. Dexter's ends in his vigilantism are complex, and involve his own need for blood, a perverted sense of justice, and penchant for control and authority, but also a need for the victim to see herself for just what she is. Dexter accomplishes this by plastering the walls of his kill room with pictures, pieces, or other reminders of those his victim has hurt and harmed. He enhances their vulnerability by binding the victim on the table naked, a symbolic act, which further reduces the victim to her object-self, to her body, and physically limits all possibilities. According to Sartre, however, such acts on Dexter's part are ornamental, because Dexter's look alone would be sufficient to cause some degree of shame in the victim.

Sartre describes a scene in which one has been caught listening at a door and looking through a peephole. When he assumed the hallway was empty, the peeper was completely caught up in the act of peeping, unaware of himself and completely directed towards the scene on the other side of the door. "But all of a sudden" Sartre writes, "I hear footsteps in the hall. Someone is looking at me! What does this mean?" (p. 349). It means that he has been seen, caught in the act and identified as a peeper. Dexter's victim's likewise assume a veil of privacy in their crimes, and if caught in the act by Dexter, they, too, react with horror, shock, and shame.

To Sartre, shame is the almost inevitable result of being seen. While in bad faith I might flee from my freedom and try to limit myself, when the other successfully identifies me as being something—a peeper, a rapist, a murderer (or even something positive, like a police officer or a loving mother)—I react with shame— shame that I am not that free and open possibility which is the mark of the human subject. In Season 5, when Lumen inadvertently watches Dexter kill Boyd Fowler, she catches him in the act and he reacts with horror, not simply because Lumen represents the threat of being caught, but also the shame of being identified as something at all. To the other, I am a mere thing in the world, I am a peeper as the table is merely a table, with no chance of escape. "Shame reveals to me that I am this being" Sartre tells us (p. 351). Shame makes me be "somebody" as opposed to an endless stream of possible otherwises, and, as such, it tries to locate my essence on par with my very existence.

"My shame," Sartre writes, "is a confession" (p. 350), and it is this confession that Dexter hopes to elicit from his victims, explicitly or tacitly. Dexter sees who the victim is, when often they have tried to hide this from the world, and he demands of his victim, through various methods, that the victim, likewise, recognize who he himself is. "Shame" Sartre tells us further, "is shame of self; it is the recognition that I am indeed that object which the other is looking at and judging" (p. 351) and that my freedom, that which demarcates me as a human subject, has its limits in a world that contains other people. The look of the other forces me to see myself from outside, from beyond myself, and to see myself as fixed, or as having a "nature"(p. 352). Dexter's victims often try to deny that they are what Dexter has identified them to be. In one sense, they are correct in that the freedom that is the heart and structure of the human subject is open to them—they could change their ways, reform. But by identifying them as a criminal, and as one unlikely to change, Dexter not only utilizes shame to objectify them based on their pasts, but to demand that they hold themselves responsible for those pasts. The fixed past and the open future create an almost insurmountable tension when brought to a head on Dexter's table.

Look at What You've Done!

This tension, between our freedom and what Sartre calls our facticity (the ways in which we are actually fixed and limited, which include the past), are identified by Sartre in an example quite relevant to Dexter. "We are readily astonished and upset when the penalties of the court affect a man who in his new freedom is no longer the guilty person he was" Sartre tells us (p. 107). A criminal who has recognized his radical freedom to not be what he was is a reformed, changed criminal. "But at the same time" Sartre goes on, "we require of this man that he recognize himself as being this guilty one" (p. 107).

Dexter's victims often plead with Dexter that they can change, that they won't do it again, and, on occasion, we might want to believe them. We might want to see Dexter let someone go. Dexter's call for shame and recognition, initiated when he begins to look, is in some ways a lack of regard for the future while a permanent bond to the past. Dexter's kills suggest that to him, the past, our actions as well as that which was done to us, shape us, take hold of us, and form us in ways that are almost impossible to break.

In Season 1, Dexter confronts the role of the past and the structures of childhood when he watches Jeremy, the young killer. Dexter sees himself in Jeremy, but he wants to believe in Jeremy's freedom to change. Thus, in Episode 3, even after watching Jeremy plot a kill (thwarted by Dexter rustling through the woods to look out on the scene), Dexter lets Jeremy go after discovering that he was raped by the man he killed at age fifteen. Dexter wants to believe in Jeremy's ability to change, to escape the path he is on. But Jeremy kills again, and then takes his own life. The past had a strong hold on Jeremy, but we cannot allow the past to excuse what he does. Every new act, every new crime, is a free choice in its own right, and it is for this reason that we must be responsible for both who we are in the present as well as who we were. To rely on a claim that this was Jeremy's nature, or his destiny, is to rob Jeremy of the very freedom that defines him as human.

Dexter's elaborately staged kills call upon the victim to feel shame, to see herself as having been fixed and limited to the designation 'evil'—not by Dexter, but by the activities and projects the victim has chosen. The demanded recognition requires each victim to accept responsibility, to recognize each decision to kill, rape, drive drunk, deal drugs, for what it was: the free choice of a free subject. In the Season 1 episode "Shrink Wrap," when Dexter kills the psychiatrist Emmett Meridian, he tells him, "I'm sorry doc, actions have consequences, and this is yours." Meridian has genuinely helped Dexter to confront the past through psychoanalysis, but whatever good Meridian could accomplish in the future, he needs to be held accountable for his past. The only way to end this bond to the past is to kill the subject who carries that past forward.

Thus, in spite of our freedom to change, the present subject is responsible for its past. Sartre explains, using the example of a grudge, that so long as the person against whom we hold the grudge is alive, we can continue to hold the grudge, even if the person is no longer the offender in the same sense in which the thief is no longer a thief. Sartre claims that "I am my past and if I were not, my past would not exist any longer either for me or for anybody, it would no longer have any relation with the present" (p. 169). In this respect, the thief, even if truly reformed, is still responsible for the thief that he was; it is only because of him that the past thief has any being at all in the present.

As Dexter suggests a connection between past actions and current consequences, Sartre too sees a shared bond of responsibility between the past, the present, and the future. I am not only responsible for my past, but the past weighs on my present and future, and is, for example, "responsible for the fact that at each instant I am not a diplomat or a sailor" (p. 173). Dexter watches and shames others into recognizing who they are and acknowledging responsibility for what they have done. But he kills them because, in spite of a seemingly limitless freedom to make other choices, what they've done is in some ways responsible for what they continue to do.

Bad or Bad Faith?

Dexter looks at criminals, identifies them as being criminals, and then shames then into recognizing what they are as he holds them responsible. He robs his victims of their freedom, of their freedom to change, to always be something else, to create the world around them based on the choices they make, and this freedom is a fundamental aspect of what it is to be human. While in bad faith we actively flee from this freedom, by seeking essential identities that limit our possibilities and help us to avoid the anguish of endless openness, we resent the one who robs us of this freedom by objectifying us. The encounter with the other brings to the fore a tension at the core of consciousness; the desire to be free and escape what I am, and the anguish I have in this freedom. Nobody better encapsulates the Sartrean tension between freedom and identity than Dexter himself.

Dexter is well aware of the various roles he takes on. "None of us," he says, "are who we appear to be on the outside, but we must maintain appearances to survive . . . all you can do is play along at life and hope that sometimes you get it right" ("Shrink Wrap," Season 1). But Dexter believes that there's one thing which he truly, fundamentally, and inescapably is: a killer. The entire show is premised on Dexter's bad faith choice, his project of vigilante serial murders. Dexter thinks he cannot escape this identity—that it is a combination of his nature and what happened to him as a little boy. Sartre would deny that there is such a powerful bond of determination, that Dexter's Dark Passenger has such control over him.

Yes, the past influences who we are and what we do, but we are always free to make other choices, to behave otherwise—first, we are, and only later do we make ourselves be something. Thus, our existence primarily and in every instance precedes our essence, which is, for as long as we are alive, open and free to change. Dexter does not yet see, though it is increasingly suggested through the series, the ways in which Harry created Dexter's murderous identity out of his past. Dexter thinks he does not have, and never had, a choice about what he does. In other words, Dexter believes his past has ultimately determined his essential identity. To deny himself the choice is, like so many of his victims, to deny that he is responsible for his actions.

We, as viewers, watch Dexter, as Dexter watches his own victims. And while Dexter looks in order to see guilt, we look at Dexter to see his innocence, to see the ways in which he might escape his chosen identity. It is our acknowledgment of Dexter's freedom, of his ability not to be forever determined by and limited to this role, that intrigues us as viewers, that allows us to sympathize—even root for—this serial killer. We believe that Dexter "is not what he is" because we begin to suspect that he is not a monster, that he might be able to escape his past, and we wonder if (or worry that) he will make an authentic choice, recognize his freedom, and abandon his murderous project. Mostly, however, we love him because he doesn't.

25
Safe Dex

DAVID RAMSAY STEELE

Arthur Mitchell, the misnamed Trinity Killer, surmises for one fleeting moment that Dexter aspires to be a vigilante ("The Getaway," Season 4). Our Dex, however doesn't want to be a vigilante, though the net result is that he acts just like one.

Well, maybe not *just* like a vigilante: occasionally saving killers from being picked up by the police so that he can have the satisfaction of slaughtering them himself isn't VSOP (vigilante standard operating procedure). But even this Dexter quirk has its helpful side: it does save the taxpayer all that expensive crap about appeals, psychiatric evaluations, and maybe in some cases, life sentences for the killers (which come with a life sentence for the taxpayers who have to feed, clothe, accommodate, and entertain them).

Dexter the Just Man

One hundred and four years before Season 1 of *Dexter*, when the word "vigilante" was still confined to westerns and was fairly obscure even there, and the term "serial killer" had not even been coined, Edgar Wallace published *The Four Just Men*. It instantly became, and remained for the next fifty years, a super-hyper-mega-bestseller, and was followed up by several sequels, both novels and collections of stories, including *The Three Just Men* (there had really only been three all along).

The Just Men are rich, well-connected (one is a European prince), ruthless, cosmopolitan individuals with secret lives and a secret plan. They ingeniously conspire to assassinate evil-doers who have somehow escaped the law. In the main story of the first book, however, their target is not an especially wicked person, merely somewhat misguided, in their opinion, about current politics. The Just Men publicly announce that they will kill the British Foreign Secretary (equivalent to Secretary of State) if a certain piece of legislation goes through the British Parliament. It does and they do. Good job, killers! Sometimes even non-evil persons may have to be eliminated, in the interest of the greater struggle against evil.

The Four Just Men is not a whodunnit but a howwilltheydoit: how can the Just Men manage to kill the illustrious cabinet minister at a precise pre-announced time, under the eyes of the entire Metropolitan Police Force and the secret service? The Just Men always keep their word to the very letter, so it's understood that if they don't succeed in killing the minister at exactly that time, they will have to abandon the attempt to kill him altogether.

If we want to understand why our cuddly monster Dex is a true hero of our time, we can begin by asking why nothing like *The Four Just Men* could possibly be a major hit in the early twenty-first century.

Both the Just Men and Dexter kill bad guys. Both the Just Men and Dexter have secret lives, respectable public faces contrasting with their clandestine callings. Both the Just Men and Dexter are dedicated, disciplined, charming, *muy sympatico*. Both the Just Men and Dexter are, if you want to get technical about it, murderers, serial killers, dangerous criminals who, if caught, would be executed. Both the Just Men and Dexter are strongly identified with by readers or viewers, who want them to keep on getting away with their killing.

As far as I know, there were no protests or complaints about the *morality* of the Just Men. I've come across several disdainful references to Wallace in writings of the 1920s, 1930s, and 1940s. Snobbish literary people dismissed Wallace, along with Agatha Christie, Edgar Rice Burroughs, and sometimes even the Sherlock Holmes canon, as vulgar and escapist. They considered this stuff to be trash, though many of the literary intellectuals who took this line still thoroughly enjoyed reading that kind of slickly-executed trash.

But I have not encountered anyone from that period saying that there is something unhealthy about encouraging millions of readers to identify sympathetically with people who cold-bloodedly break the law in myriad ways, and commit numerous murders for which, if caught, they would be executed. And this was at a time when hardly anyone doubted that such people *should* be executed.

Rooting for a Killer

When we turn to *Dexter* and our own time, things are different. *Dexter* is continually being denounced by people whose denunciations are well publicized. The Parents Television Council (PTC), which claims membership of over a million, has called for action against advertisers who support *Dexter*, and has repeatedly agitated for confining *Dexter* to cable and keeping it off the broadcast channels. Although explicitly concerned about sex, violence, and profanity in TV shows which might be watched by children, the PTC is well aware that *Dexter* does not have a higher level of sex, violence, and profanity than some other shows, but still singles *Dexter* out as the worst offender because (as their President, Timothy F. Winter, puts it) "the series compels viewers to empathize with a serial killer, to root for him to prevail, to hope he doesn't get discovered."

There must be more to it than that, though. To pick just one obvious example, since 1844, readers of *The Count of Monte Cristo* have been "compelled" by Dumas's story-telling magic to empathize with Edmond Dantes, root for him to prevail, hope he doesn't get discovered. And Dantes, the Count of Monte Cristo, like the Just Men, is literally a serial killer. What's going on here? No doubt part of the answer lies in the fact that TV is easily accessible in a way that books aren't. But there seems to be something else.

As a first stab at the answer, Edmond Dantes has a personal motive: revenge for a terrible wrong. And the Just Men had a moral purpose—though we don't know that the PTC wouldn't object to the Just Men if they were popular today. But Dexter is addicted to the thrill of slaughtering humans for its own sweet sake. He's not just a serial killer, he's a *psychotic* serial killer, *addicted* to ritual killing—or so we're told.

What's the attitude of Wallace (and presumably many of his readers) to the operations of the Just Men? It's an attitude which no thriller writer or TV scriptwriter could get away with today. The killings of the Just Men are depicted as a rational plan, and are tacitly commended, at least to the extent that the reader is expected to identify with the Just Men and hope that they keep getting away with it. Each killing is one more happy ending. The Just Men are smooth operators, fully in control. Most of their victims (with the notable exception of the Foreign Secretary in the first story) are evil characters who thoroughly deserve their fate.

In conversation, the Just Men good-humoredly compare their own notoriety with that of Jack the Ripper, then as now the most famous of all serial killers. (The Ripper is more legend than fact. The press, with the connivance of the police, conspired to pad his resume by crediting him with murders committed by several different unconnected people.)

Our Killers, Right or Wrong

What about the rightness or wrongness of what the Just Men are doing? Wallace's attitude, as storyteller, seems to be: 'There are big ethical issues here, and they add to the excitement, but we don't want to get sidetracked into debating them.' The authorial voice betrays no defensiveness, even though we're continually reminded that the Just Men have to outwit official law enforcement as well as the bad guys. The Just Men never falter in their belief that what they're doing is absolutely right. The writer seems to be saying to his readers: 'I have a story to tell, and part of the charm of my story is that you and I can imagine what it's like for scoundrels to be brought to justice. There are powerful, influential, or very slippery people who commit a lot of evil acts but are outside the reach of the law, but wouldn't it be wonderful if ruthless, glamorous persons, with efficiency and *panache*, could give these disgusting villains their come-uppance?'

Could something like *The Four Just Men* be made today, say as a TV series, and be successful? Can you imagine a show something like *Criminal Minds*, in which the heroic team is a self-appointed group of private crime-fighters, who illegally execute bad guys? To make the parallel close, suppose that the pilot episode shows our heroes assassinating the Secretary of State because she supports a piece of over-intrusive homeland security legislation—and imagine that this episode is wildly popular, with no one voicing a qualm about its propriety.

This is extremely unlikely, for two related reasons. First, any such series would provoke a storm of controversy about the choice of targets for assassination, as well as the general immorality of endorsing murder. Second, and more importantly, today's writers would be quite incapable of presenting the Just Men as entirely rational. They would be unable to stop themselves from finding the origin of the Just Men's plans in their troubled childhoods. The ideology of childhood trauma is now so very powerful. But if the writers took care to present the team of killers as victims of their demons or their 'issues', this would tend to defuse the former kind of objection. We see here how currently dominant ideology automatically pushes any acceptable vigilantism in the direction of *Dexter*.

What became of Edgar Wallace? He persuaded his employers at the *Daily Mail* (a major UK national newspaper) to serialize *The Four Just Men*, with a generous prize to readers who could guess the ending (just how the Foreign Secretary was killed). Although the book sold millions, boosted the circulation of the *Mail*, and made Wallace famous, Wallace was careless with the wording of the prize offer, so that everyone, without limit, who guessed the ending was entitled to the prize. Wallace's book sold millions but the prize competition drove Wallace himself into bankruptcy.

After that, he wrote many successful stories, including a series about "the Ringer," a glamorous revenge killer. He earned a lot of money, but always spent far more than he earned, gripped by the superstition that if he failed to spend lavishly, his run of success as a writer would come to an end. His final project was the script for *King Kong*. In 1932 he went to Hollywood to work on that movie, but quickly fell ill and died.

Wallace's Just Men are the crystallization of a common theme in popular fiction: the hero will sometimes break the law in a good cause. Sherlock Holmes, aside from such trivialities as burglarizing houses in search of evidence, sometimes lets killers go free. Unlike the irreproachable Just Men, Holmes also displays another common trait of the storybook hero: he has his Dark Passenger. His major motivation is the fascination of solving problems and if he has no criminological problems to occupy him, he injects himself with cocaine and plays inchoate dissonant chords on the violin.

The Retribution of Raffles

While Conan Doyle's Holmes mostly upheld the law, Conan Doyle's brother-in-law, E.W. Hornung, created A.J. Raffles, a proper gentleman and "the greatest slow bowler of his generation." Raffles has a public face and mingles with the rich and fashionable, but also leads a secret criminal life. He is a jewel thief constrained by an idiosyncratic code of honor.

When Raffles's confidant, accomplice, and narrator, Bunny Manders suggests that being a well-known cricketer would be a hindrance to a life of burglary, Raffles responds:

My dear Bunny, that's exactly where you make a mistake. To follow crime with reasonable impunity you simply must have a parallel ostensible career—the more public the better. . . . it's my profound conviction that Jack the Ripper was a really eminent public man, whose speeches were very likely reported alongside his atrocities. ("Gentlemen and Players")

I suppose that in this day and age we do have to mention that Bunny is a member of the male sex, and to explain that to be most revered as a cricketer in those days, you had to be a gentleman, and therefore someone who was not paid to play.

In *Mr Justice Raffles*, the great jewel thief steals no diamonds, but utilizes all his skills to bring retribution on an evil man and restitution to some of his victims. The retribution does not extend to the arch-villain's death, but, presumably sensing that anything less than death would leave the reader's sense of justice unsated, the bad guy is slain by someone else. *Mr Justice Raffles* is now the least anthologized and least reprinted of the Raffles stories, presumably because of its rather numerous unpleasant comments about the villain's ethnicity.

Enter the Bulldog

Eighteen years after the Just Men made their appearance, along came Bulldog Drummond, in stories penned by the writer who wrote under the name 'Sapper'. Drummond was the James Bond of his day, and later became Ian Fleming's major inspiration for Bond, just as Drummond's arch-villain Carl Peterson was the inspiration for Ernst Stavro Blofeld (if you're rusty on your Bond movies, he's the guy with the long-haired white cat).

Drummond in 1920 is a former British army officer who finds life dull after World War I, but then stumbles on a secret conspiracy aiming at the total ruination and humiliation of Britain. Drummond briefly considers informing the police of Peterson's foul plot and criminal deeds, but decides that he, Drummond, would be just as liable to prosecution as Peterson.

The first four Drummond novels describe Drummond's epic battle to thwart Peterson's vile schemes. Drummond has a secret life like that of the Scarlet Pimpernel. He and his friends, all rich young men who seem to have nothing more on their minds than getting sozzled in the posh London clubs, have secret lives as ferocious fighters against evil.

In *The Black Gang*, Drummond and his associates, all dressed in black, terrorize the evil-doers and run rings round the police. A vast malign conspiracy is afoot. Jews and Communists (the latter indifferently described as Bolsheviks or anarchists) figure prominently in the conspiracy, but these individuals, though degenerate and malevolent enough, are simple-minded dupes of the master-mind Carl Peterson, a German who can pass for English or American, and whose goals, aside from the obvious enormous piles of money and despotic power, include the destruction of the British Empire.

Apart from administering executions, floggings, and other punishments, the Black Gang is responsible for the disappearance of many leftist agitators and the reader wonders what has become of them. Perhaps they have been chopped into pieces and . . . well, there were no plastic bags in those days, and no cordless circular saws. On the other hand, manual labor was cheap and forensics was pretty basic. However, near the end of the book, the disappeared ones turn up, in a rehabilitation camp run by the Black Gang. Here the former subversives are made to work hard under the fist of a drill-sergeant, thus teaching them (a touch of irony here, old chap) what socialism is really all about.

In the climactic scene of *The Black Gang*, Drummond and the Gang have captured Peterson and his leading cronies. Peterson, a wizard with disguises, is in the persona of a sweet American clergyman.

[Drummond] swung round on the cowering clergyman and gripped him once again by the throat, shaking him as a terrier shakes a rat. . . . And still the motionless black figures round the wall gave no sign, . . . They knew their leader, and though they knew not what had happened to cause his dreadful rage they trusted him utterly and implicitly. Whether it was lawful or not was beside the point: it was just or Hugh Drummond would not have done it. And so they watched and waited, while Drummond, his face blazing, forced the clergyman to his knees, . . .

It was Phyllis who opened her eyes suddenly, and, half-dazed still with the horror of the last few minutes, gazed round the room. She saw . . . the Black Gang silent and motionless like avenging judges round the walls. And then she saw her husband bending Carl

Peterson's neck farther and farther back, till at any moment it seemed as if it must crack.

For a second she stared at Hugh's face, and saw on it a look which she had never seen before—a look so terrible, that she gave a sharp, convulsive cry.

"Let him go, Hugh: let him go. Don't do it."

Her voice pierced his brain, though for a moment it made no impression on the muscles of his arms. A slightly bewildered look came into his eyes: he felt as a dog must feel who is called off his lawful prey by his master.

So Drummond relents, and so (women never think about the trouble they cause by their sentimental interventions) we have another two novels in which Drummond battles the arch-fiend Peterson before finally seeing him off.

What was it that dear little Phyllis saw in hubby's eyes, and what was it doing there? We're repeatedly reminded that Drummond had nothing but wholesome fun in the Great War, cruising through No-Man's-Land in search of Germans whom he could savagely throttle. Presumably he had that look in his eyes then. And what's the big deal, since Carl Peterson is more of a threat and more of a monster than Kaiser Willy?

The incident may show feminine frailty, or it may show that even in the struggle against absolute evil, the decent Britisher is restrained by civilized inhibitions unknown to the filthy Hun. On the droll side, it seems to show that the immensely muscular Drummond takes a suspiciously long time to break someone's neck. But what it most clearly shows is that Drummond, like Dexter, has his Dark Passenger. There's a monster within, and somehow, it's for the good if that monster is sometimes let loose.

Enter the Saint

At school in England, the young boy who would later be Leslie Charteris thought carefully about his optimal future career, a career that would suit his personality and make him rich, and eventually he hit on the answer: he would become a professional burglar. The record is silent on whether he actually tried out this profession, but he was a supremely practical person and we can draw our own conclusions.

And then Charteris discovered that the writing which came easily to him was saleable. He gave up burglary for writing, and systematically developed a hero, Simon Templar, a fearsome vigilante who kills bad people ("the godless," as he refers to them, though this is his only symptom of piety), and who continually has to outwit Inspector Teal of Scotland Yard. Teal, not knowing the whole story about Templar, considers him a dangerous criminal, and to be strictly accurate, Teal happens to be technically correct.

Templar's true purpose is proclaimed early on:

> "We Saints are normally souls of peace and goodwill. But we don't like crooks, bloodsuckers, traders in vice and damnation. We're going to beat you up and do you down, skin you, smash you, and scare you off the face of Europe. We are not bothered by the letter of the law, we act exactly as we please, we inflict what punishment we think suitable, and no one is going to escape us." (*Enter the Saint*)

As a typical example, in "The Death Penalty," the Saint runs into Abdul Osman, a drug dealer and white slaver whom he's already met some years before. On that earlier occasion, the Saint had contented himself with branding both of Osman's cheeks with a nasty Arabic word. Now the story ends with Osman's death, though at whose hands remains a mystery until the very end. The Saint has no qualms about forging evidence and presenting a fabricated story to the inquest on Osman, and laying the blame for Osman's killing on another drug dealer and white slaver, who ends up being hanged for a crime he didn't commit. Thus, the Saint hoodwinks the official machinery of law enforcement into killing a man because the Saint believes he deserves it. The Saint's moniker is quite consciously ironic.

In popular fiction before World War II, "white slavery" is a code term for prostitution. Prostitutes and pimps make appearances in these stories, but these words are generally considered too indelicate. By the 1940s, for instance in *The Saint in Miami* (1944), the word 'pimp', at least, has become permissible. Both Drummond and the Saint speak in a kind of chummy public-school argot (the Saint's owing something to Bertie Wooster) which a later generation might consider somewhat campy. But the concept of camp lay in the future, and if you could've explained what it meant to the Bulldog or the Saint, you'd earn yourself at least a sock in the jaw.

The Saint is flamboyant, abrasive, and often inconsiderate of bystanders. These were the days of the great sports cars with magical names, the Hispano-Suiza and the Lagonda. The greatest of all these cars was the Hirondel, as driven by Simon Templar, terrorizing other drivers as well as pedestrians in his ruthless, high-velocity pursuit of his own brand of justice.

> Some who saw the passage of the Saint that night will remember it to the end of their lives; for the Hirondel, as though recognizing the hand of a master at its wheel, became almost a living thing. King of the Road its makers called it, but that night the Hirondel was more than a king: it was the incarnation and apotheosis of all cars. For the Saint drove with the devil at his shoulder, and the Hirondel took its mood from his. If this had been a superstitious age, those who saw it would have crossed themselves and sworn that it was no car at all they saw that night but a snarling silver fiend that roared through London on the wings of an unearthly wind. (*The Saint Closes the Case*, also sometimes titled *The Last Hero*)

Now *that's* a car. And that's what we call writing. Those who have hoped to acquire a genuine old Hirondel have been disappointed, for this make of car lived entirely in the brains of Leslie Charteris and his millions of readers.

What such passages illustrates is that we always (at least, since Lord Byron) like our heroes to have an anti-social streak. They have their Dark Passengers. If they're too utterly sane, like R. Austin Freeman's Dr. Thorndyke, they lack an essential ingredient and come across as bloodless cyphers. Charteris often described the Saint as a "buccaneer," but in later stories the Saint is co-opted by the authorities. In *Angels of Doom* (1931), he seems to be working with his old enemy, Inspector Teal of Scotland Yard, then seems to have double-crossed Teal and become an outlaw vigilante, then turns out to have been working for the Secret Service (thus outranking Teal) all along. But it wouldn't do for him to become entirely respectable and above board. Part of the mystique of the Saint is that he's a criminal, so this image is continually toyed with in subsequent stories.

The Saint never had much success on the big screen, but a fairly close imitation, The Falcon, had a good run in the 1940s (Charteris sued the RKO studio for plagiarism and made contemptuous fun of the Falcon in *The Saint Steps In*). Charteris lived in the United States, but was unable to obtain permanent residency because of the Chinese Exclusion law (which kept out people with fifty percent or more Chinese ancestry). Charteris had a Chinese father and an English mother; his real name was Leslie Bowyer-Yin. Eventually a special Act of Congress was passed, just to enable Charteris to stay in the US. But after marrying his fourth wife, the Hollywood starlet Audrey Long, he moved back to England, and lived there till his death in 1993.

Charteris wrote over a hundred lucrative books, mostly about the Saint. His last few Saint stories were mainly written by other people; he just looked them over and made a few changes before attaching his name. The writers chosen were highly competent, and the books remained excellent, but the Saint's popular appeal was waning.

Decline of the Vigilante Novel

At first glance, if we look at what happened after World War II, we may get the impression that systematic private enforcement of justice went into eclipse. Even as the word 'vigilante' became popular, the vigilante novel almost disappeared. Simon Templar was now working for the government, at least some of the time. Bulldog Drummond's fan following dwindled and his niche was filled by James Bond, a civil servant 'licensed to kill' by a government department.

Mickey Spillane's Mike Hammer and the hero of the *Death Wish* movies, played by Charles Bronson, were exceptions, but in spirit they did not go very far beyond revenge. Revenge is a form of justice and has its own rules just as onerous as any other form, but revenge is personal retribution and does not extend to punishing offenders with whom the punisher has no personal connection. Still, some revengers may graduate to vigilantism.

In the late twentieth century, private enforcement of justice is more usually presented as a fearsome threat. Harry Callahan, hero of *Dirty Harry* is sometimes idiotically called a vigilante. *Magnum Force* (1973), the second Dirty Harry movie, shows a group of cops who bump off evil-doers in their spare time. These vigilante cops are not presented at all sympathetically, and the law-abiding Callahan is compelled to waste them in order to uphold the law.

In *The Star Chamber* movie (1983), a group of judges assassinate killers who have managed to escape official justice by legal technicalities. The true plot begins when they realize they have made a mistake and their hired executioner is already on his way to kill the designated target. One of the judges, played by Michael Douglas, decides to intervene personally to protect the target. At the end of the movie, Douglas is delivering up the other vigilante judges to the official police force.

The movie's point of view is one of bland confidence that the Star Chamber, the unofficial conclave of judges, is dangerous and indefensible. It does not explore the irony in the fact that the Star Chamber has made one rare mistake and that in all its other operations it is rectifying mistakes by the official system. Nor does it confront what should be done on those occasions when the official system makes the same mistake as the Star Chamber had made: punishing the innocent. Should a judge with a conscience then intervene physically to thwart the implementation of official justice?

Despite appearances, vigilantism had not died. It had merely moved from the bookstores to the newsstands. Comic-book superheroes took over most of the illegal enforcement of justice. These new heroes have superhuman powers, not just figuratively, like the Saint's amazing agility, quick-wittedness and extraordinary reflexes, but literally. The most outstanding of the superheroes *not* to have superhuman abilities is Batman, who—like the Just Men, Bulldog Drummond, and the Saint before him—is independently wealthy.

The eviction of vigilantes from popular novels and their relegation to the disreputable underworld of comics does seem to reflect an increased hostility to vigilantism, connected with the growth of state-worship in the twentieth century, the age of totalitarianism.

Dexter, Hero of Our Time

In the early twenty-first century, the ideology of childhood trauma reached its peak in popular culture, even while psychological research had largely undermined it as scientifically acceptable.

Look at the difference between the first movie made of *Willy Wonka and the Chocolate Factory* (1971) and the remake, *Charlie and the Chocolate Factory* (2005). The first movie, following the Roald Dahl story, presents Willy Wonka as a somewhat inscrutable, interestingly dangerous, quirky, but fundamentally benign person, a formidable godlike figure. The remake depicts Wonka as a dude with serious issues, a man who worships chocolate because his father, a dentist, did something terrible to him all those years ago, as well as forbidding him to eat chocolate. The director of the remake, Tim Burton, repeatedly voiced his opinion that Wonka just has to be seen as "screwed up" and that therefore some explanation of his mental disorder is required. The explanation, of course, has to be childhood trauma—what else?

Another example is the 1997 movie, *The Saint*, with Val Kilmer, which borrows a few plot devices from Charteris but is basically about an entirely different character. The Saint of this movie has not dedicated his life to punishing bad guys, and instead of being self-assured and confident in his righteous mission, he is driven by—a childhood trauma. The Kilmer Saint is a professional thief who has become very wealthy and plans to retire after one more job. He is clever and resourceful, but helplessly possessed by an irrational compulsion, flowing from his childhood mistreatment by priests.

Childhood trauma plays the same role in modern popular culture as used to be played, in traditional folk tales, by love potions. Like a love potion, a childhood trauma compels the hero to behave in an irresponsible way, takes possession of him and leaves him no choice. These magical effects of childhood trauma are as mythical as those of the love potion, but they seem to be passionately believed in by most of today's writers.

The storyline of *Dexter* is popular because it's safe—ideologically safe. A story about someone who bumps off people for carefully calculated reasons, in pursuit of a strict code of justice, would make too many people too uncomfortable. Today's ruling ideology (at least among the intellectual class from whom scriptwriters are chiefly recruited) holds that motiveless, irrational killing is tasty, especially if it can be linked with childhood trauma, while calculated killing in a worthy cause, by a hero without hangups, is almost unthinkable, and if thinkable at all, painfully embarrassing. Every age is as straitlaced as every other, but the specific taboos change.

Dexter adroitly accommodates itself to the reigning ideology. It gives us the glamour of the Secret Life and of the anti-social 'bad boy', the narrative appeal of the supernormal hero who fights his way out of adversity and triumphs, the satisfaction of seeing the most cunning and elusive evil-doers getting their just desserts. Instead of inviting criticism or derision by having the hero take a strong moral line against the villains he executes, any questions about the rightness of the hero's cause are defined away: the hero is not responsible for his actions. To make the hero a puppet of his bloodlust seems, on the surface, outrageous, provocative, audacious. But really it's the very safest way to go.

This is not to denigrate the artistic quality of *Dexter*, which is superb. Nor is it to criticize *Dexter* on ideological grounds. We should be no more troubled by the childhood-trauma ideology of *Dexter* than by the anti-Semitism of A.J. Raffles and Bulldog Drummond, the ultra-politically-correct feminism of Stieg Larsson, or Jack London's amalgam of Marxism and Social Darwinism. Outside the context of the story, these belief systems may be criticized and rejected, while within a work of fiction or drama, they can be accepted as features of the landscape.

It was inevitable that the indestructible popular hunger for stories of unofficial justice would meet the rampant ideology of my-childhood-makes-me-do-it. It was not inevitable that the artistic result would be as intelligent, as witty, as well-plotted, and as brilliantly produced and acted as *Dexter*.

The Perps

Sᴜʟᴛᴀɴ Aʜᴍᴇᴅ is a graduate student in the Bioethics Department at Case Western Reserve University. He does research in Islamic medical ethics and the psychology of terrorists, as he is sometimes mistaken for one when going through airport security. He is at times suspected of being a psychopath and finds himself drawn to blonde women with lots of emotional baggage.

Aᴀʀᴏɴ C. Aɴᴅᴇʀsᴏɴ is a doctoral candidate at the University of California, San Diego. He is currently parlaying his experience as a blood spatter intern with Miami Metro Homicide into his dissertation on aggression and graphic violence in the slasher film.

Pᴀᴛʀɪᴄɪᴀ Bʀᴀᴄᴇ is a Professor of Art History at Southwest Minnesota State University, in Marshall, Minnesota. With co-author Robert Arp, she contributed chapters to *Lost and Philosophy* (2008); *The Ultimate Lost and Philosophy* (2010); *True Blood and Philosophy* (2010); and *The Philosophy of David Lynch* (2011). The character in *Dexter* she most resembles is Lila; not in the burn down your own studio, kidnap Rita's kids, blow up Doakes psycho way, but because of the sexy artist thing. . . .

Jᴀsᴏɴ Dᴀᴠɪs has only had intimate contact with serial killers involved with academic library budget cuts to journal subscriptions. Still, working in research evaluation at Macquarie University does have its days when he feels the "Dark Passenger" within wanting to begin a very different body count. In between preparing specimens of audit numbers with a knifepoint glint of light in his eyes, he thinks crazy thoughts like what would happen if you sped up the scenes in *Dexter* involving Daniel Licht's "Wink" music to the same tempo as "The Spear Waltz" from *Donnie Darko*? And what if a serial killer did have time-traveling powers? And why shouldn't there be a scene in a future *Dexter* episode where all the major female characters—from Jennifer Carpenter to Julia Stiles—appear together and break into a synchronized dance routine to Little Eva's "The Loco-Motion"?

PHILLIP DEEN is a lecturer in Wellesley College's department of philosophy. He has published articles on the history of American philosophy, the aesthetics of videogames, and contemporary democratic theory and has edited John Dewey's lost work *Unmodern Philosophy and Modern Philosophy*. Befitting his submission in this volume, he is a rigorously self-disciplined individual who always helps neighbors with their packages, except for that time he beat a redneck to death in a everglade shack with an anchor. You know, to relax. (It's possible he has unresolved hallucinogenic daddy issues.)

M. CARMELA EPRIGHT is an Associate Professor of Philosophy at Furman University. Her research is in medical ethics and psychiatry. As a rule she steers away from writing about psychopathy because sociopaths have consistently shown disinterest in her brilliant insights about morality. She lives with her husband, son, and two cats, one of which is named Dexter. Like his namesake, he is a serial killer; unlike his namesake he eats his prey.

ABROL FAIRWEATHER teaches Philosophy at San Francisco State, University of San Francisco and Las Positas College, all in the Bay Area. His philosophical interests include virtue epistemology, philosophy of mind and emotions, and existentialism. He has recently contributed to a volume on Facebook and Philosophy and co-edited a volume on Blues and Philosophy. His life interests include loving and listening to dusty, whiskey-bottle blues music, connecting with his dog and keeping more in touch with his emotions than Dexter.

EVERITT FOSTER is an independent scholar and film historian living in Austin, Texas. He holds an MA in military history from Texas Tech University where his thesis attempted to use films to tell a nearly complete history of the Vietnam War and the effects it has on veterans. He is currently working on a manuscript of on Eastern European cinema during the Cold War. He agrees with Dexter that pulled pork sandwiches are the perfect driving food.

REBECCA STEINER GOLDNER is a PhD student in Philosophy at Villanova University, where she works on Aristotle, Merleau-Ponty, perception and the body. Her work on the body is significantly different from Dexter's.

RICHARD GREENE is a fucking Professor of Philosophy at Weber State University. He's co-edited a shitload of books on pop fucking culture and philosophy with various assholes, fucktards, and douchebags. His favorite fucking character on Dexter is Deb. Motherfuck!

BRIAN GREGOR holds a PhD in philosophy from Boston College. He has published several essays in the areas of phenomenology, hermeneutics, and existentialism—particularly with regard to philosophy of religion, ethics, and aesthetics. Like Dexter, he is still trying to figure out what it means to be human.

DANIEL HAAS swears he didn't do it. He's a graduate student in philosophy at Florida State University and is much too busy teaching undergraduates and working on his dissertation to have made the drive all the way from Tallahassee to Miami. Oh? You say it's less than an eight hour drive which would have been ample time? And that you found a box of blood samples stored in his office? Surely, none of them match the samples taken from the murder scene. Oh, they do? Dan would like to speak to his lawyer.

ERIC HOLMES is a freelance writer and instructor of writing and public speaking. He has published articles on EC Comics and agitative rhetoric. Like Dexter, he buys a suspicious amount of black plastic trash bags, but only because he has four dachshunds to pick up after.

EWAN KIRKLAND lectures in Film and Screen Studies at Brighton University, UK. Instead of murdering criminals who have evaded justice, Ewan is compelled by his Dark Passenger to deconstruct representations of gender, race, and sexuality in popular culture.

DANIEL P. MALLOY is lecturer of philosophy at Appalachian State University in Boone, North Carolina. His research is focused on political and Continental philosophy. He has published on the intersection of popular culture and philosophy, particularly dealing with ethical issues, as well as on Leibniz, Spinoza, Foucault, Hegel, Horkheimer, and Adorno. Daniel was Dexter's neighbor for a while. When asked about it, Daniel described his one time neighbor as quiet and polite.

SEAN MCALEER is Associate Professor of Philosophy at the University of Wisconsin, Eau Claire. He likes all things Dexter: Pete Dexter's novels, Dexter Gordon's saxophone, C.K. Dexter Haven's yachts; but he likes Dexter Morgan most of all. He is currently at work on a children's book on Dexter's exploits, which has yet to find a publisher. He keeps the manuscript in a fake air-conditioner, next to the blood samples.

DEBORAH MELLAMPHY is a part-time Assistant Lecturer and Tutor in Film Studies in the School of English, University College Cork, Ireland. Her research focuses on gender transgression, star theory and collective authorship in the collaborations of Tim Burton and Johnny Depp. Her teaching interests include the horror genre, gender studies and film theory. Deborah's love of *Dexter* stems from the conversations she has about blood slides and plastic wrapping with her Dark Passenger.

NICOLAS MICHAUD teaches Philosophy at the University of North Florida. He has begun to think that Dexter's way of dealing with serial killers might be an excellent way of dealing with annoying philosophical opponents. Sadly, he has not found a way to sneak a syringe into the American Philosophical Association's conference, yet. . . . Should he ever succeed in this endeavor, however, the name if his boat will be *Cutting Remark*.

JOHN KENNETH MUIR is the award-winning author of reference books such as *Horror Films of the 1970s* and *The Encyclopedia of Superheroes on Film and Television* by day, and a dark, avenging genre blogger by night at Reflections on Film/TV (http:// reflectionsonfilmandtelevision.blogspot .com), recently named of the best 100 film study sites on the Net. John's split personality is also the driving creative force behind the independent web series The House Between (www.thehousebetween.com), which in 2008 and 2009 was nominated by Sy Fy Portal and Airlock Alpha as "Best Web Production."

MIKE PIERO is a graduate assistant in the English department at John Carroll University. His research interests include post/modernism studies, composition and rhetoric, critical theory, and blood spatter reports. During the week, he orders the chaos of his world by alphabetizing books.

JERRY S. PIVEN is sometimes mistaken for a celebrity, though he is neither an actor nor a sociopath. However, with so many actors in the family, he has had extensive fieldwork studying sociopaths in their own habitats (which naturally inspired him to compose an essay on Dexter). When not teaching philosophy at Case Western Reserve University, Dr. Piven is writing on the psychology of religion, culture, and violence, watching episodes of *Dexter* and *Futurama*, hangin' at the jazz club, and cycling insanely to flee from evil. He is the author of *Death and Delusion: A Freudian Analysis of Mortal Terror* (2004), *The Madness and Perversion of Yukio Mishima* (2004), and sundry other works on equally festive subjects. His latest work is *Slaughtering Death: On the Psychoanalysis of Terror, Religion, and Violence.*

JAMES F. PONTUSO is Charles Patterson Professor of Government and Foreign Affairs at Hampden-Sydney College (Founded 1775) in Virginia. He has lectured or taught in a dozen countries, including his latest position as visiting professor at the American University of Iraq, Sulaimani. He has published six books and more than seventy scholarly articles, reviews and essays. Although he has written extensively on popular culture, composing a chapter on Dexter is the only project that gave him nightmares.

GEORGE A. REISCH keeps tiny clippings of every article and book he has published sandwiched between glass slides and hidden in long wooden box. As Series Editor for Open Court's Popular Culture and Philosophy series, the number of samples is growing rapidly. He has also published articles about twentieth-century philosophy of science and wrote the book *How the Cold War Transformed Philosophy of Science* (2005).

RACHEL ROBISON-GREENE is a PhD Candidate in Philosophy at UMass Amherst. She is co-editor of *The Golden Compass and Philosophy: God Bites the Dust* (2009), and contributed chapters to *Quentin Tarantino and Philosophy* (2007), *The Legend of Zelda and Philosophy* (2008), and *Zombies, Vampires, and Philosophy* (2010). Rachel's Dark Passenger rides in a booster seat.

DAVID RAMSAY STEELE always pays cash for plastic sheeting and frequently "works late because something's come up." He likes Cuban sandwiches but some nights feels a different kind of hunger. Dr. Steele is the perpetrator of *From Marx to Mises* (1992) and *Atheism Explained* (2008), and co-perpetrator of *Three Minute Therapy* (1997). He has been implicated in *The Atkins Diet and Philosophy* (2005), *The New Encyclopedia of Unbelief* (2007), and *The Encyclopedia of Libertarianism* (2008). Thinking. Sometimes it sets his teeth on edge, sometimes it helps him control the chaos.

SARA WALLER is an Associate Professor of Philosophy at Montana State University. She edited *Serial Killers—Philosophy for Everyone* (2010) because she really wanted to write a chapter about Dexter. In this volume, she finally got her wish. She spends her time studying and writing about other serial killers, including cats, coyotes, and dolphins, though she suspects that these killers are utilitarian rather than deontic.

SARAH E. WORTH is Associate Professor of Philosophy at Furman University. She publishes mostly in the field of aesthetics and sometimes in the intersection of pop culture and philosophy. She contributed chapters to *Seinfeld and Philosophy* (2000) and *The Matrix and Philosophy* (2002). Because of her obsession with *Dexter*, she is going to school part time to become a blood spatter expert, so she can be as like Dexter as possible, but in a moral kind of way.

Index